Low Tide

High Tide

APALACHICOLA STATE BANK IS PLEASED TO MAKE AVAILABLE THIS expanded edition of *At the Water's Edge: A Pictorial and Narrative History of Apalachicola and Franklin County*. We recognize that this coastal region has been bequeathed to us by many generations of loyal and industrious people. These characteristics can be found in the citizens of Franklin County today. These are the people who placed their confidence in Apalachicola State Bank, a division of Coastal Community Bank, and have helped us to grow solidly over the past century.

Special thanks to authors Dr. William Rogers and Lee Willis III as well as photography editors Joan Morris and Dr. Bawa S. Singh for their tireless efforts in making this book the beautiful tribute that it is. Their careful documentation has preserved our history into something that will benefit each of us, as well as future generations.

We are proud to share this legacy and the belief that it will be treasured by those to whom it is entrusted.

Terry DuBose, Chairman of the Board, CEO

APALACHICOLA STATE BANK • 1897
A Division of Coastal Community Bank

At the Water's Edge

A Pictorial and Narrative History of Apalachicola and Franklin County

William Warren Rogers and Lee Willis III

Joan Morris *(Historical Photographs Editor)*

Bawa Satinder Singh *(Color Photographer)*

Expanded Edition
2004

THE DONNING COMPANY PUBLISHERS

In association with

SENTRY PRESS
TALLAHASSEE, FLORIDA

Dedication

For my three new grandchildren who have arrived since the first edition of this book came out in 1997: the twins, Emma and Fred Lindsey, and Benjamin Loftin Rogers. W. W. R.

For my mother, Katharine Jackson Willis, who instilled in me a love for history and for Apalachicola. L. W. III

For Joanna K. "Jody" Norman with love and gratitude. J. P. M.

For my brother, Bawa Ranbir Singh, with great admiration. B. S. S.

Copyright © 1997 and 2004 by William Rogers, Lee Willis III, and Joan Morris
Second printing 1999
Expanded third printing 2004

All rights reserved, including the right to reproduce this work in any form whatsoever without permission in writing from the publisher, except for brief passages in connection with a review. For information, write:
The Donning Company Publishers
184 Business Park Drive, Suite 206
Virginia Beach, VA 23462

Steve Mull, *General Manager*
Barbara B. Buchanan, *Office Manager*
Sally C. Wise, *Associate Editor*
Richard A. Horwege, *Editor for Expanded Third Printing*
Kevin M. Brown, *Graphic Designer*
Cassie Perry, *Graphic Designer for Expanded Third Printing*
Stephanie Danko, *Imaging Artist*
Mary Ellen Wheeler, *Proofreader/Editorial Assistant*
Scott Rule, *Director of Marketing*
Travis Gallup, Marketing Coordinator

B. L. Walton Jr., *Project Director*

Library of Congress Cataloging-in-Publication Data
Rogers, William Warren
    At the water's edge: a pictorial and narrative history of Apalachicola and Franklin County / by William Warren Rogers and Lee Willis III; Joan Morris, historical photographic editor; Bawa Satinder Sing, color photographer.
        p.   cm.
    Includes bibliographical references and index.
    ISBN 1-57864-001-6 (hardcover : alk. paper)
    ISBN 1-57864-276-0 (Expanded third printing)
    1. Apalachicola (Fla.)—History—Pictorial works. 2. Franklin County (Fla.)—History—Pictorial works. 3. Apalachicola (Fla.)—History. 4. Franklin County (Fla.)—History. I. Willis, Lee, 1973–   II. Title.
F319.A62R62   1997
975.9'91—dc21   97-13711
                                                                     CIP

Printed in the USA at Walsworth Publishing Company

Contents

Acknowledgments		6
Introduction		7
One	From Early Times to the American Period	11
Two	Antebellum Era Activities	21
Three	Commercial Activity	35
Four	Civil War and Reconstruction	41
Five	After the War	55
Six	Neptune's Bounty	71
Seven	Advance and Retreat: Uncertain Decades and a New Century	81
Eight	Popham and the Early 1920s	95
Nine	The Triumph, Decline, and Fall of the Oyster King	111
Ten	The Great Depression	123
Eleven	World War II	131
Twelve	To the End of the 1900s	149
Thirteen	The Beginning of a New One-Hundred-Year's Cycle	167
Select Bibliography		175
Index		176
About the Authors		184

Acknowledgments

WILLIAM WARREN ROGERS, LEE WILLIS, III, Joan Morris, and Bawa Satinder Singh—the people who produced this book—are indebted to a number of individuals and institutions. Without their help the volume would still be in the planning stages. We would like particularly to thank Barry Brynjolfsson—president of the Apalachicola State Bank and, although a newcomer to Franklin County, a man vitally interested in the region's history and progress—and Lee Willis, II—a lawyer in Tallahassee and a property owner in Apalachicola whose wife Katharine Jackson Willis has deep family roots in Franklin County. Thanks also go to Bernie Walton of Donning Company/Publishers, who brought out the book. Cynthia Clark and George Chapel of Apalachicola and Erica Clark of Tallahassee were especially helpful in reading drafts, assisting in the research, and providing useful advice.

We are grateful to the following people who helped in many ways to bring the project to its intended conclusion: a book of pictures and narrative between hard covers. They are Kristin Anderson, George Bradford, Harry Buzzett, Wesley Chesnut, David Coles, George and Alice Core, Kathleen Hays, Harold Jenkins, Michael J. Koun, John Lee, Martha Morris McLeod, Homer Marks, Willoughby Marshall, Woody Miley, Jimmie Nichols, Joanna Norman, Jackson Stevens, Larry Paarlberg, C. T. Ponder, Laurie McLeod Rivers, Mary Virginia Robinson, Audrey Roux, Dolores Roux, Mr. and Mrs. W. L. Speed, Phil Stanley, Faye Tarantino, Raymond Williams, Jiggs Zingarelli, and Kimberly Zingarelli.

Over the years many people have loaned photographs to the Florida State Archives to be copied for addition to the collection. We are particularly indebted to: Robert Cauthen, Russell V. Hughes, Frances Keith, Eddie Nesmith, and Lee Willis.

Research materials and helpful staff advice were always forthcoming from the Apalachicola Public Library, the Florida State University Library, the Florida Department of Archives, History, and Records Management, the Franklin County Courthouse, and the Leon County Courthouse. We thank the University Presses of Florida for permission to use in different form some of the information that appeared in William Warren Rogers, *Outposts on the Gulf Saint George Island and Apalachicola from Early Exploration to World War II* (1987). Unintended errors of act and interpretation are the sole responsibility of the narrative's authors.

Introduction

Flags symbolize sovereignty over territory. Apalachicola and Franklin County had first the Spanish, then the British, United States, Florida (1861), and Confederate. Since May 20, 1865, when Florida surrendered, the stars and stripes has flown over the peninsula. The Porter family, one of Apalachicola's oldest, was loyal to the Confederacy, but was not anxious to have their home used for target practice during the Civil War. A local story claims that they hung a Belgian flag outside their residence to indicate neutrality. Even so, Belgium does not claim that its national flag was ever an official standard for Apalachicola.

Geography is essential to understanding the city and county, which had an impressive river, bay, and sound. All three, like the town, bore the euphonious name of Apalachicola. The word means "those people residing on the other side," and comes from *Apalachicolas*, the name the Spanish gave to Indians living along the river's lower extremities. They spoke the Hitchiti language, were of Muskogean stock, and a part of the Lower Creeks.

Apalachicola Bay opens into the Gulf of Mexico and is protected by three barrier islands–Dog, Saint George, and Saint Vincent. The United States acquired Florida from Spain by the Adams-Onis treaty of 1819, and Congress created the Florida Territory in 1822. A port town, first called Cottonton, then West Point, and by the 1830s Apalachicola, was established on the Bay's western side. To the north stretched a delta formed by the river that contained tupelo trees, sabal palms, and endless stands of cypress, live oaks, and various hardwoods. Vast forests of heart pine trees dotted adjacent lands.

The small town prospered. In 1835 the U.S. Supreme Court ruled in favor of a private company that claimed surrounding lands known as the Forbes Purchase. Reorganizing as the Apalachicola Land Company, it proceeded with land sales. The main deterrent was the shallow harbor, but that did not prevent Apalachicola's growth. By 1832 the town became county seat for the newly created Franklin County. Florida's Native Americans surrendered their claims by a series of treaties and many were removed to the West. Those that remained, including the Seminoles, disappeared into the Everglades.

Apalachicola became a cotton city and a way station for trade. The port received goods, especially cotton, from upriver farmers and planters in Florida, Georgia, and Alabama and trans-shipped cotton bales to American and international ports. A center of deposit, sale, and distribution, Apalachicola shipped manufactured goods and supplies upriver to inland merchants and planters, and became the third largest cotton port on the Gulf after New Orleans and Mobile. In 1860 Galveston, Texas, supplanted it for third place.

Apalachicola's wealth was shared by merchants and cotton factors, steamboat owners and river traffic personnel. Brick warehouses were constructed, and during the winter and early spring the town was the scene of frenzied activity. A dramatic exit of commission merchants, ship captains, and others came during the summer months. The exodus resulted from the seasonal decline in shipping, lasting until late fall.

The Civil War brought drastic changes in 1861. The city's busy stores and warehouses, its rival Whig and Democratic newspapers, banks, militia companies, academies, churches, and diverse population (including a few slaves and free persons of color) were affected. Apalachicola was no longer a colorful and untypical Southern town with many Northern characteristics. Nearby St. Joseph, a bustling city founded in 1836, had been decimated by a hurricane in the late 1830s and the destructive yellow fever epidemic of 1841. Even without an economic rival, Apalachicola suffered as it endured a bitterly contested war.

Sectional questions concerning those over slavery, combined with Republican Abraham Lincoln's election as president in 1860, pushed the nation into armed conflict.

The only federal installations near Apalachicola were the lighthouses on Cape Saint George and Dog Island. Soon the Confederate Congress created an army and began enlisting troops directly. Florida's Civil War governor John Milton disagreed and wanted to control the troops as a state army. Milton also wanted to defend Apalachicola, which was blockaded by the federal East Gulf Coast Blockade Squadron. Early successes at running the blockade soon became rare. Southern hopes of using the Apalachicola River as a passage for Confederate ships under construction at Columbus, Georgia, proved unsuccessful. Yet, putting obstacles in the river and mounting cannon along the high riverbanks north of Apalachicola saved Columbus. Markers, buoys, and lighthouse equipment were removed from the barrier islands. Apalachicola was protected by four local militia companies and a regiment of state troops.

Within the year the Confederates abandoned the islands, and by 1862 Apalachicola was poorly armed and undermanned. The few supplies available in stores sold at exorbitant prices. Citizens began to "refugee" north to such places as Bainbridge and Thomasville in Georgia. No additional soldiers arrived, and those present were moved out of town and upriver. Half of the civilians fled, and, undefended, Apalachicola was left with about five hundred civilians. On April 3, 1862, U.S. military forces landed at Apalachicola, and the Union commander declared the town captured. The city became a no man's land, and those remaining had to cope and survive.

For the remainder of the war Apalachicola saw scattered units of Southern troops drift in and out; federal raiding parties appeared sporadically. By 1864 Apalachicola's citizens felt abandoned. Late successes in Florida at Olustee and Natural Bridge did nothing to prevent Union victory. On April 1, 1865, Governor Milton went to Sylvania, his plantation near Marianna, and shot himself to death. In Virginia Lee surrendered to Grant on April 9, and Columbus fell to General James H. Wilson whose army swept east from Alabama. The war was over.

After 1865 Franklin Countians accepted hard times, but never faltered in their affection for their homeland. Saint George and the other barrier islands had several owners, but except for the lighthouse attendants and their families there were few permanent residents. Dr. Ray V. Pierce of Buffalo, New York, bought Saint Vincent in 1907, and the island remained in his estate until 1948. Pierce made it a game preserve. Thomas Orman purchased Little Saint George in 1861, and the property was kept in the family. In the postwar years George Sinclair emerged as Saint George Island's major owner. Dog Island was largely controlled by Benjamin L. Curtiss, who sold parcels of it.

Franklin County returned to maritime commerce, especially shipping cotton, although Apalachicola's shallow harbor remained a major problem. The potential of the seafood and lumber industries attracted little immediate interest. Apalachicola remained isolated despite having a river and the Gulf of Mexico for a front door. Roads were inadequate, there were no railroads, and no bridge to connect the town and the rest of Florida. Yet, the county's diverse population maintained political and religious tolerance. Despite the Democratic majority, many Northerners were Republicans and there was limited political discord. There was racial tolerance, but the new black citizens remained second-class citizens for many years. Reconstruction was a difficult period. While much of the nation celebrated the centennial year of 1876, Apalachicola and Franklin County languished.

Changes came with the burgeoning timber industry in the 1870s. Supplying the demand for lumber led to moderately successful efforts to revive Apalachicola's harbor and to build new shipping facilities at Carrabelle, established in the 1880s. Apalachicola businessmen began agitating for a railroad and secured a charter, although the line never received sufficient funding. Efforts to obtain additional monies for deepening West Pass failed. Apalachicola was still a sleepy down-at-the-heels town. In 1880 the county's population was 1,904 fewer than it was in 1860.

Later, Franklin County saw the creation of two new towns: Carrabelle and Eastpoint. Twenty-two miles east of Apalachicola the Carrabelle River empties into Saint George Sound. Dog Island is six miles away. To the north lay an almost impenetrable swamp known as Tate's Hell. The area between the coast and the swamp was a popular camping ground for saltwater and freshwater fishermen and hunters. The natural harbor there and adjacent East Pass were deeper than those at West Pass and Apalachicola. When a hurricane toppled Dog Island lighthouse in 1873, a new structure, Crooked River light, was built on the mainland near the sound. As the timber industry grew, a permanent settlement began. Oliver Hudson Kelley was the man responsible.

Kelley, a native of Boston, Massachusetts, and an employee in the U.S. Bureau of Agriculture, is best known as the founder of the Grange, a farm organization. As an early developer, he came to Florida and purchased land. He moved his family into his hotel, Island House, that was managed by his niece, Carolyn Arrabelle Hall. Kelley named the new community by combining her names into Carrabelle. Lumber mills began operations, people moved in, stores were opened, and by 1878 there was a post office. The Carrabelle, Tallahassee, and Georgia Railroad was opened to Tallahassee in 1893, the same year that Carrabelle was incorporated.

Eastpoint was founded as a combined economic and religious effort. In the mid-1890s a group of Nebraska families decided to migrate south. The group sent Thomas Brown to Georgia and North Florida to find a home for them. The latter-day explorer duly went and, on returning, reported his findings. The families rented two rail cars and arrived at Columbus, Georgia, in 1896. They bought a nearby plantation and established a communal Christian Commonwealth. The experiment was satisfactory, although the Brown family felt alienated. After visiting Florida again, Brown gathered his family, plus five other families, and two single men and left. They built three barges, and the thirty-four people (plus their animals) comprised a strange flotilla that successfully floated down the Chattahoochee and the Apalachicola Rivers. Reaching Apalachicola in eleven days, they purchased land across the bay where they disassembled the barges and used the wood to help build houses. The next year they were joined by Harry C. Vrooman, a Harvard graduate, lecturer, and Congregational minister who had been at Columbus. Vrooman organized a collectivistic organization called the Co-workers' Fraternity. Meantime, Brown concentrated on truck farming. He raised vegetables and sugar cane and sold syrup under the brand name Bay Croft.

Eastpoint lacked Apalachicola and Carrabelle's natural advantages and grew slowly. By the twentieth century it became significant as a fishing village and profited from the timber industry. Eastpoint would become the mainland anchor for two bridges, both named for politician Bryant Patton, built to Saint George Island, the first in 1965 and the second in early 2004.

From its founding Apalachicola became famous for its oysters and, later, for other shellfish—shrimp, crab, and scallops. A sponge industry lasted from the 1870s into the early twentieth century. A large variety of saltwater and freshwater fish was always available, and whether the objective was commercial or recreational the desire could be filled. The seafood industry began as a local noncommercial enterprise, but starting in the 1880s it became a full-scale industry that has given Apalachicola, Carrabelle, Eastpoint, and Franklin County a unique way of life. The industry has always been vulnerable to the competing forces of weather and of man. In the twentieth century William Lee Popham became Apalachicola's most flamboyant figure in the seafood industry, the development of Saint George Island, and recreation. Known as the Oyster King, his dramatic career is traced within this book.

Apalachicola and Franklin County in the twentieth and twenty-first centuries faced new developments. Unforeseeable circumstances altered the area and the nation—two world wars, other conflicts in Asia, and a long-lasting rivalry with Soviet Russia. Franklin County and the nation suffered through the 1930s, a decade-long economic depression. Yet, in 1935 the John Gorrie Bridge was opened and linked Apalachicola to the largest part of Florida.

The area boomed during World War II. The civilian economy recovered from the Great Depression, and the military maintained the Apalachicola Army Air Field. Camp Gordon Johnston, just east of Carrabelle, trained thirty thousand men in the art of amphibious warfare. The post–World War II decades ushered in a new era. At the century's end Apalachicola, free from the noise and congestion of city life, became increasingly attractive. The barrier islands with their dazzling white beaches, were magnets hard to resist. A new John Gorrie bridge was opened in 1989.

The state and The Nature Conservancy became active agents in purchasing land in the county. Meanwhile, private corporations and companies became more active. After Ed Ball, manager of the St. Joe Paper Company, the largest landowner in Franklin and nearby counties, died in June 1981, the company was reorganized into smaller units. One of them, the St. Joe Company, concentrated on land sales and developing environmentally sensitive tracts of land in Franklin, Gulf, Bay, and other counties. More and more people became temporary and permanent residents.

America's awareness of ecological problems found full reception in Florida, especially in the state's growing western counties. The concern triggered laws at all levels to protect the delicate balances of nature in Franklin County. Real estate prices rose as acreage and lots were in demand. Many people purchased older homes, remodeling them into attractive residences. Real estate companies vied with each other, and the St. Joe Company pursued a development plan on a grand scale. There was a strong desire to enjoy the benefits of sand and sea, but no one wanted the pollution of the environment. Controlling the flow of water on the tri-river system that emptied into Apalachicola Bay and the Bay itself remained unresolved for the states of Florida, Georgia, and Alabama.

Such was the challenge of the twenty-first century for Apalachicola and Franklin County: to preserve the beautiful and the pristine at all costs, while carrying out needed programs of protection, improvement, and modernization. The task would be difficult, but the alternative was unacceptable.

This 1703 French map names the sites: St. Joseph, Cide San Blas, Isle St. George, Isle St. Catherine and St. Marie d'Apalache. Courtesy of the Florida State Archives.

One

From Early Times to the American Period

Persons "earnestly desiring to flee from the hardships of depression, unemployment, hot summers, cold winters, floods, dust storms, drought, 'Hard Times,' and financial lack" should move to the Apalachicola area, William Lee Popham wrote in the bleak year of 1935. Popham—preacher, poet, novelist, Chautauqua lecturer, politician, oyster king, and promoter—died in 1953. Were he alive at the end of the twentieth century, Popham would have seen many of his dreams come true and others on the verge of being fulfilled. Yet long before Popham left his imprint, Apalachicola had been an important part of Florida's colorful past.

Apalachicola's maritime setting has dominated its history. A ship plying its way landward toward the north Florida coast would, on penetrating the shallow coastal waters of the Gulf of Mexico, first sight a land mass: the barrier island of Saint George. A narrow, elongated sliver of indented land containing 10,840 acres, it stretches some thirty miles and lies two to three miles off the mainland. At St. George waves roll onto broad white beaches that become sand covered dunes held in shifting place by sea oats and various coastal vegetation. Beyond that are palmetto and pine forests, magnolias, small hammocks of live oaks, plus the ubiquitous scrub oaks and bushes that grow in the porous soil. Wide tidal marshes characterize the bayside shoreline facing the mainland.

The western one-third of the island (2,300 acres) has historically been known as Little St. George Island and was divided physically from the larger, eastern portion by a passage known as West Gap or New Inlet. Periodic hurricanes caused the division, although silt filled in the gap from time to time and the islands became one. Permanent division came in 1957 when the United States Army Corps of Engineers opened Bob Sikes Cut (named in honor of Congressman Robert L. F. Sikes). The cut's purpose—shortening the time required for fishing boats to reach the open Gulf from Apalachicola—was achieved, but within a generation a more environmentally sensitive society would not have permitted the project.

The western end of Little St. George Island widens abruptly into an elbow, then narrows into a thin section of grasses, trees, and sand. Known as Cape Saint George, the elbow was the site of a lighthouse built in 1852. Periodic storms caused yet another division at the extreme western end of Little St. George Island. There a few acres, depending upon nature's caprices, varied between being joined and being separated.

Big St. George, or, more simply, St. George, has 4,039 acres and contains all of the island east of Little St. George. At the island's extremity, East Pass divides it from Dog Island, known on some late seventeenth century maps as *Isles Aux Chiens*. The origin of the name is unclear, but Dog Island's 2,000 acres extend seven miles and form a barrier island for the fishing and lumbering town of Carrabelle, founded in 1877. East Pass was not utilized extensively by commercial ships entering Apalachicola Bay until the last decades of the nineteenth century.

West Pass separates Little St. George Island from St. Vincent Island. Yet another barrier island, St. Vincent has 12,358 acres and the appealing winglike shape of a giant marine plowshare, gracefully and forever cleaving the waters of the bay and Gulf. St. Vincent Sound separates it from the mainland and opens on the west to the Gulf through narrow Indian Pass and widens on the

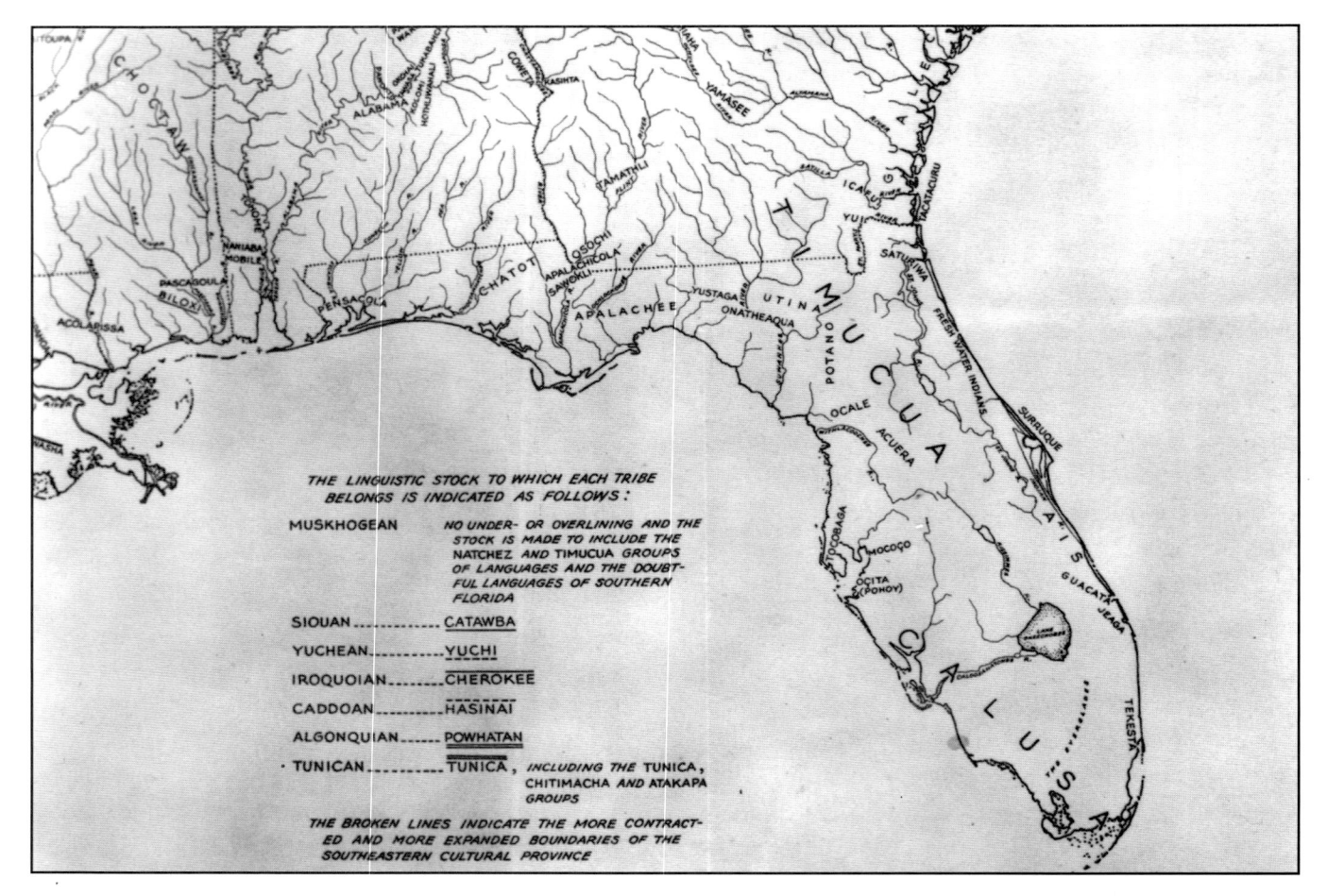

The Spanish explorers found about 8,000 Apalachee Indians farming, hunting and fishing in Middle Florida between the Apalachicola and the Suwanee rivers. Courtesy of the Florida State Archives.

east into the expanse of Apalachicola Bay. West Pass was the main commercial entrance to the bay during the antebellum period.

St. George Island, flanked by Dog Island and St. Vincent Island, dominates the barrier chain that protects the mainland. Appearing on early maps as "San Jorge," it and the nearby water and land formations were apparently named by early Spanish explorers. All of the barrier islands are bounded on the south by the Gulf of Mexico. On the mainland across from St. George Island the pearl gray and sometimes rust red Apalachicola River empties into the bay at a point of deep incursion and creates an inner expanse of water known as East Bay. The town of Apalachicola, founded in the 1820s, is situated on the river's western bank. Fresh river water flows into East Bay creating a true delta: a complex of swamps, bayous, winding creeks, and streams such as the East River, the Little St. Marks River, and the St. Marks River. To the east, Apalachicola Bay becomes St. George's Sound and extends past St. George and Dog Islands. Eastpoint, not formally established until 1898 and not connected to Apalachicola by a bridge until 1935, is situated on the mainland across the bay.

The large sweep from Indian Pass to beyond Dog Island is from one to fourteen miles in width and thirty-six miles long. Containing 204,320 acres, it is commonly called the Apalachicola Bay area. From the beginning, white visitors and settlers were impressed by the region's two major characteristics: the teeming abundance of marine life, especially oysters, and the shallow waters.

Apalachicola had its beginning in the early 1820s. Seat of government for Franklin County, established February 8, 1832, Apalachicola moved from small hamlet to significant shipping center and became Florida's leading port. One authority has transcribed the appealing word to mean "those people residing on the other side," and notes that the Apalachicola Indians spoke the Hitchiti language. They were of Muskogean stock and a part of the Lower Creeks. Other meanings have been suggested for Apalachicola (was it, as some contend, a Choctaw word connoting "allies?") which has various "official" spellings over a period of time.

By the time the Apalachicola River empties into the bay it has flowed one hundred six miles from the town of Chattahoochee located on Florida's northern boundary. Near there the Chattahoochee River moving southwest out of Georgia, joins the smaller, less powerful Flint to form the Apalachicola. By then the Flint River has come from its origins north of Albany, Georgia (194 miles from Apalachicola). The storied Chattahoochee River that originates in the hills of north Georgia, wanders southeast until it reaches a fall line near Columbus, 262 miles form Apalachicola Bay. It then plunges abruptly south, a watery demarcation between Alabama and Georgia, to intersect in Florida with the Flint

Alvar Núñez Cabeza de Vaca, one of the few survivors of Narvaez's 1528 expedition, wrote about the odyssey and mentions reaching an island that is believed to be either Dog, St. George or St. Vincent Island. Courtesy of the Florida State Archives.

and form the Apalachicola River. Seasonably, the Chattahoochee is navigable from Columbus to the sea, while the Flint is navigable from Albany.

Various other rivers, such as the sometimes navigable Chipola River flowing southeast through west Florida, feed into the Apalachicola. The fresh, constant current bears the river to the waters of the bay, and, early on, created there a strategic place for exporting and importing. Apalachicola became the major trading mart for an extensive agricultural kingdom whose hinterland included three large river valleys in Florida, Alabama, and Georgia. The strong pull of the river to the bay's saline waters soon carried the flow of commerce, and by the 1830s steamboats had the power to

Pánfilo de Narváez's 1528 expedition landed in the Tampa Bay area and moved north into the Apalachee country. These were probably the first Europeans in the area. Courtesy of the Florida State Archives.

In 1539 Hernando De Soto landed at Tampa Bay and marched north to the Apalachee-dominated region. Courtesy of the Florida State Archives.

DeSoto sent an exploring party west from the winter camp at Tallahassee and it is probable that the expedition along the Gulf sighted or visited the mainland and islands around Apalachicola Bay. Courtesy of the Florida State Archives.

navigate upstream and create a double flow of trade. The geographical setting determined the character and culture of Apalachicola. Franklin County had only a limited agricultural base but Apalachicola, although isolated from much of Florida, became the focus, the economic conduit for a large portion of the lower South. As a bustling trade center, the port was a door to cities throughout the United States and the world. It was an anomaly to much of Florida. Its people and their pursuits were different. Incongruously, Apalachicolans had not only the provincialisms and attractive manners of southerners, but a cosmopolitanism and world view that made them and their place unique.

As for the earliest settlers, some scholars estimate that aboriginal Indians from Siberia crossed the land mass linking Asia with North America at least forty thousand years ago. Some of them migrated to Florida and developed a life of surprisingly advanced culture. The earliest Spanish explorers found a Florida containing an estimated twenty-five thousand Indians. The Apalachees—about eight thousand farmers, hunters, and fishermen—were the major tribe of Middle Florida, the area between the Apalachicola and the Suwannee rivers. The less numerous Apalachicola Indians were concentrated nearer the coast. The identity of the first Europeans to reach Apalachicola or the barrier islands is unknown. Ponce de Leon discovered Florida in 1513 but returned to Havana, Cuba, without having gone that far west or north. Alonzo de Pineda was among other Spaniards who followed, and in 1519 was responsible for mapping the entire Gulf coast.

Pánfilo de Narváez was probably the first European to sight the area. After landing with an expedition in the Tampa Bay area in 1528, Narváez moved north into the Apalachee country. Experiencing strong resistance from the Indians, the invaders constructed rough boats at present-day St. Marks and headed west along the shoreline. Narváez and most of his men perished before their journey ended in Mexico, but Alvar Núñez Cabeza de Vaca, a survivor, recorded the cruel odyssey. He mentioned reaching an island near the shore and making a brief stop there. It is believed that the place was either Dog, St. George, or St. Vincent island.

In 1539 Hernando de Soto landed at Tampa Bay and marched north to the Apalachee-dominated region. De Soto sent an exploring party west in 1539 while he

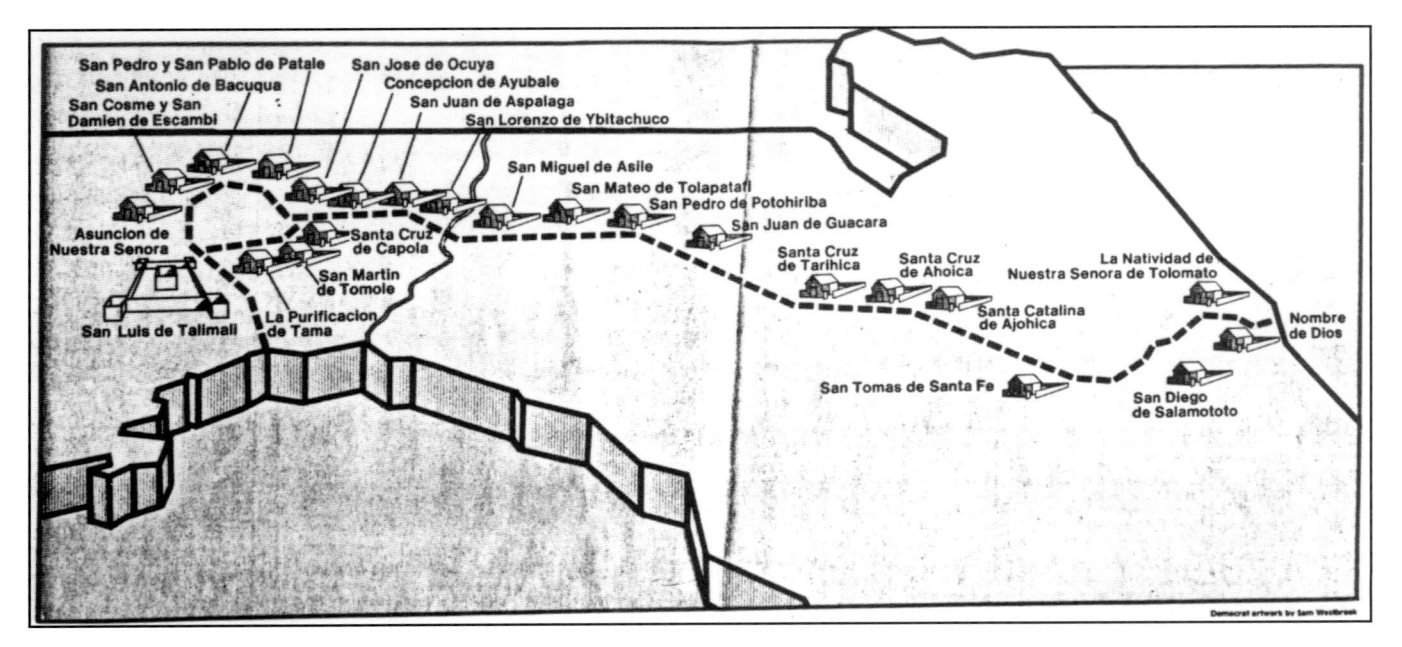

From their outpost of St. Augustine, the Spanish built missions up the Atlantic coast and inland to the Apalachee country. By 1680 there were over fifty missions, but none were located near the mouth of the Apalachicola River. Courtesy of the **Tallahassee Democrat.**

and his men wintered in the vicinity of the future Tallahassee. It seems probable that the expedition along the Gulf sighted or visited the mainland and islands around Apalachicola Bay. The Spanish settled the Atlantic coast but not the Gulf coast in the sixteenth century. On the east they faced French encroachments, but Pedro Menendez de Aviles repulsed them in a series of fierce engagements. From their outpost of St. Augustine, founded in 1565, the Spanish built missions up the Atlantic coast and inland to the Apalachee country. By 1680 there were over fifty missions but none were located near the mouth of the Apalachicola River.

In the last half of the seventeenth century Spanish Florida faced threats from the rising colonizing powers of England and France. The British moved from their base at Charleston, South Carolina, south and west to the Apalachicola and on the Mississippi River. In 1704 Governor James Moore of Carolina and his Indian allies raided the Apalachee Country wreaking havoc—missions were destroyed and the Apalachee Indians were enslaved or driven out. The French moved southward from their settlements on the St. Lawrence River and the Great Lakes into the Mississippi Valley. By 1682 Robert Cavelier Sieur de La Salle had discovered the mouth of the Mississippi River. He claimed the river and its vast environs for France and named the region Louisiana in honor of Louis XIV. Fearing French expansion to the east, Spain had Andres Arriola establish a tenuous strongpoint near Pensacola in 1698.

Ultimately, Spain and her Indian allies were unable to defend Florida, and it fell victim to international rivalry and wars of imperialism. A declining Spain lost out to the English and French. Time grew short for the House of Bourbon in 1733 when James Oglethorpe founded Georgia for the British. English power

Spain ceded the Florida peninsula to the United States by the Adams-Onis treaty of 1819, but the actual transfer did not occur until 1821. Courtesy of the Florida Department of Commerce.

Indians of Creek culture moved from Georgia and Alabama into north Florida and gradually became known as Seminoles or "runaways." Escaped slaves were welcomed by the Seminoles and an important relationship developed. Courtesy of the Florida State Archives.

increased, and in 1763 culminated in victory over France and her ally Spain in the French and Indian War (the Seven Years' War). The important Treaty of 1763 gave England territorial gains from France and from Spain the British got Florida, possessed by the Spanish for two hundred fifty years.

Florida did not flourish under British control but the new owners made St. Augustine the administrative capital of British East Florida and assigned Pensacola a similar role for British West Florida. In addition, English became the common language, place names were added, and the economy was improved. British rule in Florida only lasted twenty years and the Union Jack was hauled down after the American Revolution. Spain got Florida back as a result of her role as ally to the American colonies in their struggle for independence. Spain's second period of ownership was short-lived: from 1781–1819. In that year Spain ceded the peninsula to the United States by the Adams-Onis treaty. The actual transfer of control did not occur until 1821. The United States, anxious to acquire more contiguous territory, had made blatant encroachments. Americans defined Florida's northern boundary to their territorial advantage, complained that Florida was a harbor for runaway slaves, and denounced Spain for inefficient administration. Further, they criticized Spain for permitting Indian raids across the international border. Indians of Creek culture had made sporadic migrations from Georgia and Alabama into north Florida and gradually became known as Seminoles or "runaways." They also developed an important relationship between blacks, the Creeks, and the Seminoles in Florida.

Meantime, the United States became involved in the Napoleonic wars of Europe. The nation's motive for war was the result of European violations of American neutrality. Legitimate grievances were given added power by territorial ambitions (nationalistic Americans desired territory in Canada and Florida). The result was a declaration of war against Great Britain. Spain hoped that during the War of 1812 she could retain Florida and made alliances with the Creeks and Seminoles. Even so, the English used the Gulf coast as a military base. When the Creeks attacked the frontier of southwest Alabama, the United States retaliated and the Creek War followed. Andrew Jackson, with his frontier troops and Indian allies, crushed the Creeks at the Battle of Horseshoe Bend in Alabama. In the Treaty of Fort Jackson (1814), Old Hickory, now a military hero, imposed a humiliating treaty, forcing the Creeks to surrender extensive lands in southwest Georgia and Alabama.

Jackson extended his exploits to include ending British threats against Mobile by seizing and then evacuating Pensacola. From there he moved on to his brilliant victory at New Orleans on January 8, 1815. The war ended with the Treaty of Ghent on January 8, 1815 but Florida remained an issue of dispute. Spain could not control her province, and Jackson made a controversial return in 1818 that set off the First Seminole War (actually a continuation of the Creek War). His invasion was successful and while the origins were of doubtful legality, its accomplishment was the final pressure point that Secretary of State John Quincy Adams used to persuade Spain to give up Florida.

When the United States acquired Florida, what would become of Apalachicola, the barrier islands, and

Comte de Castelnau's drawing of the Creek or Muskogee town called Iola, or Iolas, on the Apalachicola River. Courtesy of the Florida State Archives.

much of the interior countryside was part of the Forbes Purchase. In 1776 three loyal Englishmen—William Panton, Thomas Forbes, and John Leslie—found refuge in St. Augustine. They had previously dealt with the Indian trade in South Carolina and Georgia. In St. Augustine they established the trading firm of Panton, Leslie, and Company. The company soon flourished in its economic relations with the Indians due to the owners' friendship with Alexander McGillivray, a gifted man, part white and part Indian, who had great influence with the southern Indian nations. Panton, Leslie, and Company transferred its headquarters to Pensacola and expanded its business operations. When Spain regained possession of Florida the efficient firm was permitted to keep its trading privileges. By 1802 John Forbes (Thomas's brother) and Panton's nephews,

After the United States' war with Britain ended in 1815, Spain could not control Florida and Andrew Jackson made a controversial return in 1818 that set off the First Seminole War. Courtesy of the Florida State Archives.

James and John Innerarity, were admitted as partners. The company continued to grow (one branch store was located twenty miles up river from Apalachicola Bay at Prospect Bluff), and began accumulating debts from the

17
Apalachicola and Franklin County, Florida

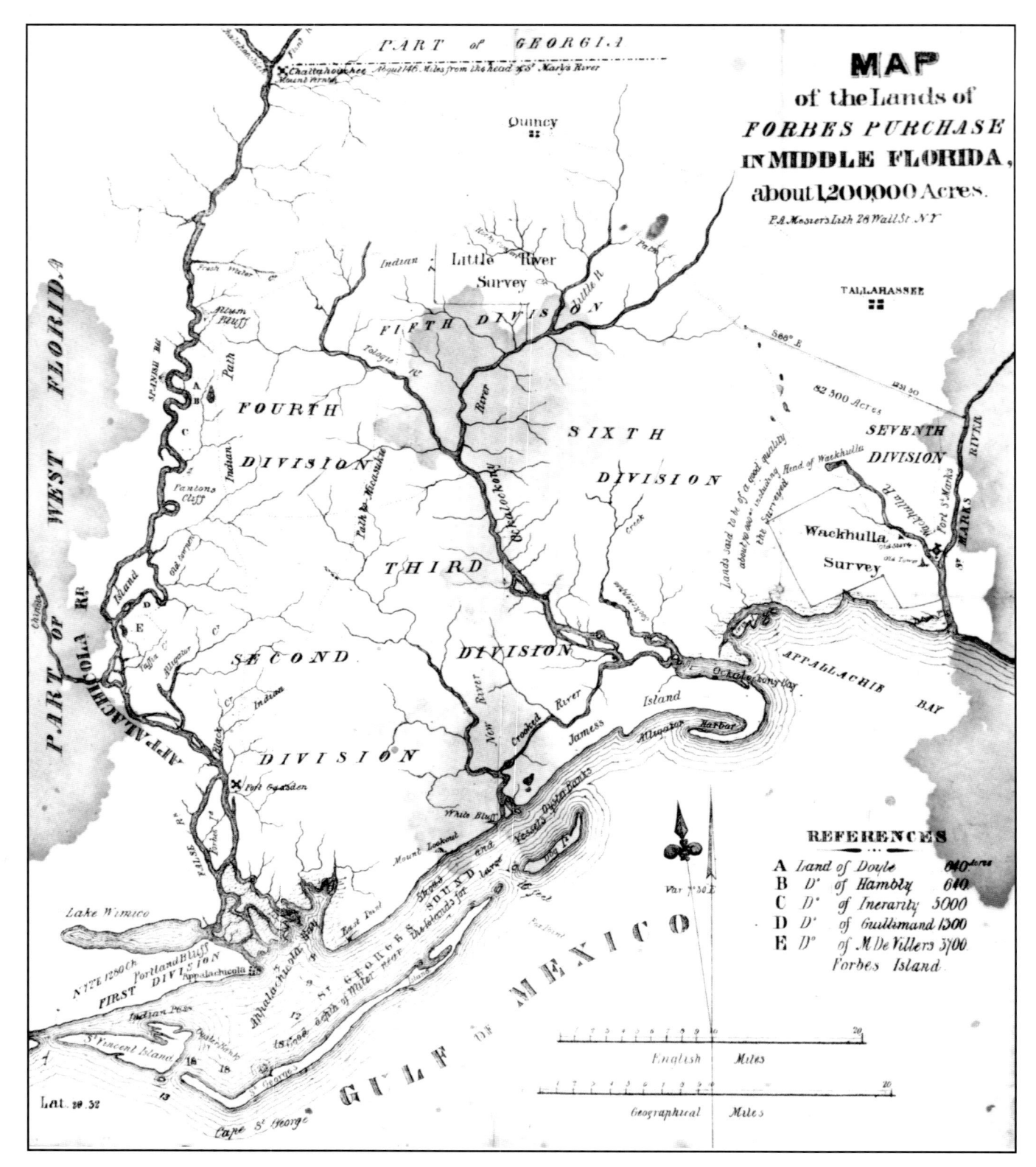

When the United States acquired Florida, John Forbes and Company claimed about 1.5 million acres of land. Courtesy of the Florida State Archives.

William Panton, Thomas Forbes, and John Leslie established an Indian trading firm in St. Augustine. The company, Panton, Leslie and Company, flourished and transferred its headquarters to Pensacola to expand its business operations. Courtesy of the Florida State Archives.

William Augustus Bowles, a British loyalist who married an Indian and lived with her people, was a business rival of Panton, Leslie and Company and schemed to bring the firm down. Courtesy of the Florida State Archives.

Indians. Jealous business rivals, including William Augustus Bowles, a British loyalist who later married an Indian and lived among her people, schemed to bring the firm down. The remarkable Bowles envisioned himself as heading an independent nation in Florida. His schemes in the 1790s damaged the property of Panton, Leslie, and Company but ended in Bowles's capture, escape, recapture, and death in 1796.

The United States was another economic rival to the firm. After McGillivray died in 1794 and William Panton in 1801, John Forbes headed the company. Unable to collect its debts, the firm received Spain's permission to take land as payment. The first transaction came in 1804 when the Indians turned over many acres of land between the Apalachicola River and the Wakulla River on the east and between the Gulf on the south and an unspecified line on the north. Shortly afterwards, the firm became known as John Forbes and Company. In another treaty of cession in 1811 the Indians expanded the initial grant and in 1818 the Spanish government ceded acreage to cover the company's losses during the War of 1812. The last agreement was nullified by the Adams-Onis treaty. With the retirement of Forbes, the task of management fell to the Innerarity brothers. Then in 1819 the firm's property was sold to Colin Mitchel, representing his three brothers and the trading firm family of Carnochan and Mitchel (headquartered in Savannah and Darien, Georgia). John Forbes and Company claimed about 1.5 million acres of land when the United States acquired Florida. That claim would be disputed as Florida and Apalachicola entered a new era.

By 1821 President James Monroe had set up a customs district that stretched from Cape Florida to the Apalachicola River and vessels began entering Apalachicola harbor through West Pass to take on cargoes of cotton. Courtesy of the Florida Parks Service.

Two

Antebellum Era Activities

DESPITE PROPHETS OF DOOM—THE Apalachicola Bay area was low and unhealthy, it swarmed with flies, gnats, and insects, and was surrounded by marshes and malaria—by 1821 President James Monroe had set up a customs district that stretched from Cape Florida to the Apalachicola River. Vessels began entering Apalachicola harbor through West Pass and taking on cargoes of cotton. With Charles Jenkins as collector, the District of Apalachicola was created in 1823 while he established his residence at the mouth of the river. A small settlement grew up and was described by an upriver Georgia newspaper, the Bainbridge *Southern Spy* of July 28,1829, as a village "rapidly improving. We think it will be a place of a great city in due time. Many of the eastern vessels now come there and bring with them many of the good *notions* of the Eastern people—and for which they can get in a few years, as much good Georgia and Florida sugar, as they wish."

Elsewhere the new territory of Florida (created March 30, 1822) had problems of its own. Because a permanent, centrally located capital was needed to replace Pensacola and St. Augustine, Governor William P. Duval, acting on the authority of the Legislative Council, appointed Dr. William H. Simmons of St. Augustine and John Lee Williams of Pensacola to select a site. Coming by land from the Atlantic Ocean port, Simmons rendezvoused in the fall of 1823 with Williams at St. Marks, an old Spanish settlement dating from a Spanish stockade of 1680. Williams had a much more difficult journey by boat and land from Pensacola. The men and their parties explored the surrounding area and finally selected Tallahassee, an overgrown Indian village and former site of a Spanish mission. Tallahassee, an Indian word meaning "abandoned fields" or "old fields," was officially named in 1824 and incorporated in 1825.

New towns began to rise in Florida as commercial and plantation centers, ports, and military bases. Trade increased at Apalachicola—coming downriver were hogsheads of sugar, lumber, staves, cedar, live oak timbers, hides, and cotton. By the spring of 1828 the steamboat *Fanny* penetrated to Columbus, Georgia and with increased trade, the settlement at the Apalachicola's mouth grew. Known at first as Cottonton, the name became West Point for geographical reasons and was incorporated in 1829. Neither the intendant (mayor), his four man council, nor the general populace liked the name and bombarded by petitions, the Legislative Council changed it in 1831 to Apalachicola.

Ownership of the Forbes Purchase land remained uncertain as the firm of Carnochan and Mitchel sought clarification from Congress. The company had difficulty selling its lands without clear title, and all the while, squatters were moving in. Mitchel and his partners petitioned the U.S. District Court of Middle Florida to validate their claim but were denied. As late as 1830 the status of Apalachicola, the barrier islands, and the entire Forbes Purchase was uncertain. Even so the creation of counties went forward—Jackson, Washington, and Franklin (with Apalachicola as county seat.) Legal status on paper did not immediately mean courts—county, common pleas, admiralty, superior. There were long intervals between court sessions, not to mention the absence of a jail, courthouse, or ways to control gamblers.

Yet growth continued, as Apalachicola expanded from the riverbank west and north and to the bay's

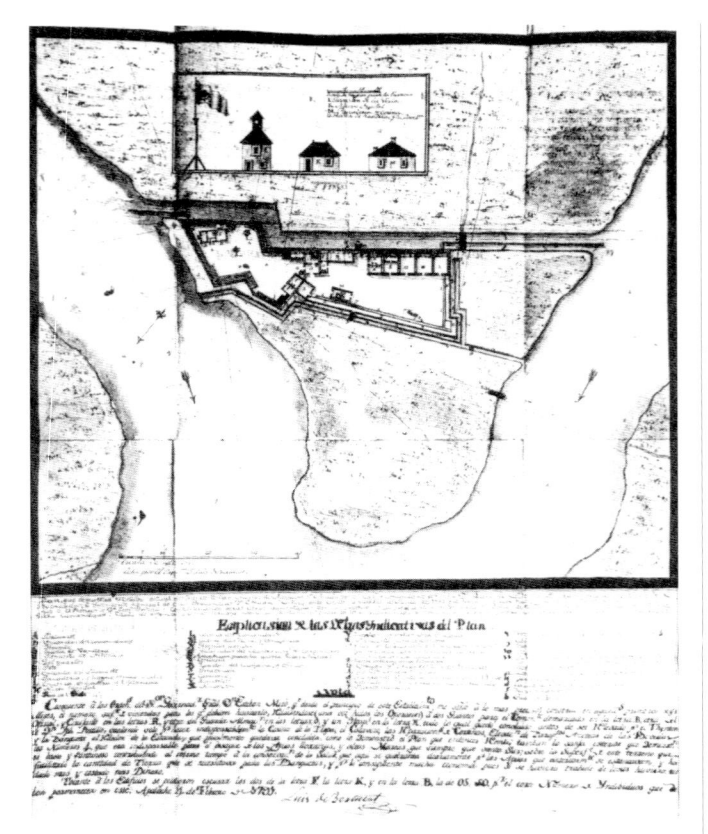

In the fall of 1823 Dr. William H. Simmons of St. Augustine and John Lee Williams of Pensacola rendezvoused at the old Spanish settlement of St. Marks and, acting on the authority of Governor William P. Duval and the Legislative Council, chose the Indian village of Tallahassee as the capital of the territory. Courtesy of the Florida State Archives.

Resenting the terms of the Treaty of Payne's Landing (1832) and led by Osceola, and others, the Indians resisted in the drawn out Second Seminole War (1835-1842). Courtesy of the Florida State Archives.

Coacoochee (Wildcat) was one of the Seminoles who led his people in resistance against the terms of the Treaty of Payne's Landing and the Treaty of Fort Gibson (1833). Courtesy of the Florida State Archives.

shoreline on the south. Wharves were built, and there was construction of churches, schools, homes, stores (dry goods, groceries, clothing), hotels, and warehouses. A real but macabre sign of permanence was the laying out of a cemetery. Still Apalachicola could not become a major port until physical order came, town government was reorganized, the Creek Indians in the Chattahoochee River valley were moved west, and the intense rivalry of the neighboring town of St. Joseph was overcome.

Indian removal proved to be one sided. As a territory, Florida had about five thousand Indians. The Indians had surrendered their lands in the Forbes Purchase and only a few lived around Apalachicola Bay. The Treaty of Moultrie Creek in 1823 shortchanged the Seminoles who traded their north Florida lands for

The Creeks had been removed from the state by 1837, and Apalachicola became the port of shipment for the farmers and planters who replaced them. Courtesy of the Florida State Archives.

inferior acreage in the south. Six of their leaders received small reservations north of the Forbes Purchase and near the Apalachicola River. The Indian Removal Act of 1830 passed by congress and implemented in Florida by the Treaty of Payne's Landing (1832) and the Treaty of Fort Gibson (1833) transferred the Indians to lands west of the Mississippi River. Resenting such terms and led by Osceola, Caocoochee (Wildcat), and others, they resisted. What followed was the drawn out Second Seminole War (1835—1842). The Indians were finally removed and a few disappeared into the Everglades, a sad ending to a conflict that discredited the United States and seriously slowed the growth of Florida.

Chattahoochee gained from its strategic site linking Alabama and Georgia with Florida, as well as east and west Florida, and a federal arsenal was built at the crossroads town. Courtesy of the Florida State Archives.

In Georgia, the Chattahoochee River Valley helped determine Apalachicola's prosperity. There and elsewhere in the state Indian lands were acquired from 1735

Richard Keith Call, protégé of Andrew Jackson, and powerful Florida politician, was the government's chief lawyer in the Supreme Court case involving the Forbes Purchase. Courtesy of the Florida State Archives.

to 1835 through a controversial series of agreements and treaties. Following the Treaty of Fort Jackson in 1814, the Upper and Lower Creeks made other cessions after 1818. By 1827, the Creeks had ceded all their lands in Georgia. After losing most of their lands in Alabama by the Treaty of Fort Jackson, the Creeks were forced into other unfair agreements and by 1837 had been removed from the state.

Apalachicola became the port of shipment for the farmers and planters who replaced the Indians. Merchants in developing river towns such as Eufaula, Alabama, relied on goods obtained from Apalachicola. None was more important commercially than Columbus. The Georgia town was incorporated in 1828 and soon established powerful economic ties with the Gulf port. If the Chattahoochee River was the connection for Eufaula and Columbus, the Flint was the link for the southwestern Georgia trading towns of Bainbridge and Albany. Bainbridge, site of an Indian village, became an exchange center and military outpost known as Fort Hughes. After Decatur County was created in 1823, the settlement was renamed Bainbridge and designated as the seat of government. Albany lay northeast of Bainbridge and was named for the capital of New York, a trading city on the Hudson River. Alexander Shotwell, a Quaker from New Jersey, purchased the town site, but young Nelson Tift of Connecticut was the real founder of Albany in 1836. That same year Tift and his companions brought a stock of goods up from Apalachicola on the steamer *Mary Emeline*. By 1837 Tift's firm had shipped its first cotton to the bay port and under his leadership, Albany became the county seat and leading town in southwest Georgia.

In Florida, Chattahoochee gained from its strategic site. Located where the Chattahoochee and the Flint joined to form the Apalachicola River, the town linked Alabama and Georgia with Florida as well as east and west Florida. A federal arsenal was built at the crossroads town and by the time it was incorporated in 1834, several Apalachicola merchants owned warehouses on its landings. Even so, Quincy, located nineteen miles to the

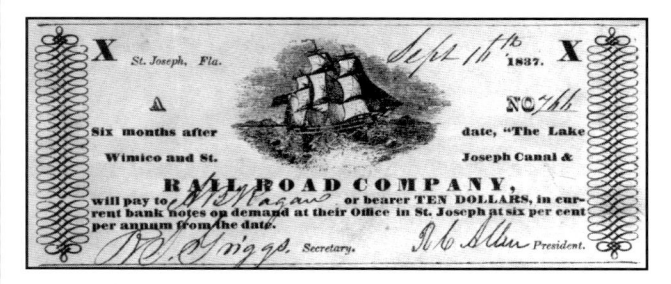

Money issued by the Lake Wimico and St. Joseph Canal and Rail Road Company, rechartered in 1835 from the old Chipola Canal Company of 1828. Courtesy of the Florida State Archives.

A replica of the engine of Florida's first railroad, the Lake Wimico and St. Joseph Canal and Rail Road Company, which opened in September 1836. Courtesy of the Florida State Archives.

east, was larger, the county seat, and the social and economic center for the prosperous agricultural county of Gadsden. Marianna, the major town in Jackson County, lay twenty four miles west of Chattahoochee. Located on the Chipola River, Marianna was founded in 1827 and carefully laid out by the Scotsman Robert Beveridge and his associates. The river wound southeast sixty miles before joining the Apalachicola fifteen miles above the bay. The Chipola's waters were clear and pure, but shallow, and falls impeded commercial traffic. Yet flatboats hauling cotton and logs to the bay generated considerable trade.

St. Joseph was chosen as the site for Florida's 1838 constitutional Convention. Courtesy of the Florida Parks Service.

A huge roadblock was opened for the region in March 1835. Colin Mitchel and his associates had pressed their land claims since 1831 but the U.S. government kept delaying. Finally John Marshall, speaking for the majority of the Supreme Court, ruled in favor of the claimants. In his last decision on the bench, the chief justice caused consternation to Richard Keith Call—the government's chief lawyer, protege of Andrew Jackson, and powerful Florida politician—by declaring that the Forbes Purchase was private property. The proprietors moved quickly to reform themselves as the Apalachicola Land Company. With visions of large profits, the company proposed a new town plan and reorganization for the carelessly structured village. Some older residents fearing they would be victimized, contemplated moving nearby to a proposed town on St. Andrew Bay outside the Apalachicola Land Company's property. Added inducements to move were the local shortcomings of a shallow bay, winding channel, all encompassing jungle growth, and generally unhealthy conditions.

The old Chipola Canal Company of 1828 was rechartered in 1835 and 1836 as the Lake Wimico and St. Joseph Canal and Rail Road Company. Most of its subscribers were natives of Apalachicola but there were a number from Columbus (men anxious to control their own port) and Tallahassee (wealthy speculators such as Benjamin Chaires, Florida's first millionaire.) Their plan was to have steamboats bound downriver turn west into the Jackson River that flowed into the Apalachicola at a bend called Pinhook. From there a few miles north of the bay, they would enter a large bayou known as Lake Wimico, cross it and connect with a canal that terminated at a port on St. Joseph Bay. The ships would thus avoid altogether the last and most hazardous miles of the journey downstream. Apalachicola would be bypassed and its economy strangled. Engineering problems made the plan unfeasible and it was replaced with one calling for a railroad. Construction was begun in 1836 and in September Florida's first steam railroad, running the eight miles from St. Joseph Bay to Lake Wimico, was opened. Construction of houses was

In the late 1830s a series of damaging hurricanes struck St. Joseph, but the final calamity came in 1841 when the town was decimated by a yellow fever epidemic. Courtesy of the Florida State Archives.

Purchasers of lots along Apalachicola's Water Street, in the land sales of April 1836, were required to build sturdy wharves and to construct three-story, fireproof, brick buildings. Courtesy of the Florida State Archives.

begun in the spring of 1836 and the new town of St. Joseph came into being.

An intense rivalry began. Dinsmore Westcott, who in 1835 had established the *Advertiser*, Apalachicola's first newspaper, moved to St. Joseph and set up the *Telegraph* (later the *Times*) to trumpet the new town's advantages. Cosam Emir Bartlett was brought in by the Apalachicola Land Company to edit the *Gazette,* and the fiery editor poured invective on St. Joseph and encomiums on the older town. Gabriel Floyd, port collector, tried surreptitiously, but unsuccessfully, to get the customs office moved to St. Joseph. No sooner was the latter incorporated in 1836 than the citizens there demanded that it be made the county seat. The Legislative Council agreed but the U.S. Senate overruled the change. As a compromise, Calhoun was created as a new county with St. Joseph as its seat of government. By 1838 the town was chosen as the site for Florida's constitutional convention and some Saints even suggested moving the territorial capital to St. Joseph.

Spokesmen for each town dealt wholesale in praise and denunciation. Much of the bile was genuine but it was partly exaggeration and citizens of the towns visited each other and were friendly. By 1840 the Saints pointed to their jockey club and race course but despite the show, survival depended on establishing a viable connection between St. Joseph Bay and the Apalachicola River. Lake Wimico proved too shallow for steamboats and Iola, a new settlement, was built on the river's west bank. The St. Joseph to Iola line, a second railroad, was begun. Before it was completed in November 1839 St. Joseph had begun to decline. Upriver tradesmen refused to pay shipping charges twice: on the railroad as well as on the steamboats. They declined to equate railroad fees with the lightering charges required in Apalachicola Bay. St. Joseph never matched Apalachicola in the shipment of cotton and the Apalachicola Land Company refused to work out any compromise.

In the late 1830s a series of damaging hurricanes struck St. Joseph but the final calamity came in 1841 when the town was decimated by a yellow fever epidemic. There were many deaths and survivors moved away, many returning to Apalachicola. The storms and sickness were much less severe in Franklin County. St. Joseph was practically deserted by the summer of 1841. The boom town died

There were 1,030 persons living in Apalachicola when the city issued this 6 1/4 note in 1840. Courtesy of the Florida State Archives.

Dr. Alvan W. Chapman settled in Apalachicola in the 1830s. He abandoned medicine for botany and earned a wide reputation through his research and scientific papers. Courtesy of the Florida State Archives.

after only a few years from a combination of overexpansion, hurricanes, and disease.

The triumphant Apalachicola Land Company held a series of lot sales in April 1836 but permitted local citizens to buy property before the public got its chance. The company had laid off its property well and in the best sense of civic good, provided the town with streets, squares, and lots for public use. Included were a courthouse, cemetery, and churches. The channel was deepened from anchorage to wharves. Purchasers of lots along Water Street fronting the river were required to build sturdy wharves and to construct three story, fireproof, brick buildings. H. A. Norris, a civil engineer from New York, drew the original plans. From its headquarters on the corner of Chestnut and Water Streets, company officials conducted a lively business. The Tallahassee *Floridian* of August 27, 1839 declared that "Apalachicola is a proud specimen of American enterprise."

Still, apparent success such as early lot sales in Apalachicola of $443,800, began to decline. A financial panic that hit the country in 1836 had struck hardest in Florida, a territory characterized by unsteady banking practices and crippled by the Second Seminole War. Apalachicolans came to distrust the Apalachicola Land Company and there were lawsuits over taxes, grumbling over high rents and short term leases, and inevitable attempts to foreclose lapsed mortgages. In Apalachicola the demands for lots dropped dramatically.

Conditions were worse in the rest of the Forbes Purchase where no mineral lands were discovered and where for the most part, agricultural lands were poor. Dreams of sea island cotton being produced on the barrier islands vanished. Fortunately for the company, the Forbes Purchase contained vast stands of virgin pine, while cypress crowded the swamps and various other trees, including live oaks, grew lavishly and in great profusion. Despite the presence of seemingly inexhaustible timber resources the company's expenses exceeded its income. Ever hopeful, officials continued to issue notices of public sales as late as 1843.

Apalachicola itself had to struggle to survive. A place of commerce, the town had little manufacturing and Franklin County had limited farming and therefore few planters and slaves or even small farmers. Apalachicola was a cotton town dependent on a crop produced many miles away and aside from local needs, satisfied the requirements of people far from its environs. Apalachicola had 1,030 persons in 1840, 1,562 in 1850, and 1,906 on the eve of the Civil War, although it was by then Florida's sixth largest town. The mayor and town council raised money by taxing real estate and businesses. There were sale taxes and special taxes as

Through his efforts to combat yellow fever and other diseases John Gorrie, a young Apalachicola physician, noted how a fever patient benefitted from a drop in room temperature. He invented an ice-making machine and developed a process for cooling a room artificially. Courtesy of the Florida Department of Commerce.

Apalachicola's geographical setting made it vulnerable to hurricanes. St. George and the other barrier islands always took the first storm surge—as in 1837, 1842, 1844, and 1850—and then the destructive rains, winds, and tides hit the mainland. One benefit was that a hurricane, usually called a gale in the nineteenth century, often deepened the harbor channel. Violent winds from a hurricane in 1851 washed away the lighthouse on Cape St. George. It was rebuilt but another storm in 1856 destroyed the beacon at nearby Cape San Blas. The destructive hurricanes caused the deaths of people as well as destroying ships, property, trees, and crops.

Crippling fires were sometimes the work of arsonists but also broke out for other reasons, including hurricanes. A fire company chartered in the early 1840s battled heavy odds. The town marshal required citizens to keep their chimneys repaired and businesses to possess fire buckets. After all the storms and fires Apalachicola rebuilt and expanded its interior and coastal shipping.

As a port Apalachicola developed a reputation that, depending on someone's point of view, was open and friendly or unrestrained and wicked. Besides their overworked town marshal, citizens depended on the services of all white males between eighteen and fifty to patrol the streets after nine o'clock each night. The patrol had wide arrest powers over all races and the right to whip slaves. At one point in 1837 the people petitioned congress for judicial aid. As late as 1839 there was neither a courthouse nor jail.

As a trading town Apalachicola had a number of banks beginning with the Commercial Bank of Apalachicola established in the 1830s. It is unclear how many actually opened but chartered in the antebellum era were the Bank of Apalachicola, Franklin Bank, Marine Insurance Bank of Apalachicola and branch offices of banks in other Florida towns and Columbus.

well as poll taxes on white males, free persons of color, and slaves who hired out their labor. The Irish were the leading immigrant group (most of them lived in a bucolic workingmen's section called "Irishtown") and were followed in number by the English, Germans, and Italians. Sicilians and Italians were the most numerous oystermen and fishermen. Sectional sophistication came from Pennsylvanians, New Yorkers, and New Englanders. Many of them were temporary residents who lived in Apalachicola only during the business season (fall to spring) and they controlled the port's shipping traffic.

A model of Dr. John Gorrie's ice machine, issued patent no. 8,080 in 1851. Courtesy of the Florida Department of Commerce.

The Western Bank of Apalachicola was chartered a month after Florida seceded from the Union.

Antebellum Apalachicola had two important men of science, John Gorrie and Alvan W. Chapman. A young physician from South Carolina, Gorrie was mayor and a strong spokesman for the Apalachicola Land Company. Through his efforts to combat yellow fever and other diseases, Gorrie noted how a fever patient benefitted from a drop in room temperature. He invented an ice-making machine and developed a process for cooling a room artificially. Unfortunately Gorrie died in 1855 and was never able to secure

Christ Church, organized in 1836, was chartered by the Legislative Council as Trinity in 1857. Courtesy of the Florida State Archives.

The white pine church was shipped in sections from New York and assembled in 1838-1839. Courtesy of the Florida State Archives.

enough financial backing to market his pioneering work in air conditioning. A native of Massachusetts, fellow physician and friend of Gorrie, Chapman settled in Florida in the 1830s. Noting the abundance of botanical specimens in the vicinity of Apalachicola he abandoned medicine. Soon his scientific papers and research brought him into contact with fellow botanists and earned him a wide reputation. His monumental *Flora of the Southern United States* appeared in 1860 and he continued his research until his death in 1899.

Cultural life was not neglected. A local library association was chartered in 1840. Novels were serialized and local poets published their works in the town's newspapers. Books could be purchased at several stores and the town had a full time portrait painter. There was an active local historical society as well as an agricultural society. In 1848 large crowds enjoyed contests of speaking skill and logic staged by the debating society. Few towns of comparable size were so well served by newspapers, some highly partisan although most were oriented toward commerce. The previously noted Bartlett's *Gazette* was the only daily paper published in territorial Florida during 1839–1840. Other pre–Civil War journals included the *Courier*, the *Apalachicolan*, and most important, the *Commercial Advertiser*, established in 1843. Whatever their quality at least the *Watchman of the Gulf* and the *Star of the West* had colorful names.

Some young people attended schools in other towns although Apalachicola had private schools by the

Although the Methodists held services as early as 1839, they did not organize until 1844. Courtesy of the Florida State Archives.

1840s. The best known was the Apalachicola Academy opened in 1848 by Samuel J. Bryan and his female assistant. For two terms of twenty-two weeks each, boys and girls attended classes that were conducted in separate rooms. Franklin County commissioners carried the division further by enclosing and dividing the playground.

Laws required revenue from the sale of public lands to be set aside for education but Franklin County did not benefit because it had no public land. To its credit Franklin provided education for poor people. Florida did not develop a true secondary public school system before the Civil War. Yet in 1860 Franklin County had four "common schools" with four teachers and 182 pupils. Support came in part from local taxation. A high percentage of young white boys and girls were literate but state law prohibited blacks from being taught to read and write. On occasion, educated blacks and whites violated the restriction.

Whatever its reputation for wickedness Apalachicola had a number of churches. First were the Episcopalians. Christ Church, organized in 1836, was chartered by the Legislative Council as Trinity in 1857. The Rev. Charles Jones, the first rector, held services in a white pine church that had been shipped in sections from New York and assembled when it arrived. Although the Methodists held services as early as 1839 they did not organize until 1844. In 1839 Methodist minister Peter Haskew divided his time between the Apalachicola Mission and the St. Joseph Station and filled his appointments in hotels and private homes (sometimes the Episcopalians loaned him Trinity.) Baptist churches, although formed in Florida in 1821 were not organized at Apalachicola until 1848. From the beginning black members were permitted freedom in the white church and were noted for their intelligence and piety.

The first Catholics were the Spanish explorers of the sixteenth century but regular church services came in 1845 when the Rev. Timothy Birmingham began serving churches in Columbus, Georgia and various missions, including one at Apalachicola. St. Patrick's was completed in 1853 under the leadership of the Rev. Patrick Coffey who had taken charge of the mission. Irish, Italian, and other families supplied the membership.

Fearful of slave insurrection, although Franklin County had only five hundred twenty in 1860, whites would not permit slaves to worship separately with their own pastors. Most southern denominations, including those in Apalachicola, held separate services for blacks in white churches under white supervision. At Trinity slaves occupied special balcony pews but heard the same sermons as whites. Black Baptists outnumbered whites by 1848 and had their own church. Local white pastors conducted the services with the assistance of black ministers.

Apalachicola's churches worked to improve community morality and by the mid-1840s the Apalachicola Temperance Society held regular meetings in the Methodist church. Temptations were strong and the editor of the Apalachicola *Commercial Advertiser* declared on April 11, 1846 that he sided with the teetotalers: "God give them the strength of resolution to resist the temptations they must encounter! Ice, sugar, wine, and Madeira!"

There was abundant evidence that the atmosphere in Apalachicola was at the very least convivial. Some of the flourishing hotels shocked the pious, although the hostels became more sedate as the town itself matured. Notable hotels included Mansion House where a band played in a flower–scented garden, Sans Souci, and City Hotel. The Mechanics & Merchants Exchange featured oysters and billiards and many hosted stately dinners, celebrations, and formal balls. The sporting crowd patronized hotel barrooms and their private rooms for roulette, poker, and faro. Depending on one's tastes and the size of their pocketbook, Apalachicola's hotels could accommodate their guests.

As will be seen, Apalachicola was emphatically a business town but there were diversions. There were well attended theatrical performances by the 1840s. Boat races drew spectators but horse races were more popular. A track, the Franklin Course, hosted an annual five–day meet where blooded horses from Florida and surrounding states raced for purses of up to nine hundred dollars and bettors put their money down. Apalachicola was part of a circuit that included surrounding towns. The meets, complete with jockeys dressed in racing silks drew fashionable patrons (and some not so fashionable).

Several military companies were formed in Franklin County—the Alaqua Guards, City Cavalry, Apalachicola Guards and City Dragoons. The units and interest in

The Franklin Course at Apalachicola hosted an annual five-day meet where blooded horses from Florida and surrounding states raced for purses up to nine hundred dollars. The meets drew fashionable patrons and bettors. Courtesy of the Florida State Archives.

them typified the martial spirit exhibited in other Southern towns and locales. The members provided the protection needed on the frontier (Apalachicola's units fought in the Second Seminole War) but mostly the members joined for the comradeship, love of military drill and competition, and to gain any political advantages that might accrue. Nowhere was the bristling display of military tactics and resplendent military dress more evident than during the Fourth of July celebrations. Without question Independence Day was the major holiday. It brought out besides competing military companies, representatives of various societies, clubs, fraternal groups, and even the City Hospital and the Marine Hospital. The Declaration of Independence was always read and followed by an Orator of the Day. There was a formal dinner hosted by one of the hotels and the formal toasts to the nation's heroes (mainly southerners such as Andrew Jackson), states, territories, towns, counties, the various virtues, and most importantly, to women occupied hours. Many celebrants had difficulty finding the banquet room's exit on the conclusion of the celebration.

Cruising the area's waterways, picnicking, swimming, outings to the barrier islands, especially St. George Island, helped pass the time. The bountiful area yielded impressive hunting and fishing rewards with minimum expenditure of effort. Some citizens might complain about their area but, save for the slaves, most thought they lived in paradise.

New crop cotton in November was a welcome sight and bales filled the warehouses and were frequently lined along Water Street until they could be loaded on steamships. Courtesy of the Florida State Archives.

Three

Commercial Activity

APALACHICOLA'S COMMERCIAL ACTIVITIES were fourfold: receiving goods from upriver producers, shipping goods upriver to merchants and individuals, exporting and importing goods in the coastal trade, and exporting and importing goods in the international trade. As a significant way station of deposit, sale, and distribution, Apalachicola bustled with activity during the winter and early spring. Then from late spring to late fall the town closed down and its permanent residents went into a relaxed hibernation. Non–permanent residents went back to the North and those locals who could afford it fled the lowland fever season for the upcountry and the mountains.

New crop cotton in November was a welcome sight and activity picked up. Bales filled the warehouses and were frequently lined along Water Street. Merchants operated cotton presses that compacted the unwieldy bales into sizes convenient for storing and shipping. Some complained of local conditions but most people, certainly the cotton buyers, welcomed the steady stream of steamboats that came in. There was such a stirring that in 1858 a Georgian wrote to his hometown paper (the Bainbridge *Argus*, March 10) about the port: "There is a good deal of 'Yankeedom' in this place....all hands are at work and always at it is the motto here."

Slaves and the town's few free blacks were important workers. Local and state laws pertaining to slaves although restrictive in language were only sporadically enforced. Free blacks competed with white laborers and so did slaves who hired themselves out, paid their masters part of their earnings, and kept the rest. In the cruel world of slavery being black was hard but life was better in Apalachicola than on cotton plantations. By 1860 the sectional crisis had reached the point that saw harsher slave laws enacted and free blacks who were transients (mostly sailors) were not permitted to come into town.

The harbor was vital to the town's welfare and was a subject of constant concern. West Pass, the most used entry point, accommodated ships drawing twelve feet of water. The vessels anchored three miles from town and were served by lighters. East Pass had greater depth but ships were forced to anchor ten miles from the wharves. The Apalachicola Land Company dredged the harbor in 1836. In the 1830s the federal government responded to petitions by appropriating funds to remove obstructions from the Apalachicola River and to deepen the channel in the bay and St. George Sound. Even so, silt deposited by the river kept the bay from becoming a deep–water harbor. Despite these impediments the port grew because much of its trade was coastwide and carried on in shallow draft vessels. In 1842 the port shipped 48,070 bales to domestic markets and 38,794 abroad.

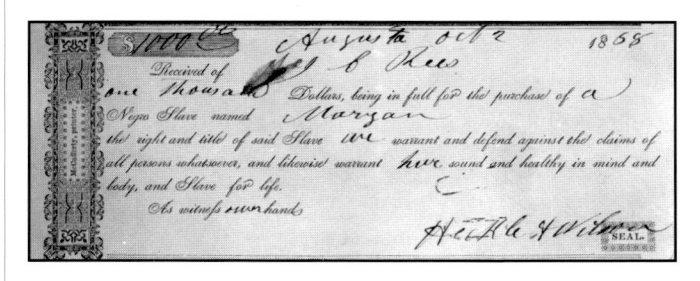

Slaves and free blacks were important workers, and life for blacks was better in Apalachicola than on cotton plantations. Courtesy of the Florida State Archives.

There were variations but the overall pattern was simple: tri-state farmers and planters shipped their bales to Apalachicola; there merchants or factors (who were paid commissions for their services) received, handled, and shipped the cotton. Sometimes the factors were bypassed and the steamboat took the cotton directly to a vessel in the harbor. The ships (square-rigged vessels of three masts, barks, brigs, and especially schooners) in the harbor had arrived earlier loaded with consumer goods. Schooners enjoyed wide use in the harbor as lighters and in the Cuba trade. The steamboats were also used in the coastal trade and as packets, lighters, and riverboats.

Typically a vessel arrived from New York on the first leg of a commercial odyssey. The second leg began with the departures from Apalachicola to Liverpool or a European port. The final leg began after the unloading abroad and the onloading of passengers and foreign goods for the return to New York. There were a number of differences in this pattern including a direct return to Apalachicola loaded with salt in ballast or manufactured goods. Local merchants often sailed to northern cities to select goods for their Apalachicola stores.

Because of its strategic location, St. George Island with its lighthouse was important to Apalachicola's economy. Federal money to maintain the building physically and pay for a keeper was appropriated annually and was a subject of much importance. Money was first appropriated in 1831 for a lighthouse and for placing buoys in the bay between the island and the river's mouth. Acquiring land for the light involved complicated negotiations with the Apalachicola Land Company (the federal appropriation required only that the lighthouse be built outside of the town's limits but within a radius of fifteen miles.) Port Collector Gabriel I. Floyd assumed a new responsibility as superintendent of lights. Floyd held out for building the light at Cape St. George but was overruled by financial considerations. Construction began at the western tip of Little St. George in the spring of 1833 and was completed by the end of the year. The $12,000 structure at West Pass was brick, sixty-five feet high, and had a dwelling house. It was poorly located and had a series of inefficient keepers, none of whom could keep the light lit. Collector Floyd was never satisfied.

As international trade increased, a deeper entrance was needed and in 1837 money was appropriated to build a lighthouse and dwelling on the western end of Dog Island. Construction was completed in 1838 and the forty-eight-foot-high light, which could be seen for thirteen miles, was more functional than the light at West Pass. At the latter Hiram Nourse became superintendent in 1842 and, backed by town fathers such as David G. Raney, sea captains, and the chamber of

This lumber schooner, taking on cypress at Carrabelle, probably departed for Liverpool or a European port, unloaded and took on passengers and goods for New York where some passengers and goods were unloaded and others were substituted for the trip back to Florida. Courtesy of the Florida State Archives.

commerce, sought removal of the useless West Pass lighthouse. Pressure paid off and in 1847 Congress appropriated $8,000 for a light on Cape St. George. The Apalachicola Land Company sold between six and eight acres to Samuel W. Spencer, the new superintendent. Ambiguity as to who actually owned the land was settled in 1847 when the Florida legislature deeded the land to the United States. Lanterns and lighting apparatus were taken from the old light house at West Pass and one at St. Joseph. Work on the beacon and dwelling produced a sixty-five foot structure. Lighted on

December 20, 1848, its beam could be seen fifteen miles at sea.

Trouble came with a new superintendent who, besides being physically sick, had to cope with a powerful gale in 1850 that damaged the structure. There was no breakwater protection and an even worse hurricane in 1851 sent Cape St. George (and other district lights) crashing down. Rebuilding was begun at the same site but the structure was increased to seventy–five feet, moved further inland, and given a stronger foundation. The structure was functional and served the added benefit of being a meeting place for social occasions and fishing and hunting outings.

Even the so called routine business of entering and leaving the port at Apalachicola was complex. The harbor pilots were top seamen. In their small, fast schooner, a pilot and his one–man crew cruised for up to two weeks or so off St. George Island waiting for customers. When more than one ship converged simultaneously a pilot could still bring in several a day. Leaving his companion with the schooner, the channel–wise pilot boarded the ship and giving decisive commands to the crew, brought the vessel safely in. The fee depended on the ship's draft and whatever its specific purpose, the harbor pilot guided it to the exact place for transferring goods. The possibility of fires added danger to the job.

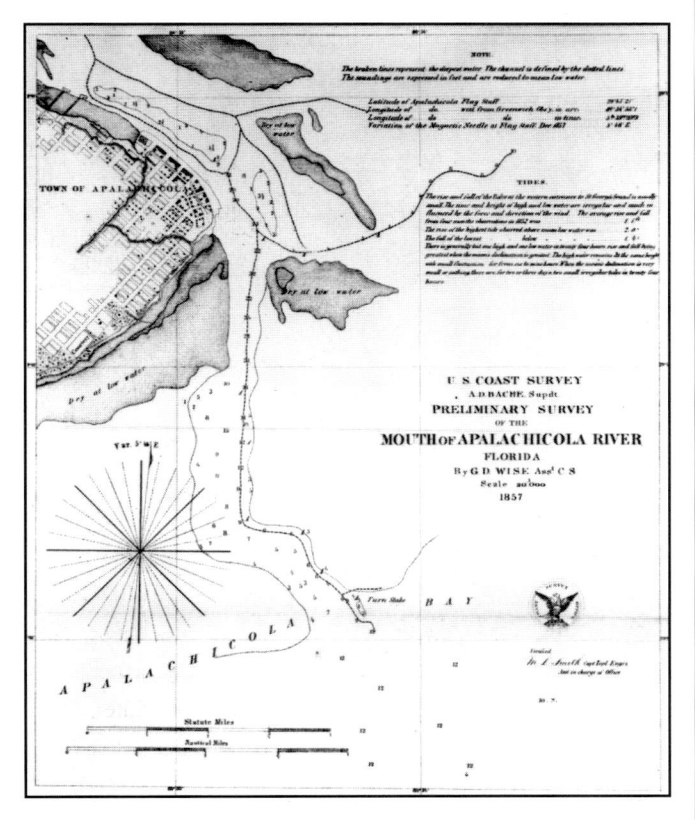

A lighthouse built on the western tip of Little St. George in 1833 was poorly located and in 1837 money was appropriated to build another on the western end of Dog Island. An 1851 hurricane sent the Cape St. George light crashing down and it was replaced by this 75-foot structure in 1852. Courtesy of the Florida State Archives.

Map of the mouth of the Apalachicola River, based on an 1857 survey by G. D. Wise. Courtesy of the Florida State Archives.

In general, the port's international trade was in foodstuffs (bananas, coconuts, spirits, and especially salt), while the coastal trade supplied manufactured goods. Food and drink also came from American ports but a bewildering variety of supplies—everything from ice to machinery—was imported from New England and the Middle Atlantic states. During the business season regularly scheduled packets, such as the Charleston and Apalachicola Line, followed a timetable that, far from perfect, served its purpose. Steamboats engaged in the domestic trade but their important function was to serve the Apalachicola–Chattahoochee–Flint river system. At least one hundred thirty steamers were on the rivers between 1828 and 1831 and sixty-four listed Apalachicola as their home port. Eight vessels were built in Apalachicola and twelve others along the Chattahoochee and Flint but most were constructed on the Mississippi and Ohio rivers.

The steamboats were designed for both freight and passengers. Most were side–wheelers because they were more powerful and maneuverable than stern–wheelers and could be docked more easily. The river system was dangerous: rocks and snags, fires (there were no holds and deck cargoes were vulnerable to sparks from the burning wood used as fuel), and explosions. Accidents were frequent and there was considerable loss of lives and much destruction of cargoes (usually inadequately insured or not insured at all—rates were understandably high). For example in 1840 six people were killed when the *Leroy's* flue collapsed between Chattahoochee and Iola. Apalachicola had three marine insurance firms before 1860.

River conditions determined the prices and the amount of trade and despite complaints about unfair freight rates and inflated costs, Apalachicola developed an extensive inland trade. Cotton was the most important commercial item but there was trade in timber, corn, rice, and tobacco. Still, the port's percentage of the cotton produced in the hinterland dropped from 80 percent in 1850 to 43 percent in 1860. A similar decline occurred in the shipment of other produce and some Apalachicola commission merchants were forced out of business.

In a decade of expanded commercial activity in the South, the decline could not be explained as one outsider tried in terms of an inert citizenry. The reasons were multiple and serious: low water caused by a lack of rain; inadequate attention to removing obstacles in the rivers; limited federal and state funding to dredge the harbor, which was filling up with silt; and most

At least one hundred thirty steamships were on the Apalachicola-Chattahoochee-Flint river system between 1828 and 1831, including the **Hardtimes** *shown at an Apalachicola wharf piled high with cotton and other goods ready to be put aboard. Courtesy of the Florida State Archives.*

important, increasing competition from railroads. Lines in Florida, Alabama, and Georgia were laid in the 1850s and significantly diverted traffic from Apalachicola. When newly opened textile mills in Columbus began using cotton from Muskogee and surrounding counties it reduced the amount shipped to Apalachicola. Franklin County had no diversified economy to ameliorate the crisis. There was no agriculture to speak of and little manufacturing. On November 25, 1856 the Bainbridge *Argus* noted with objective and deadly honesty, "Blow out the Flint and Chattahoochee rivers and what would be the condition of this flourishing city?" It would soon be deserted and its streets overgrown with sea weeds and bushes.

The undoubted potential of seafood could not be exploited because it was highly perishable and no real export market was established. The extensive oyster beds mainly enjoyed local fame, although by the 1850s such pioneers as John Miller and Joseph S. Lawrence were shipping some oysters in bulk in the shell. Timber offered another possibility of great wealth but transportation problems and inadequate industrial equipment and techniques held it back.

Sadly, the volume of trade in Apalachicola harbor dropped. At least two hundred eighty-seven vessels anchored there in 1842 alone and from 1837 to 1850 the

David G. Raney was one of Apalachicola's leaders. Courtesy of the Florida State Archives.

town was, after New Orleans and Mobile, the Gulf's third largest port. Newly opened cotton lands in Texas boosted Galveston to that position in 1860, although in that year Apalachicola's total value of goods handled exceeded $14 million. More of the cotton shipments from Apalachicola went to domestic markets rather than abroad but the port had an important international trade and shipped sea island (long staple cotton) to Europe in large quantities. Local leaders such as David G. Raney, William G. Porter, and Thomas G. Ormond never gave up on their town.

For that matter, political conditions that resulted in the Civil War kept Apalachicola from benefiting from governmental attention at all levels. Such attention would have improved transportation by roads and rails and possibly made connections with the town. Certainly the harbor and river would have received added efforts at improvement. The citizens were anxious to do what was necessary to continue and expand the town's prosperity. The same could not be said for the Apalachicola Land Company. Title rights were achieved by the Supreme Court decision of 1835 but bureaucratic delays tied up real possession of the almost 1.5 million acres until 1842. After the success of early lot sales in Apalachicola nothing went right for the company. Ten separate surveys established the fact that most of the property was practically valueless. Despite the timber, most of the lands were unsuited for agriculture and were lacking in any mineral resources. Over the years the company's organizational structure underwent many changes in personnel, the number of officers, and voting procedures. Facing rising debts and no income, the company paid its own debts in land and finally had to surrender land to pay county taxes. Finally, large parts of company property were sold at public auctions at the courthouses in Apalachicola and Tallahassee. Most of the sales were completed by 1861 and the land usually went for a few cents on the acre. The Apalachicola Land Company, with its wilderness kingdom larger than Rhode Island, finally failed because it had poor land and, as the southern expression had it, was land poor.

By 1860 Dog and Saint Vincent islands had been sold to private individuals. St. George had been surveyed in the late 1840s and again in the mid–1850s. The island had gone into a receiver's hands along with the Apalachicola Land Company but source titles were lost when the Franklin County Courthouse burned in 1874 and destroyed land records. No one was concerned with owning St. George until Reconstruction and then only a few persons expressed interest. Despite the failure of the land company and the reduction in town trade, Apalachicola had hope for the future in 1860. Yet the Civil War was about to begin and would bring changes of short and long term importance.

This Ordinance of Secession was signed on January 10, 1861 after McQueen McIntosh of Franklin County introduced a resolution declaring the right of secession and of the convention to take that step. Courtesy of the Florida State Archives.

Four

Civil War and Reconstruction

AFTER THE ELECTION OF ABRAHAM Lincoln and the Republicans in 1860 Florida followed the lead of South Carolina and on January 10, 1861, became after Mississippi, the third state to secede. At the secession convention in Tallahassee, McQueen McIntosh of Franklin County introduced a resolution declaring the right of secession and of the convention to take that step. Florida formally joined the Confederate States of America, formed in Montgomery, Alabama, in February. The state gave its allegiance to a new country under the leadership of President Jefferson Davis of Mississippi.

Florida's Democratic governor Madison Stark Perry was succeeded in October by another Democrat, John Milton, a native Georgian, who lived with his family on Sylvania plantation in neighboring Jackson County. Milton became a strong Civil War governor, protective of Florida's interests but loyal to the Confederacy. Some critics claimed his county's geographical proximity to Franklin County gave him an unusual interest in Apalachicola's welfare. In fact the town's strategic location made it a factor in both Union and Confederate strategy.

Anticipating war, Governor Perry began accepting militia companies for the state's defense in November 1860 and initiated the reorganization of Florida's state troops. In January, Florida used military force to seize the federal arsenal at Chattahoochee, Fort Marion at St. Augustine, and Fort Clinch on Amelia Island. The United States retained possession of federal forts at Pensacola and Key West throughout the war, although Confederate military actions at Pensacola almost caused the Civil War to begin in Florida instead of at Fort Sumter in Charleston's harbor.

Anticipating the war, Governor Madison Starke Perry began accepting militia companies for the state's defense in November 1860 and initiated the reorganization of Florida's state troops. Courtesy of the Florida State Archives.

In January Milton appointed William Chase commander of Florida's troops. Chase occupied Pensacola and prepared for battle. Then in February a legislative act established Florida's Civil War militia and made it subject to a six months' call to active duty. Once the Confederate congress established an army in March, General Braxton B. Bragg took command in the Pensacola area. Answering a call from the Confederate

Florida formally joined the Confederate States of America and gave allegiance to a new country under the leadership of President Jefferson Davis and his cabinet (left to right): Attorney General Judah P. Benjamin; Secretary of Navy, Stephen M. Mallory; Secretary of Treasury, C. S. Memminger; Vice President, Alexander H. Stephens; Secretary of War, Leroy P. Walker; President Davis, Postmaster, John H. Reagan; and Secretary of State, Robert Toombs. Courtesy of the Florida State Archives.

Answering a call from the Confederate War Department for additional troops, Florida supplied five hundred men who were mustered into service on April 5, 1861 at Chattahoochee arsenal and placed under the command of Colonel James Patton Anderson. Courtesy of the Florida State Archives.

After President Lincoln declared a blockade of all Confederate ports, implementation of the order followed, but it was 1862 before Apalachicola came under the jurisdiction of the East Gulf Coast Blockade Squadron. Courtesy of the Florida State Archives.

War Department for additional troops at Pensacola, Florida supplied five hundred men. They were mustered into Confederate service on April 5, at the Chattahoochee arsenal and placed under the command of Colonel James Patton Anderson. Company B was Captain William E. Cropp's Franklin Volunteers. Later the War Department's request for troops rose and Confederate authorities began enlisting soldiers directly instead of receiving them through the governor. Milton strongly dissented because he wanted to maintain the militia's integrity and keep the troops under the governor's control as a state army.

Governor Milton insisted on protecting the port of Apalachicola and the river system stretching into the interior of Alabama and Georgia. St. George, St. Vincent, and Dog Islands became the front line of defense. A blockade by Union forces was inevitable. To break it, construction of gunboats was begun in the hinterland, at Columbus and Saffold, Georgia. Obstacles were placed in the river and batteries were established at key places to prevent an attack on the interior. Union strategy called for a blockade and if possible, using Apalachicola as a base to send military expeditions up river. Geography made this difficult: the bay, the depth of the passes, the river channel, and the multitude of exits to the Gulf. The federal fleet's inadequacies also impeded enactment of the scheme. After President Lincoln declared a blockade of all Confederate ports, implementation of the order followed. Still it would be 1862 before Apalachicola came under the jurisdiction of the East Gulf Coast Blockade Squadron (EGCBS). The squadron's duties were multiple: capturing outbound and inbound blockade runners, destroying salt works, convoying, protecting Union sympathizers and "contrabands" (runaway slaves), and staging amphibious raids. The EGCBS's jurisdiction extended from Cape Canaveral on the east to St. Andrew Bay on the west and its ships were watchdogs of the eastern part of the Gulf, the northern coast of Cuba, and the Yucatan Channel.

On June 11, Lieutenant T. Darrah Shaw, commander of the steamer *Montgomery*, moved carefully through West Pass and appeared in the bay. There Shaw received a three–man delegation from Apalachicola who appeared under a flag of truce. He gave the locals an official statement announcing that Apalachicola was under blockade. Neutral and foreign ships were permitted several days to clear the port. Northern hopes that only one ship was needed proved unrealistic. Lieutenant Shaw had to guard the exits at St. Vincent Sound and Indian Pass as well as at St. George Sound and the eastern end of Dog Island. The largely ineffective blockade was improved in August when reinforcements arrived with the steamer *R. R. Cuyler* and its 111–man crew. Even so, the Union ships were deep–water vessels and their usefulness was limited. Protection for expeditions into the bay, the sounds, and to the mainland was beyond the blockaders' range. When prizes were taken, they had to be burned. Still, in the coming months more blockaders arrived, this time in the form of shallow–draft steamers.

All the while the people of Apalachicola strengthened their defenses. The buoys and markers and the lighthouse equipment at Cape St. George and Dog Island were removed. Appeals for military support to Governor Milton, who passed them on to Secretary of War Leroy Pope Walker, brought no results. Local men

Taking a blockade runner was a military assignment, a patriotic act, and a profitable endeavor. Seized ships and their cargoes became prizes of war that were sold and the proceeds shared by the officers and crew of the ship that took the prize. Courtesy of the Florida State Archives.

One of the duties of the East Gulf Coast Blockade Squadron was the destruction of the salt works that dotted the Florida coast manufacturing the salt necessary for the preservation of meat and the health of the troops. Courtesy of the Florida State Archives.

Protecting "contrabands" (runaway slaves) was another of the duties of the blockading squadron. This drawing shows the United States bark **Kingfisher** *picking up escapees off the coast near St. Marks. Courtesy of the Florida State Archives.*

formed four voluntary companies. A public subscription bought two cannons (thirty four pounders) from the state and a battery was erected on the waterfront. The main land defense was a state regiment, the Florida Fourth Infantry, mustered into service on July 1, 1861 and placed under the command of Colonel Edward Hopkins. A political enemy of Governor Milton, Hopkins was a hapless commander, scarcely drilling his troops and allowing dissipation and heavy consumption of alcohol. Later Methodist minister Simon Peter Richardson who served as chaplain, remembered in his book, *The Lights and Shadows of Itinerant Life* (Nashville, 1900, p. 172), "The general and all the field officers but myself drank."

On a larger scale Governor Milton's relations with Confederate Brigadier General John B. Grayson, commander of Middle and Eastern Florida, were better. Unfortunately, Grayson was in the late stages of tuberculosis. Meanwhile Colonel Hopkins decided to defend Apalachicola by erecting a battery, Fort Davis, together with a ramshackle barracks on St. Vincent Island. The battery was unable to prevent a federal force from entering Apalachicola Bay in August 1861 and burning the *Finland,* which was there to receive a cargo of cotton. The incident alarmed local citizens as well as Governor Milton who used it to obtain more defensive weapons from Confederate officials and the assignment of Navy Lieutenant August McLaughlin to the Apalachicola area.

The people were disturbed by the transfer of the port's defenses to St. Vincent Island. Camp Retrieve, about a mile from town, became the only protection. It was manned by a company of voluntary artillery and two companies of undrilled infantry, a total of under a hundred invalids and "exempts." There were only five other companies stationed along Florida's Gulf coast. The governor and various citizens sent pleas for help to Secretary of War Judah B. Benjamin. Milton did what he could: he provided for entrenchments and breastworks around the town's land approaches, got Hopkins assigned to St. Vincent Island, and put Colonel

Richmond F. Floyd in command at Apalachicola. The truth was that Confederate officials in Richmond assigned Apalachicola, as well as the rest of Florida, a place of low priority in the overall war effort. On his own initiative Milton got some of St. Vincent's men and cannons brought back to the mainland. Colonel Floyd restored discipline and instituted regular drills. Morale improved and the military force was increased. An artillery expert was brought in and military and civilian authorities cooperated in strengthening surrounding defenses.

Governor Milton clung to his idea of keeping the state militia independent of Confederate control. When the consumptive General Grayson died in October 1861, Milton tried to secure Colonel Floyd as his replacement but the assignment went instead to General John H. Trapier. Ineffective as a commander, Trapier at least got along with Milton. Across the Georgia line at Saffold (Decatur County) a plan to assume the offensive took the form of construction begun on the ill–fated wooden gunboat *Chattahoochee*. The first year of the war ended with an air of cautious optimism and a sense of unreality for Florida and the South. In Apalachicola there was price speculation but no real hardship. The Apalachicola River was open to people and freight. Supplies were becoming depleted but some luxuries were still available. The blockade prevailed off the barrier islands but it was still largely ineffective.

All of that changed soon. The Gulf Squadron assigned new ships to the area and the Union fleet's maneuverability and strength were increased. Soon there was a rise in the number of outbound and inbound ships that were captured. Taking a blockade runner was a military assignment, a patriotic act, and a profitable endeavor. Seized ships and their cargoes became prizes of war that were taken to Key West, dealt with by admiralty courts, and sold. Proceeds were shared by the officers and crew of the ship that took the prize. Ever the patriot, Governor Milton attempted to force blockade runners to bring in cargoes needed for military use rather than the more profitable luxury items such as dry goods, coffee, and cigars. The governor was correct in questioning the motives of those engaged in unregulated traffic but he could do little other than make verbal and written protests. At least Milton had the satisfaction of getting the remaining forces on St. Vincent Island transferred back to the mainland and Colonel Hopkins reassigned to Fernandina.

Although Governor John Milton wanted to maintain the militia's integrity and keep the troops under his control as a state army, the Confederate authorities began enlisting soldiers directly. Courtesy of the Florida State Archives.

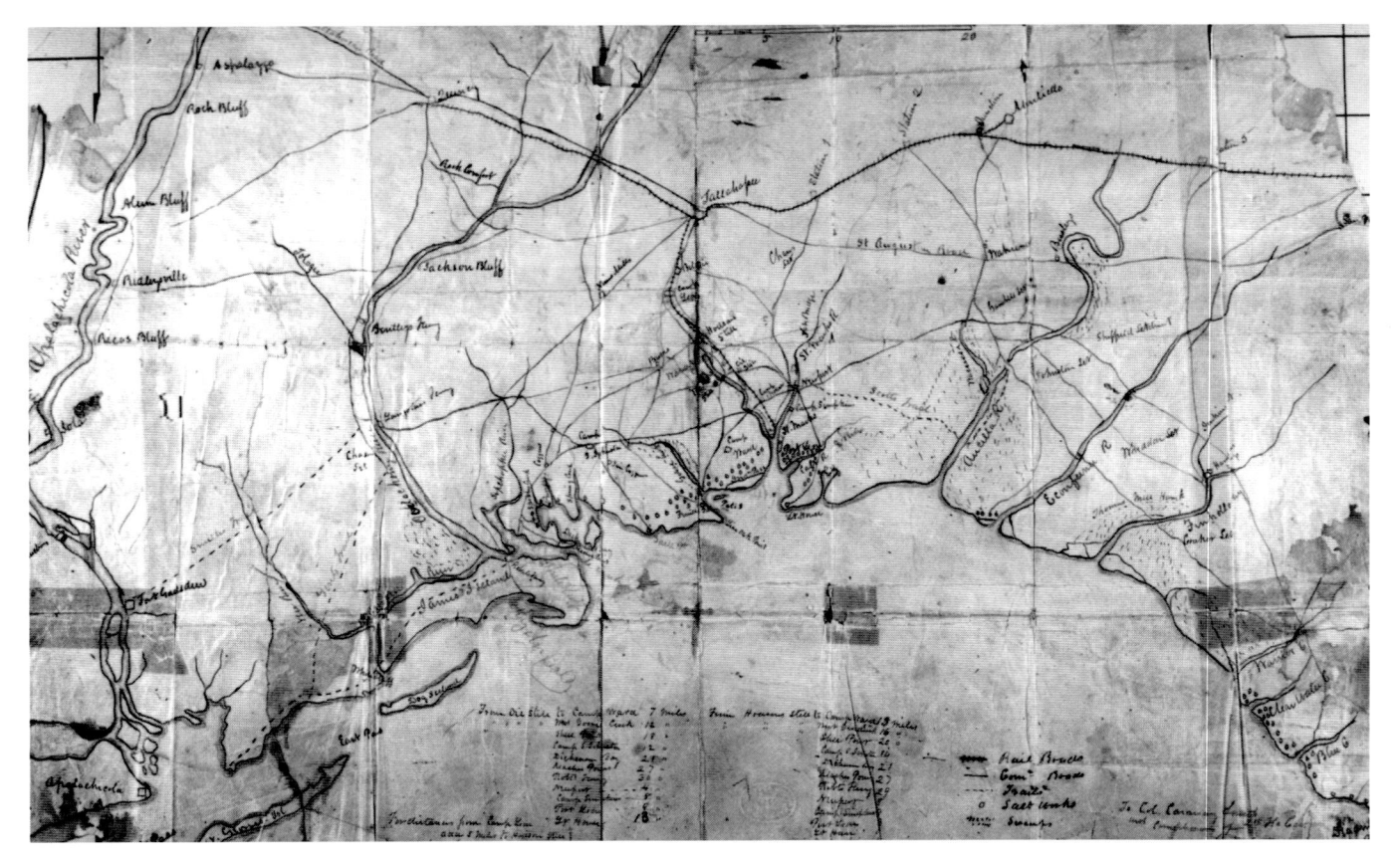

This mid–1860s map of the area from Apalachicola to Deadman's Bay, hand drawn by Union soldier George Washington Scott, has fine detail including roads, trails, and railroads. Courtesy of the Florida State Archives.

By November 1861 pressure from the EGCBS forced the remaining Confederates on St. Vincent to return to the mainland. Union forces took control of St. George and Dog Islands. No personnel were stationed there permanently but they used the islands and the lighthouses as recreational areas. Occasional landing parties came ashore to gather firewood and the Confederates countered with raids that failed in attempts to ambush them. In 1862 H. S. Stellwagen, commander of the steamer *Mercedita,* took over the EGCBS. The sailors found blockade duty monotonous and dull and they welcomed diversion. Supply ships bearing food, water, ammunition, books, pay, and letters from home were always welcomed. According to reports from Confederate deserters, Union sympathizers, and escaped blacks the blockade runners were still successful. Yet the blockade's net continued to tighten.

Apalachicola was directly affected by Confederate and Florida military policy early in 1862. Florida's secession convention reconvened and acting as a legislative body, ordered the dissolution of the state troops by March 10. Milton dissented sharply but without result. If Colonel Floyd's Fourth Florida regiment of state troops disbanded and failed to enlist in regular Confederate units, Apalachicola would be undefended. It was improbable that other troops would replace them. The civilian front deteriorated even as defensive positions declined. Few goods were available, prices were exorbitant, and many citizens began to "refugee." Like southerners in similar situations elsewhere, they began leaving for safer climes.

Governor Milton maneuvered desperately—governors in Alabama and Georgia did not respond to his appeal for troops and General Robert E. Lee at Savannah (commander of coastal defenses for South Carolina, Georgia, and Florida) regretfully declined a similar appeal. Lee asked for even more Florida troops to serve the Confederacy out of state. Milton then appeared personally at Apalachicola and persuaded some troops to stay beyond the March 10 deadline and others to go over into Confederate service directly. Otherwise, as Mayor J. N. G. Hunter put it, what would fifteen hundred women and children, wholly unprotected and unable to refugee, do? General Lee relented and ordered the assignment of troops left in Florida to Apalachicola.

It was too late. The secession convention made belated and unsuccessful efforts to aid Apalachicola leaving Governor Milton and Colonel Floyd no choice but to remove artillery defenses and other ordnance up river to Ricco's Bluff (fifty-one miles away). The town was evacuated by the military. Elsewhere in Florida Cedar Key was attacked and Fernandina and St. Augustine were occupied by the federals. Jacksonville was occupied for the first of four times by blue–clad soldiers. Over half of Apalachicola's civilians followed the military exit—bound elsewhere in Florida or to Georgia and Alabama. Apalachicola had no more than five or six hundred people left and some of them were openly supportive of the United States. A few men formed a military force but it had no power to resist an enemy.

Hearing conflicting reports about the situation in Apalachicola, Commander Stellwagen ordered Lieutenant Trevett Abbot to go to town and investigate. With a cutter, a whaleboat, and an armed crew, Abbot approached by way of West Pass. The Federals landed at a wharf with a flag of truce and were met by four men: the mayor, two others, and Father Miller, the Catholic priest. There were no Confederate military personnel present. Abbot demanded a surrender, promising no armed attack and protection of private property for those who took a loyalty oath. The townsmen replied that no one would take the loyalty oath other than some resident foreigners who had no stake in the war's outcome. At that, the federals returned to the *Mercedita*. After some consultation it was decided to launch an attack. Six boats (one bearing a howitzer) led the way and were followed by Stellwagen with two armed gigs. They moved directly on the port and captured a sloop in the harbor. Three boats were left at

Seafood became the vital staple during the war and it was both ironic and sad that the people of Franklin County could not avail themselves of the wild cattle and hogs that multiplied and flourished on St. George and St. Vincent Islands. Courtesy of the Florida State Archives.

Apalachicola and the other five moved upriver where they took five other vessels and towed the prizes to Apalachicola. Six vessels had been taken without a shot being fired.

All eight Union boats then converged on Apalachicola. The citizens waited but when no one offered to surrender the town, Stellwagen declared it captured. He then made a few conciliatory remarks. Commander Stellwagen reported later that the people had expected burning and pillage and were surprised at the gentle treatment they were given. The federals did not have enough troops to occupy Apalachicola permanently. Stellwagen knew that fishing helped feed the people and he allowed them to keep their oystering and other boats. Warning them that any future aid to the Confederacy would bring his men back to town, Stellwagen ordered a salvo of shrapnel fired into the air and he and his men returned to their ships.

The entire Federal encroachment took less that thirty six hours. The town had been captured and abandoned at the same time and for the rest of the war remained open and occupied by a greatly reduced civilian population and no military personnel. As the war continued the people had to find ways to survive. They proved practical and adept at coping with adversity.

Apalachicola became an outpost of the Confederacy. Guerrillas and scattered units of cavalry moved in and out for the rest of the war. Federal raiding parties appeared sporadically looking for Southern soldiers, cotton, and sailors from blockade runners. The civilians supported the Confederate cause although there were exceptions. For the most part loyalists kept discretely silent although some, such as native New Englander Dr. Alvan W. Chapman, were exceptions. Unionist Chapman and his Confederate wife reached an accommodation: she refugeed to her home in Marianna and he remained in Apalachicola. After the war they happily reconciled.

Life was difficult in Apalachicola and most people went quietly about their affairs. A public safety commit-

On February 20, 1864 the battle of Olustee (called Ocean Pond by Southerners) near Lake City occurred and resulted in the defeat of the northern forces. Courtesy of the Florida State Archives.

tee was appointed by Governor Milton to check on disloyal citizens but it accomplished little. More important was the weekly arrival of a steamer bearing a load of cornmeal. Starvation was avoided because of the large number of oysters and fish in the bay. Most days were routine although the Porter family alerted Confederates hiding in nearby swamps when Union raiders were in town by placing a rain barrel on their roof.

With Apalachicola neutralized, military action shifted upriver. In Georgia construction on the *Chattahoochee* went slowly but expectations remained high. Confederate officials considered the defenses at Ricco's Bluff and elsewhere deficient and in late 1862 placed batteries and obstructions (heavy chains that caught trees and debris and blocked transportation) at the Narrows above Apalachicola and at Rock Bluff below Chattahoochee. Some officers aboard the blockaders favored occupying Apalachicola and staging an expedition against Columbus but the plan was not activated. The blockade improved and there was no need for the incursion. A combined water and land skirmish by a few townspeople and some visiting Confederate troops against Union forces in the fall of 1862 became an easy victory for the North. At about the same time General Howell Cobb took command of the Middle District of Florida which included Apalachicola. Cobb completed the placement of river obstructions although Governor Milton appealed in vain to President Davis to order the occupation of the town, removal of the river barriers and the reopening of contact between the port and Columbus. To do so, Milton argued, was sound military strategy and would be a humane act for Apalachicola's citizens. Neither side had real reason for alarm. The blockading ships were incapable of going upriver, even had there been no obstructions and the latter prevented the *Chattahoochee* (even if it had been completed) from coming downstream.

As 1863 began some people in Apalachicola maintained secret contact with Confederate units but mostly they went through the processes of day to day living. The Union navy honored the requests of contrabands and some whites to be taken away. Sick civilians were treated on the ships by navy doctors and sometimes the physicians visited patients in town. Seafood became the vital staple and it was both ironic and sad that the people could not avail themselves of the wild cattle and hogs that multiplied and flourished on St. George and St. Vincent Islands.

Although the East Gulf Coast Squadron had been neglected when compared to other more glamorous commands, its strength was increased to seven ships. The results were evident in the number of ships captured and in the testimony of Thomas Orman, a pioneer settler and leading citizen who had purchased Little St. George Island in 1861. Orman denounced some blockade runners as selfish exploiters and claimed that they invited Union attacks and the possible destruction of Apalachicola—he noted that three out of four blockade runners were captured.

In 1863 Confederate forces faced crippling defeats on the battlefield. Southern civilians suffered shortages and the presence of Union occupation forces. Florida

In February and March 1865 most of the ships newly assigned to the blockading squadron went east to participate in what became the Battle of Natural Bridge, near St. Marks. The amphibious operation was poorly executed and if the resulting Confederate victory had little effect, it was a psychological boost to the South. Courtesy of the Florida Parks Service.

After Governor John Milton, deeply depressed over the loss of the war, shot himself to death on April 1, 1865, Abraham K. Allison, president of the Florida Senate, became acting governor. Courtesy of the Florida State Archives.

emerged as the principal supplier of salt. To supply the crucial item many saltworks of varying size were built along the coast from St. Andrew Bay to Cedar Key. The EGCBS was kept busy destroying them and though they were quickly rebuilt, in the end the squadron was successful. Other action came in 1863 when Apalachicola was raided and ammunition and cotton were seized. The Union raiders also picked up alarming rumors that the *Chattahoochee* at Saffold and the *Muscogee* at Columbus were nearing completion. In May the blockaders captured the *Fashion* and seized its cargo before it could make a run through Indian Pass. Planning to retaliate, Confederates towed the *Chattahoochee* downstream to the obstacles, hoping to pass them, proceed to Apalachicola and recapture the *Fashion*. The *Chattahoochee* was unable to pass the bar at Blountstown and in attempting to return upstream the inexperienced crew made errors in the engine room and blew it up. The result was the death of seventeen men (three of them drowned) and the sinking of the ship. The vessel was later raised and taken to Columbus for repairs. With the loss of the *Chattahoochee*, the Union forces were free to exploit their position. Before they could do so an out of season hurricane wrought non–partisan destruction to the area. Between twenty and thirty people were killed. The May gale also damaged property, destroyed trees and crops, killed farm animals, ruined saltworks, scattered Union coal supplies stored on St. George, and sank or crippled several ships.

By the summer the East Gulf Coast Squadron resumed its raids on the saltworks and made occasional entries into Apalachicola. Milton remained Apalachicola's champion. Although he could not per-

Brigadier General Edward M. McCook was sent to Tallahassee to receive the surrender of Confederate forces in Florida. He took formal possession on May 20, 1865 and raised the U.S. flag over the Capitol. Courtesy of the Florida State Archives.

Confederates paroled

With the end of the war veterans and people who had refugeed returned home and Apalachicola became a clearing house for captured machinery of war and cotton. Courtesy of the Florida State Archives.

suade the Confederate civil and military officials to reoccupy the town, they agreed with him that completing the ironclad *Muscogee* at Columbus was important. It could result in the ship's descending the river, relieving Apalachicola, and breaking the blockade. Highly improbable, the scenario was theoretically possible because the federal forces had been so successful, the fleet was reduced to three ships. Their crews spent much leisure time oystering, fishing, and enjoying the islands' beaches.

As 1864 began the townspeople had fewer supplies and felt abandoned. Some were shaken in their loyalty to the Confederacy. Because Apalachicola was neither within Confederate lines nor those of the United States, its citizens, if not suspect, were restricted in their travel to other parts of Florida. Whatever hopes locals had for deliverance by the *Muscogee* from the constrictive grip of the blockade ended when the heavy weight of the ironclad prevented it from being launched. Even so, Apalachicolans joined other Floridians in celebrating a notable southern victory in the winter of 1864. After occupying Jacksonville for the fourth time, Union troops began moving west across Florida hoping to divide the state, obtain supplies, and deprive southern armies of cattle and agricultural products. The strategy included setting up a separate state government for Unionists. On February 20, the battle of Olustee (southerners called it Ocean Pond) near Lake City occurred and resulted in the defeat of the northern forces.

Lieutenant G. W. Gift, erstwhile commander of the *Chattahoochee,* hoped to repeat the Olustee victory on a smaller scale in the Apalachicola area. The plan was for Gift and a small crew to stage a raid on the *Adela* at East Pass and the *Somerset* at West Pass and break the blockade. Increasing his mosquito fleet to seven and his men to one hundred and sixteen, Gift crossed into Florida. The Confederates bypassed the obstructions on tributary streams and successfully reached St. George Sound. They waited for a dark night to attack the *Adela*. When provisions ran low a detail sent to obtain more at

An Apalachicola reunion of Confederate soldiers in 1916 included, at far left, the grandson, son and daughter-in-law of later judge Roderick D. McLeod (back row at left). Courtesy of the Florida State Archives.

Apalachicola learned that Union sympathizers had betrayed them. Lieutenant Gift decided to abandon the venture but as his men retreated west across the sound, a storm approached. Gift's boat and another craft attempted to reach Apalachicola across the open bay while the remaining five boats hugged the shore, a cautious ploy that delivered them safely to the town. The two boats on the bay were forced by high waters to land at St. George Island. The boats and all their supplies were lost and the men barely reached shore. In Apalachicola a federal expedition met the bulk of Gift's command but the southerners were able to escape into the dense undergrowth. Two days later Gift and his men were picked up by two boats dispatched from Apalachicola. They were spotted by a Union craft and one of the boats was captured. Gift and the others escaped. Thus did the only real attempt to break the blockade (bold but probably foolhardy) end in failure.

Naval officials were disturbed enough by Gift's raid to strengthen the blockade and gather additional data on the estuarine system. As for the southern forces, at Columbus repairs on the *Chattahoochee* were almost complete, there was work on a torpedo boat and, to the surprise of many, the *Muscogee* was actually launched. All of that offset earlier news in the fall of 1864 that Brigadier General Alexander Asboth, a fearsome Hungarian fighting under the United States flag, had led a successful cavalry raid across north Florida. Asboth won the battle of Marianna over gallant but outmanned opposition before returning to his base at Pensacola with contrabands, prisoners of war, and livestock.

At the bay, American forces waited for a Confederate assault that never came. Meantime the EGCBS staged a successful raid up the Apalachicola, capturing prisoners and burning supplies at Ricco's Bluff. In February and March 1865, the blockading squadron was assigned more ships and most of them went east to participate in what became the Battle of Natural Bridge, near St. Marks. The amphibious operation was sound but poorly executed and if the resulting Confederate victory had little effect, it was a psychological boost to the South. Yet the Confederacy had lost the war and a despairing and realistic Governor Milton turned down a plan from Georgia's Governor Joseph E. Brown to stage a joint attack down the Chattahoochee–Apalachicola Rivers and break the blockade. Milton left his office in Tallahassee on what was supposed to be a routine visit to his plantation. Instead, the deeply depressed governor shot himself to death on April 1. No less than any soldier on the battlefield, Milton was a casualty of the war. He was succeeded by Abraham K. Allison, president of the Florida Senate, who became acting governor.

In short order the Confederate capital at Richmond was abandoned and on April 9, General Lee surrendered to General Ulysses S. Grant at Appomattox Courthouse in Virginia. In Georgia the citizens of Columbus were confronted with the powerful cavalry forces of General James H. Wilson. He and over thirteen thousand men had just staged a raid that took them out of north Alabama south to Selma where they won a battle and captured the town before moving east to engulf Montgomery. After the first capital of the Confederacy surrendered without a fight, Wilson's men moved east against Columbus. The city fought against overwhelming odds and was captured on April 16.

Wilson's men destroyed military installations. Two weeks from being battle ready, the hard–luck *Chattahoochee* was set on fire and left to drift helpless in the river. Wilson and his men moved next to Macon where General Howell Cobb capitulated on April 20. Governor Brown formally surrendered Georgia's remaining military forces in early May.

Florida was in the department of General Joseph E. Johnston, commander of the Army of the Tennessee. Johnston signed a convention of surrender with General William T. Sherman in North Carolina on April 26. From his Macon headquarters General Wilson sent Brigadier General Edward M. McCook to Tallahassee to receive Florida's surrender. McCook arrived in the capital, paroled prisoners, and took charge of government property.

In Franklin County the citizens could not believe the Civil War was over. The remaining three ships of the East Gulf Squadron were removed in early June when a military post was established at Apalachicola. The much disliked General Asboth arrived from Pensacola with black and white soldiers and took charge of 944 bales of cotton. Apalachicola was a broken down, decaying town. Yet soon buoys were placed in the harbor and the lights at Cape St. George and Dog Islands were put back in operation. Veterans and people who had refugeed returned home. Apalachicola became a clearinghouse for captured machinery of war and cotton. Certain properties were seized including 1,560 acres on Little St. George Island although the ownership was only temporary. Asboth soon yielded his command to Colonel S. S. Zulavsky of the Eighty–Second U.S. Colored Infantry.

Some Union forces vacated the town in late July. One New York soldier who hated the Gulf coast heat was happy to leave. He could not understand how anyone could live there but admitted that the levee was covered with bales of cotton, the wharf was crowded with people, and there was little ill will. Units of the black Eighty–Second remained at Apalachicola until September 1866. There were few racial incidents and, in fact, various soldiers were disciplined for leaving their posts to socialize in town. The population which had always included northerners and natives of other countries, was cautious about the future. Lack of capital was the big problem but the river, the bay, and the town were still there. The fish and oysters were as plentiful as ever and the region's timber was virgin. The war had come to an end and that alone offered reason for hope.

After the war Apalachicola and the country turned once again to maritime commerce, especially the shipment of cotton from these Water Street warehouses. Courtesy of the Florida State Archives.

Five

After the War

BECAUSE FRANKLIN COUNTY HAD LITTLE pre–war farming, there was no post–war agricultural destruction to recover from. Apalachicola and the county turned once again to maritime commerce, especially the shipment of cotton. The commercial potential of the fishing and timber industries were deferred to the future and the barrier islands' recreational possibilities remained local. Apalachicola achieved a surprisingly easy transition to peacetime conditions and there was even temporary prosperity. Yet the development of a deep water port never occurred. East Pass and West Pass, despite local efforts, never received adequate state or federal funding for significant improvements and the limitations of a shallow harbor remained. Had the funds been appropriated, the area's future would have been different. As it was, the irony of history would prove cruel: Apalachicola, with river access to the heartland of the Deep South and with the Gulf offering unlimited national and international trade, became isolated. An inadequate road system (lack of a bridge across Apalachicola Bay until 1935 diminished contact even with the rest of Florida), the absence of railroads, and insufficient support for improving the harbor and river system meant steady deterioration.

As for the islands, from the Civil War to 1900 there were several owners of St. George Island and Little St. George Island. Thomas Orman and his family owned most of Little St. George and George Sinclair held at least one–third of St. George. When Sinclair went broke his brother William Sinclair bought it at a public auction for $20. Benjamin Curtis emerged as the major owner of Dog Island. St. Vincent Island was sold at public auction in 1868 for $3,000. The purchaser was George Hatch, former mayor of Cincinnati and a banker who had married the widow Elizabeth Wefing of Apalachicola. Her son George F. Wefing lived on the island with the Hatches. After Hatch died in 1875 there was litigation over debts and who owned St. Vincent although Elizabeth Hatch achieved control in 1887. She sold the island in 1890 to former Confederate general Edward P. Alexander and his estate held it until 1907. In that year

In 1907 Dr. Ray V. Pierce, a patent medicine manufacturer from Buffalo, New York, became the owner of St. Vincent Island. Courtesy of the Florida State Archives.

Dr. Pierce and his family used St. Vincent Island during the winter months and converted it into a game preserve, importing sambar deer, zebra and other exotics. Courtesy of the Florida State Archives.

Dr. Ray V. Pierce, a patent medicine manufacturer from Buffalo, New York, became the proprietor. He and his family used the island during the winter months and converted it into a game preserve, importing sambar deer (native to India) to go with the plentiful indigenous animal life. Except for the brief interim in the 1920s, St. Vincent was part of the Pierce estate until 1948.

The war was lost but Franklin countians took heart immediately after the Civil War. Transition and recovery seemed certain. The Freedman's Bureau, a federal agency established to aid blacks in their adjustment to freedom, returned property without litigation to its original ex–Confederate owners. The area's cos-

In 1866 Apalachicola shipped more than 100,000 bales of cotton. That year at least 135 large vessels entered Apalachicola. Courtesy of the Florida State Archives.

mopolitan heritage reduced sectional and racial discord and while the Democratic party controlled politics, personality rather than political affiliation determined local elections. Protestant sects held numerical superiority in religion but ethnic groups provided diversity and there were numerous Catholics and Jews. Soon blacks set up their own churches.

Socially, Apalachicola never returned to the wide open ways of the antebellum era. Even so, if a more narrow interpretation of morality prevailed, held over was respect for one's privacy, and people concentrated more on recovering from the war than on policing their neighbor's conduct. Still a local ordinance reinforced a state law that closed stores on Sunday and applied to all.

Local businessmen, old and new, reopened or opened stores and resumed economic contact with Columbus merchants in the cotton trade. In 1866 Apalachicola shipped more than a hundred thousand bales of cotton. A line of steamers cleared port every two weeks for New York. That year at least one hundred thirty five large vessels entered Apalachicola. Henry Brash, a native German, arrived in 1865 to open a store that dealt in sponges, lumber, and real estate for the next forty years. By 1867 river traffic had five steamers making weekly trips to and from the port, trade picked up with New Orleans and, nearer home, with Tallahassee and Quincy. The bright picture changed quickly though. Navigational inadequacies caused a drop in trade. A new bank in Apalachicola languished because of the increasing political problems of Reconstruction. Competition from east–west railroads north of Florida (especially the Atlantic and Gulf Railroad that linked Bainbridge and Savannah) diverted trade from the port. Local entrepreneurs were devastated and by 1869 the economic boom was over. Apalachicola was a place of such limited trade that the occasional arrival of a steamer from upriver brought a crowd of curious townsmen to the wharf. No relief was forthcoming and by 1876, the acclaimed Centennial

In 1882 the Pennsylvania Tie Company was sold and renamed the Cypress Lumber Company. Under the local management of A. S. Mohr, the company's importance for Franklin County lasted into the 20th century. Courtesy of the Florida State Archives.

A. B. Tripler's Pennsylvania Tie Company moved logs down the Apalachicola River in rafts of 150 cypress logs or more, and something like 250 feet in length, to be cut into cross-ties. Courtesy of the Florida State Archives.

James N. Coombs triumphed over the seeming handicaps of being from Maine, a Union army veteran, and a Republican to establish a store and this sawmill in Apalachicola in the early 1880s. Courtesy of the Florida State Archives.

Apalachicola and Franklin County, Florida

Year, the people of Franklin County had little to celebrate.

George Sinclair was an example of adversity. He bought his St. George Island property back from his brother for $500 and paid $20 to erase the claims of a private company. Shortly, Sinclair died and his family took over until the island property was obtained by Horace H. Humphries in 1881 who bought it at public auction. He gained 4,980 acres for $20. Still, the hope that springs eternal became reality in the rise of the timber industry. As early as 1870 the firm of Snow, Richards, and Harris had a lumber mill and it was this expanding industry that quickened the economy and helped revive Apalachicola as a port.

Earlier efforts in the lumber business had failed due to the human problems of mismanagement and lack of money and to the natural problems of fires. Now, these were overcome especially by A. B. Tripler's

The Coombs family lived in the town's most impressive house, built by George H. Marshall, Apalachicola's premier builder. Courtesy of the Florida State Archives.

The supply of timber from the area's swamps and forests seemed endless, and the market worldwide. Courtesy of the Florida State Archives.

Local leaders including John G. and George H. Ruge led a drive to secure a railroad in the mid-1880s to ship lumber, oysters and fish to northern and western markets. Courtesy of the Florida State Archives.

Pennsylvania Tie Company that cut crossties from cypress logs easily obtainable in the Apalachicola River swamps. The company was sold in 1882 and renamed the Cypress Lumber Company. With headquarters in Maine and under the local management of A. S. Mohr, the company's importance for Franklin County lasted into the twentieth century.

James N. Coombs triumphed over the seeming handicaps of being from Maine, a Union army veteran, and a Republican to establish a store and sawmill in Apalachicola in the early 1880s. He had various partners, northerners and southerners but none more important than Charles H. Parlin. The latter had precisely the same background as Coombs and together the two joined forces and expertise to establish what became the Franklin County Lumber Company. Parlin and his wife Elizabeth Grady of Apalachicola, moved twenty two miles west to the new town of Carrabelle where the lumber company had its mill. Coombs was a businessman of rare talent who had other financial interests including banking. He was faithful to his party but turned down offers to run for governor and devoted himself to his family and to business. Locals easily forgave him his birth, over which he had no control and his politics, which in a Democratic state was no threat. He became a leading citizen. It seemed fitting that the Coombs lived in the town's most impressive house, built by George H. Marshall, Apalachicola's premier builder.

Other mills of note were the Kimball Lumber Company and C. L. Storrs and R. F. Fowler's operation. By 1890 the town of Carrabelle was the center of sawmills and a naval stores industry of importance. The supply of timber from the area's swamps and forests seemed endless and the market was worldwide. Europe and South America demanded hewn logs, Mexico needed railroad ties, and northern markets wanted sawed pine lumber and shingles. New Orleans was the primary market for cypress lumber. Apalachicola's shipping capabilities were strained beyond capacity and there was a major drive to make it a deep–water port.

Efforts to obtain private, state, and federal money to deepen the channel from the bay's entrance to the mouth of the Apalachicola River and to the city wharves, and to remove snags and overhanging trees from the river met with some success but there was never enough money. From 1877—1888 most of the lumber was shipped through West Pass and funds to deepen it were never appropriated. After 1888 commerce shifted to East Pass, Dog Island Cover, and Upper Anchorage where the water was deeper, permitting larger vessels to enter. Both Carrabelle and Apalachicola used the pass. The problem was that lumber had to be lightered twenty miles across the bay and along St. George Sound, a treacherous and expensive process. Local business leaders such as Coombs and Grady, as well as the Ruge brothers, John R. and George H., and W. T. Orman, led a drive to secure a railroad. As the terminus for a rail line, Apalachicola could not only ship its lumber but begin to export oysters and fish to northern and western markets.

In 1885 a group of townspeople secured a legislative charter for the Apalachicola and Alabama Railroad. The state provided a generous grant of land and the

J. E. Grady operated a ship chandlery and grocery store next to a bank. Courtesy of the Apalachicola State Bank.

As the timber industry increased so did the amount of money in circulation, but Apalachicola remained small. Courtesy of the Florida State Archives.

With more money in circulation the town could afford some of the items available in Hoppe's Jewelry Store. Courtesy of the Florida State Archives.

incorporators planned to build northward, crossing the Pensacola and Atlantic Railroad in Jackson County, and extending to the Alabama line to make connections there. The needed funds could not be secured and the line was never constructed. Desperate Apalachicolans, led by John F. Grady, president of the Apalachicola Board of Trade, worked with officials in Columbus and other river towns to obtain federal money. Despite legislature memorials, pressure on local congressmen and the congressional Committee on Rivers and Harbors, and surveys by the U.S. Army of Engineers, an insufficient sum of $20,000 was obtained. In 1900 the Apalachicola and Columbus Deep Water Association was formed but its lobbying activities also failed.

There were three doctors and a dentist, all of whom operated drugstores. Courtesy of the Florida State Archives.

Until this structure was built in 1892 to house public records, the forty room Curtis House was a full-time hotel and part-time theatre and courthouse. Courtesy of the Florida State Archives.

There was even talk of separating from Florida, joining Alabama and getting that state to make Apalachicola a deep–water port. The plan generated little other than talk but the activity led to an expanded movement for an intracoastal waterway that would achieve large significance later. Besides the natural passes, some people advocated making an artificial cut across St. George Island. Although never serious rivals of Pensacola for the shipment of lumber, Apalachicola and Carrabelle had an industry that remained a mainstay of the county's economy for decades.

In the 1880s Apalachicola was a somewhat shabby, somnolent town. If possible, hinterland agriculture had declined. At 1,791 persons, the population was less than it had been in 1860. The town had few hygienic services but many unpaved streets. Local hauling was accomplished by slow moving drays (they also doubled as hearses). The timber industry increased the amount of money in circulation but Apalachicola remained small. People bought their meat daily from Philip Schoelles, the leading butcher. Cool lager beer was available at

FULLER HOTEL.
S. JENKINS, Prop.
APALACHICOLA, FLORIDA.
Rates, $2.00 per Day. Cuisine First-class. First-class Rooms and a First-class Service. Porter meets all Steamers.

There were two Apalachicola hotels run by blacks. The Fuller Hotel was run by Mary Aldin Fuller and her husband until his death, and then by Mary until her death in 1905. Courtesy of the Apalachicola State Bank.

Members of one of the town's black organizations, Hannah's Court H. J. J., No. 11, lined up for a portrait. Courtesy of the Florida State Archives.

A. F. Meyer's saloon and groceries at A. J. Murat's store. Other merchants included John Cook, H. L. Grady, R. H. Porter, and George F. Wefing. There were three doctors and a dentist, all of whom operated drugstores and a handful of lawyers competed for business. The forty–room Curtis House was a fulltime hotel and part–time theatre and courthouse until a structure for housing public records was built in 1892. There were a number of newspapers but the most important was the *Times* established by Henry Walker Johnston in 1866.

Gathering oysters at low tide. Courtesy of the Florida State Archives.

A local photographer beside mounds of oyster shells. Courtesy of the Florida State Archives.

Homes on the outskirts of Apalachicola, provided for black mill workers. Courtesy of the Florida State Archives.

Blacks occupied the status of second class citizens, and segregation, including separate schools, was institutionalized. Courtesy of the Florida State Archives.

A hurricane in 1873 toppled the lighthouse on Dog Island and it was replaced by a new one, shown here under construction on the mainland, a quarter-of-a-mile off the sound and known as Crooked River lighthouse. Courtesy of the Florida State Archives.

In addition to the lighthouse four beacons protected the ships in St. George Sound. Courtesy of the Florida State Archives.

Johnston continued as editor until his death in 1922. He was succeeded by his son, Herbert K. "Duke" Johnston who became a great promoter of the region and especially of St. George Island.

Blacks were worse off than the whites but they persevered. They established black churches and, no less than whites, enjoyed baseball, picnics, and going on excursions. The town's two–man police force had racial equality: a black and a white. There were two hotels run by blacks, the Spartan Jenkins (which catered only to whites) and the Fuller, run by Mary Aldin Fuller and her husband. When he died she took over and operated the hostelry until 1905 when her death was memorialized by an outpouring of black and white tributes to her at the African Methodist Episcopal church. Blacks occupied the status of second class citizens and while segregation was institutionalized, vindictive racism was not a problem. Black citizens enjoyed St. George Island, maintained personal relationships with whites and were such recognized leaders of entertainment that when whites held a dance, especially a square dance, they hired black musicians. Several black music makers (Theodore Jones, Sam Hill, and William Henry Hall) became local celebrities because of their skills with the fiddle, triangle, accordion, and tambourine. In a time of hard work and little money, square dances added pleasure to life.

Twenty–two miles east of Apalachicola the Carrabelle River empties into Saint George Sound. The river is formed about four miles from its mouth by the confluence of New River and Crooked River. Directly across the sound, about six miles, lies Dog Island. On the mainland to the north swamps and forests were home to cypress and other timber, as well as snakes, alligators, deer, bear, and other wild animals. Land and

Investors, both northern and local, obtained several state railroad charters in the 1880s but financial difficulties interfered and it was 1893 before the Carrabelle, Tallahassee, and Georgia Railroad Company completed a line to Tallahassee. Courtesy of the Florida State Archives.

In 1873 Oliver Hudson Kelley founded a town where the Carrabelle River enters St. George Sound. He built the Island House hotel managed by his niece Carolyn Aarrabelle Hall, and it was in her honor that Kelly named the community: Rio Carrabelle. Courtesy of the Florida State Archives.

water birds, migratory and native, were in profusion. Part of the area was called Tate's Hell, named for Cebe Tate of the Sumatra community who got lost there in the 1880s but emerged later to tell a story of being in hell. Saltwater and freshwater fishing were good at the mouth of the Carrabelle and the site was a favorite camping spot for hunters and fishermen before the Civil War. By 1855 a few settlers, notably McGregor Pickett for whom Pickett's Harbor was named, had moved in. Because of the natural harbor (deeper than Apalachicola's making East Pass a better entry than West Pass), it was inevitable that a town would be established there. The emergence of the lumber industry speeded the process. Despite a crippling hurricane in 1873,

Naval stores, lumber and seafood were exported from Apalachicola, Carrabelle and Eastpoint by steamships like the Rebecca Everingham, *reputed to be one of the most beautiful boats on the Apalachicola River. She was built at Columbus, Georgia in 1880, and her home port was Apalachicola. She burned in 1884. Courtesy of the Florida State Archives.*

Eastpoint was founded under the leadership of David H. Brown (back row left) and his family who came there with others in 1896. Courtesy of the Florida State Archives.

Naval stores, shown here on the Carrabelle waterfront, added to the local economy when Hampton Covington established a large export company in the late 1890s. Courtesy of the Florida State Archives.

With the aid of David Brown, Harry C. Vrooman bought a large tract of land and set up a cooperative colony, the Co-Workers' Fraternity, at Eastpoint. Workers owned their own land, but all profits from lumbering, fishing, and manufacturing, such as this cane syrup mill were shared. Courtesy of the Florida State Archives.

The founders of the community at Eastpoint had started an earlier collective in Georgia. After their decision to move south, they constructed two barges, loaded up their belongings and began the voyage down the Chattahoochee River. They used the wood from the disassembled barges to build their homes. Courtesy of the Florida State Archives.

Oliver Hudson Kelley founded a town where the Carrabelle River enters St. George Sound. The lighthouse on Dog Island, toppled during the hurricane, was replaced by a new one, built on the mainland, a quarter-of-a-mile off the sound and known as Crooked River lighthouse (finally put into operation in 1895).

A native of Massachusetts, Kelley moved to Minnesota where he farmed. Later he worked as a clerk for the U.S. Department of Agriculture and won fame as the founder of the Patrons of Husbandry, better known as the Grange. The order included women and promoted improvement for farmers through social activities and cooperative economic endeavors. In the Midwest the order became a political force but not in the South where the Democratic party brooked no divisive forces that would threaten white supremacy and a return to

The steamship Crescent City *made Eastpoint a stop on its daily trip to Carrabelle, delivering supplies, mail and passengers. Courtesy of the Florida State Archives.*

The Eastpoint post office opened in 1898 and soon there was a school and a church. Courtesy of the Florida State Archives.

Three of these Eastpoint students celebrating George Washington's birthday are daughters of David H. Brown. Courtesy of the Florida State Archives.

Picking strawberries on David Brown's successful truck farm, about 1900. Courtesy of the Florida State Archives.

The Flatauer building, built by Gilmore & Davis of Tallahassee, was part of the economic surge based on timber and the recognition of the potential of the seafood industry. Courtesy of the Florida State Archives.

Republican rule. The Grange was especially active in the 1870s and early 1880s, attracting thousands of farm families.

The Grange existed in Florida but not in Franklin County and Kelley's interest there was as a land speculator and developer. Kelley saw the Gulf coast's possibilities for commercial shipping and for seafood and timber. He believed correctly that the area's weather and beaches were natural attractions for vacationers and permanent residents. In 1877 Kelley bought 1,920 acres from Benjamin Curtis, owner of Dog Island, as well as other property and a sawmill. Kelley moved his wife and four daughters to the community where he built Island House hotel. It was managed by his niece Carolyn Aarrabelle Hall who was a national officer in the Grange. More important to the people Kelley enticed to the area was Carolyn's ability to cook and her good looks and outgoing personality. Kelley named the community in her honor: Rio Carrabelle. The small town grew with the timber industry and soon boasted a general merchandising store, a post office, and a newspaper (the *Gazelle*). A ferry service was established with Apalachicola and lasted until 1929.

Kelley and various investors attempted to establish rail connections with Tallahassee and provide the lumber industry with an outlet to Jacksonville. If a proposed thirty–eight mile line from Tallahassee to Thomasville, Georgia, was built Carrabelle would also have a connection to Savannah and northern markets. As the Gulf terminus, Carrabelle would open New Orleans, Cuba, and South American ports to Middle Florida and South Georgia. Joined by northern investors and a few southerners, Kelley and others obtained several state charters for lines in the 1880s but financial difficulties interfered. Finally, the Carrabelle, Tallahassee, and Georgia Railroad Company completed a line to Tallahassee in 1893. A severe national depression followed and prevented an extension to Thomasville. The line was sold in 1902 to the Georgia, Florida, and Alabama Railway Company. The plans were of less immediate success than hoped for but the railroad had an important economic impact.

Later, Kelley and his family moved to Washington, D. C., where he maintained his Carrabelle interests until his death in 1919. The town progressed, moving from a population of 482 in 1890 (it was incorporated in 1893) to 923 in 1900. Hampton Covington established a large naval stores export company, adding a flourishing turpentine market to the town's lumber mills and its growing seafood industry.

For years Eastpoint was a geographical description of the land that lay across the bay from Apalachicola but there was no town there. It was the connecting point for Apalachicolans headed east to Tallahassee and other places. Scattered settlers lived there before the Civil War. Cat Point, the area's southern extremity, was four miles from St. George Island and marked the end of Apalachicola Bay and the beginning of St. George Sound. A town was founded under the leadership of David H. Brown and his family who came there with others in 1896. Brown had gone with his wife Rebecca Wood and his infant son, Herbert G., from his native Virginia in 1884 to the Great Plains. There he affiliated with other rural families who were members of the Farmers' Alliance. The Alliance was a farm group that specialized in promoting the cause of farmers through social, educational, and economic activities (including cooperative buying and selling). In the West and South members of the Alliance later became the nucleus of the People's or Populist party. After the national election of 1896 which saw the Republicans triumph over Democrats and Populists, the latter declined as a political force. Discouraged, Brown and his friends were determined to leave Nebraska for the South.

Brown was sent into the region to find a suitable site. After visiting Georgia, he came as far south as Apalachicola where he talked at some length with several people, especially with Samuel E. Rice, Sr., a large landowner also prominent in the seafood business. Brown returned to Nebraska and made his report. In 1896 a group of seventy–five people pooled their resources and came by rail (they chartered two freight cars) to Georgia. The migrants settled near Columbus, formed themselves into the collectivistic Christian Commonwealth, and prepared for a future of work and shared rewards. They named their Muscogee County settlement Commonwealth and soon had a post office, public school, farm, and depot. The colony was based on the principles of the Farmers' Alliance and also emphasized religion, although its members belonged to various denominations and sects. The Browns were dedicated Quakers.

Georgia was satisfactory but not what some of the settlers wanted and once again Brown made a trip to the Gulf coast. He visited Eastpoint, liked what he saw and returned to Commonwealth where he convinced five families and two single men (thirty–one in all) to move. They constructed two barges, loaded up their belongings, and in the spring began a strange but successful voyage down the Chattahoochee River. Entering the Apalachicola River, they continued south and after a journey of eleven days reached Apalachicola on April 15. Contacting Rice, they purchased a small amount of land across the bay at Eastpoint. Rice helped them cross to a place called Godley's Bluff. The colonists disassembled the barges and used the wood to build their first homes. Larger tracts were bought the next year when Harry C. Vrooman, a late settler at Commonwealth, arrived and took the lead. Vrooman was a Harvard graduate and a former pastor of a Congregational church in St. Louis, Missouri. He was one of six brothers, all active in social reform. Discarding the Christian Commonwealth name, the settlers bought land from Rice in 1899 and with the aid of Brown, Vrooman set up a cooperative colony, the Co–Workers' Fraternity. Its members were actually members of two colonies: one was concerned with religious and philosophical study and the other with production. Workers owned their own land but all profits were shared in what they hoped would be a profitable venture in lumbering, fishing, and manufacturing.

A post office was opened in 1898 and soon there was a school and a church. The *Crescent City* made the village a stop on its daily trip to Carrabelle with supplies, mail, and passengers. Despite this the colony did not attract many people. The settlers were farmers but the land was not rich and they had little experience in fishing. Vrooman continued to preach and the business part of the colony was renamed the Southern Co–Operative Association. Still, Eastpoint lacked Apalachicola and Carrabelle's strategic location. Although there were exceptions, Brown prospered as a truck farmer, Eastpoint remained more a community than a town, a stopping place. Eventually, seafood and timber became important but for the present it remained a noble experiment, one founded by dedicated men and women.

As Apalachicola was lifted from economic drift by the natural resource of timber and as Carrabelle and Eastpoint came into being, the seafood industry's potential found recognition and exploitation. Apalachicola and Franklin County moved to participate in one of the world's most historic means of livelihood.

Oysters, like these shown on St. Vincent Island at low tide, became the Apalachicola area's first important seafood industry. Courtesy of the Florida State Archives.

Six

Neptune's Bounty

A VARIETY OF MARINE LIFE FLOURISHED IN the waters (fresh, brackish, and salt) surrounding Apalachicola and offered the possibility of commercial fishing on a profitable basis. There were natural oyster beds from Indian Pass all the way to Dog Island. The Apalachicola River's fresh water—warm, brownish, and filled with nutrients—emptied endlessly into a bay guarded by barrier islands. In such a sanctuary oysters flourished and it was also a nursery where young shrimp matured prior to entering the sea. Within the area there were blue crabs and many fish: kingfish, catfish, flounder, spotted weakfish (sea trout), bluefish, red snapper, mullet, skipjack, and pompano. Menhaden, a nonfood species but useful for bait and for making oil and fertilizer, were also present. The Apalachicola estuarine system was home to eighty-five species of freshwater fish and one hundred twelve species of saltwater fish.

The Gulf's deeper waters were filled with marketable fish and sports fishermen were attracted to the king tarpon. A large supply of sponges was discovered among the reefs off Dog and St. George Islands and the historic business of sponging became briefly important. Beyond that, the Apalachicola River and the creeks and rivers, as well as lakes and ponds, abounded in bream, trout, bass, and many other varieties of freshwater fish.

Indians had always fished for leisure and more important, to secure food. They were copied by European and then American settlers. By the 1870s outsiders from noncoastal Florida, Georgia, and Alabama began coming to the Gulf coast to camp out and fish in late summer and fall. They arrived as individuals and in family groups over the primitive roads, eager to taste fresh fish, and on leaving, took barrels of salted fish home. Locals in Franklin and Wakulla counties developed a profitable industry in selling their visitors fish, especially mullet which were plentiful. Mullet were aesthetically appealing as flashing silver streaks that by strength and instinct broke the water surface with bold leaps.

All of Florida, in fact, contained many fish and by the late 1880s regulation of the industry shifted from individual counties to the state. Unfortunately, the Florida Fishing Commission, created in 1889, was underfunded. Policing the growing industry shifted temporarily back to the counties but changes came in the twentieth century. In 1913 the Shell Fish Commission was created and became part of the Department of Agriculture and a Department of Game and Fish was established to oversee freshwater fishing. Then in 1915 responsibility for enforcing all saltwater fishing was placed in the hands of a Shell Fish Commissioner. The first commissioner, T. R. Hodges, and the fishermen of Franklin and other Gulf coast counties had a stormy relationship.

Oysters became the Apalachicola area's first important seafood industry. The oyster, which changes its sex, releases sperm or eggs; the sperm floats away in the currents and forms a dense white stream that disperses in the water. The eggs are dispelled and fertilization takes place in the sea. Within hours the fertilized eggs develop into tiny larvae (spat). The microscopic-sized oysters swim actively about propelled by cilia (whisker-like hairs); as they swarm by the thousands in surface waters, the oysters are swept away from the home oyster bed by currents and tides. Within two weeks the small oyster grows a shell and sinks to the bottom; a powerful foot enables it to crawl about seeking a hard, clean surface known as cultch (or culch); it quickly expels a stream of cementlike substance from a special gland, and, rolling over, presses its left shell into the adhesive material. In this manner the young oyster plants itself and has no further power of movement. After the attachment, the spat continues to develop and within two weeks the oyster measures one–fourth inch. Depending upon conditions, the oyster becomes marketable in from two to five years. Apalachicola Bay was the perfect area for the process to take place. Among other area advantages, while the water temperature fluctuates with the season, it never gets cold enough to cause the oysters to hibernate.

Oysters eat microscopic plants and organic matter in the water above the bottoms where they live. Ingestion of food comes from filtering—an oyster can strain twenty-six quarts of water an hour through its gills. Once past the developmental process (90 percent are destroyed), the oyster still faces natural enemies: various crabs, starfish, leeches, snails, and boring sponges. The fragile oyster bed can be destroyed by disease, excessive salinity, and fresh water as well as sudden changes in water levels. The twentieth century brought the deadly menace of pollution.

People cherish oysters not for their beauty but for their eating qualities. The Japanese and Chinese attempted oyster culture thirty centuries ago, and the ancient Greeks and Romans supplemented natural beds by transplanting British beds to the Mediterranean Sea. English settlers in America found them on the Atlantic coast as far north as Maine and once Connecticut depleted its natural grounds, oysters were imported annually from the Chesapeake Bay for planting and marketing. By the 1860s Americans increased cultivation by imitating the French method of placing clean surfaces (tiles, shells, brush) near beds of spawning oysters to provide the shellfish with clean cultch. Other methods of increasing quantity, growth, and time of maturity were also tried.

Apalachicolans had the evidence of history—visually there were the numerous shell mounds left by the Indians and in prose there were the numerous accounts of oysters by previous explorers and travelers—but more importantly, they knew about oysters from their own experiences eating them; raw, steamed, fried, as stew, and as components of other dishes. Sold locally as early as 1836, oysters were being packed in barrels and shipped to neighboring states and northern markets by the 1850s. Left mainly pristine during the Civil War, the area's oyster beds were in prime condition in the 1870s. Then firms such as Joseph C. Messina and Company, Yent and Alexander, John Miller, and Joseph Segras became dealers in "oysters and fish." In 1881 a state law awarded exclusive commercial rights in designated waters to individuals making proper applications to plant oysters. The water in various bay area beds contained differing amounts of salinity, giving each bed a local fame for tastiness and locals set to the tasks of planting and harvesting by tonging, hogging, and, least of all, dredging.

The oysterman reached his particular bar early in the morning and without ceremony began tonging. The essentials of his trade were a boat, tongs, a culling board, culling iron, and a drag anchor. The pair of long, double–handled rakes with double vise–grip prongs enabled him to reach nine or more feet, scrape shells from the beds and bring the oysters to the surface. A skilled tonger used the laborious and inefficient method with dexterity, coordination, and stamina to extract the

Left mainly pristine during the Civil War, the area's oyster beds were in prime condition in the 1870s, then firms such as Joseph C. Messina and Company became dealers in "oysters and fish." Courtesy of the Florida State Archives.

The water in various bay area beds contained differing amounts of salinity, giving each bed a local fame for tastiness, and locals set to the tasks of planting and harvesting by tonging, hogging, and least of all dredging. Courtesy of the Florida State Archives.

maximum volume possible. An oysterman's income was dependent on prices, over which he had limited control, and on how many oysters he tonged, which, to the extent of his skill, time, and hard work, he did control. Adroit and rapid culling was equally vital. As oysters were brought up they were placed on the troughlike culling board that extended across the boat. Once the hard board was full, the tonger took the culling iron and with rapid strokes broke off small oysters and extraneous material and returned the culled matter to the water.

The hogging technique was uncomplicated but limited. It took place at low tide when the oyster beds were exposed and consisted of walking out and picking them up by hand. Dredging came into use when canning oysters became popular and was not used to gather oysters that were shipped raw or in the shell. Although more productive than tonging, dredging harmed the beds. The system involved dragging a dredge or wire basket across the bars to knock the oysters loose. One problem was that physical injury was done to the

The hogging technique was uncomplicated but limited. It took place at low tide when the oyster beds were exposed and consisted of walking out and picking them up by hand, as this couple is doing on a St. Vincent Island pond. Courtesy of the Florida State Archives.

beds and another was that many oysters fell into surrounding mud and died. A state law of 1885 forbade the use of dredges in natural oyster beds and twentieth century legislation prohibited the use of dredges altogether.

The name Ruge is important to the oyster industry. Herman Ruge, a native of Hanover, Germany, migrated to Apalachicola in the 1840s and established a hardware store and machine shop. His two sons, John G. (born in 1854) and George H., worked with their father. In 1885 the family business became the Ruge Brothers Canning Company with John, who was also a real estate man, emerging as the primary partner. Through the technique of pasteurization, the Ruges became Florida's first successful commercial packers and John gained attention as an early advocate of planting oyster shells near the beds to provide places for the spat to settle when spawning.

Other prominent oyster industry pioneers included Stephen Ewing Rice, a native of Huntsville, Alabama, who came to Apalachicola in 1882. With the aid of his two sons, Stephen E., Jr., and Rob Roy, he founded a large oyster packing company. Joseph Messina, a native of Apalachicola, took over the Bay City Packing Company in 1896 and expanded his oyster packing business to include a variety of profitable seafood products. Messina's trademark was "Pearl Brand."

There were many small dealers in Apalachicola by the twentieth century as well as larger ones such as the Apalachicola Packing Company of Steven E. Rice, Jr. The industry included the men who manned the boats, shuckers who worked in the oysterhouses, and a number of employees in two canneries. Despite Shell Commissioner Hodges's enforcement of a state license tax and a privilege tax, a storm in 1903, and the threat of a federal law to forbid shipping oysters other than in their shells, the industry became well established. In 1915 lumbering was Franklin County's number one industry but fishing and oystering ranked second and Franklin led the state in oyster production.

Sponging dated to several centuries before the Christian era and down to the 1840s the world's supply of sponges came from the Mediterranean Sea. Then the French began importing them from the Bahamas and sponge beds were found in the Florida Keys. By 1849 there were shipments from Key West to New York City and the sponge industry's major source was the Keys. By the 1880s and 1890s the sponge industry shifted to beds discovered further north in the Gulf of Mexico and Greek spongers, using Tarpon Springs as their base, dominated the trade.

The sponge (which bears no resemblance to the market product) grows on the sea bottom and reproduces asexually. It has a slimy, solid, fleshy body varying in color from brown and black to grayish yellow. Although varying in appearance, the sponge is traversed by numerous chambers and canals and most resembles

Herman Ruge, a native of Hanover, Germany, migrated to Apalachicola in the 1840s and established a hardware store and machine shop. His two sons worked with him and in 1885 the family business became Ruge Brothers Canning Company. Courtesy of the Apalachicola Library.

Joseph Messina, a native of Apalachicola, took over the Bay City Packing Company in 1896, and expanded his oyster packing business to include a variety of profitable seafood products. Messina's trademark was "Pearl Brand." Courtesy of the Florida State Archives.

Several varieties of sponge were found off Florida's Gulf coast: yellow, grass, wire and, the most valuable, sheepswool. Courtesy of the Florida State Archives.

beef liver. Once the soft, fleshy matter is removed, the skeleton is dried and becomes the familiar sponge. Several varieties were found off Florida's Gulf coast: yellow, grass, wire, and sheepswool (the most valuable).

The industry evolved in Florida from men wading into shallow waters and plucking the sponges to more sophisticated methods as sponges were found in deeper waters. Apalachicola became involved with the discovery of sponge beds in the reefs off Dog Island. By 1879 local seafood men outfitted ships for expeditions that lasted up to a month. A mother ship, where the sponges were cleaned and strung up to dry and then stored below, carried several twelve-foot-long rowboats whose two–man crews took the sponges by hooking.

In the 1840s sponge beds were found in the Florida Keys. By the 1880s and 1890s the sponge industry shifted to beds further north, and Greek spongers dominated the trade. Courtesy of the Florida State Archives.

The sponge industry evolved from men wading into shallow waters and plucking the sponges to more sophisticated methods as sponges were found in deeper waters. By 1879 local seafood men outfitted ships for expeditions that lasted up to a month. A mother ship carried several 12-foot-long rowboats whose two-man crews took the sponges by hooking. Courtesy of the Florida State Archives.

As late as 1900 a dozen or more sponge boats still operated out of Carrabelle and Apalachicola.

Typically, a sculler (oarsman) and a hooker (diver) searched the area in their small dinghy. In waters averaging about twenty-four feet in depth, the hooker, using a glass-bottomed wooden bucket thrust a few inches below the water's surface to achieve a telescopic effect, spotted the beds. Upon the hooker's signal, the sculler maneuvered the dinghy into position. The hooker brought up the sponges with his pole, a one-and-a-half-inch thick, fifteen to forty-foot-long sharp-pronged tool. The rake-like pole had two to five tines (teeth) set at right angles to the shaft. The mother ship's boats kept sponging until there was a full cargo and then the ship returned to port.

Markets were at St. Marks, Tarpon Springs, and Key West. At Apalachicola, as elsewhere, the buyers inspected the catch and made sealed bids. The ship's crew shared the profits. Then successful bidders shipped the sponges to firms in New York, Baltimore, San Francisco, and St. Louis. At first the money was good but bad weather in 1902 muddied the waters and the sponge ships returned from the reefs with greatly diminished catches and sometimes empty. With time the known beds became depleted, operating expenses increased, and the market declined. It revived in 1905 but became more dangerous with the development of diving gear

At Apalachicola as elsewhere the buyers inspected the catch at a sponge exchange, and made sealed bids. The ship's crew shared the profits, and the successful buyer shipped the sponges to New York, Baltimore, San Francisco, and St. Louis. Courtesy of the Florida State Archives.

that extended the sponging to deeper waters. Gradually, Franklin County businessmen withdrew from the trade and were replaced by Greek divers and ships from Tarpon Springs.

Shrimp were plentiful in the bay area but their potential was not developed in the nineteenth century. Sicilian immigrant Mark Salvador (Anglicized from Sollecito Salvatore) began the first important shrimping around 1900 in northeastern Florida at Fernandina. The industry was a by-product of his seining operations and in 1902 the innovative Salvador, using a power-driven boat with a haul seine, worked in deep water and increased his catch. Other developments such as the otter trawl permitted the industry to expand before World War I.

The strangely concocted shellfish have complicated larval stages: eggs are hatched offshore in a twenty-four-hour period; the slow moving, minuscule shrimp then

Sponging diminished between 1902 and 1905. Gradually, Franklin County investors withdrew from the trade and business slowed down in Apalachicola. Courtesy of the Florida State Archives.

View of the Apalachicola pier, about 1906, showing the low and high tide marks. Courtesy of the Florida State Archives.

Sicilian immigrant Mark Salvador began the first important shrimping around 1900 at Fernandina. By 1902 he was using a power-driven boat with a haul seine in deep water to increase his catch. Courtesy of the Florida State Archives.

By 1897 shrimp sold locally in Apalachicola, although many fishermen threw them back into the water when they found them in their nets. Courtesy of the Florida State Archives.

move shoreward to shallow waters, taking up an existence on the bottoms of grass flats; they develop rapidly during the nursery period and move next to the bay's deeper reaches; when they reach about four inches, the shrimp migrate again to offshore waters, complete maturation, and spawn.

By 1897 shrimp sold locally in Apalachicola, although many fishermen threw them back into the water when they found them in their nets. While there was a market by 1900, as late as 1919, a state law regulating the industry still referred to them as "Salt Water Crawfish." In the 1920s the industry moved down Florida's east coast, around the peninsula to the Apalachicola area, extended further west in the Gulf coast to Texas, then back to the Tortugas and across to Campeche, Mexico. Pink shrimp were the largest and most important but white and brown shrimp became commercially important and all three varieties were found near Apalachicola. Local shrimpers used shallow–water boats and seldom ventured far out to sea. When shrimping became bad, the owners tied their boats up or switched to catching blue crabs for the local market. Later, crabmeat became a full–scale industry itself. Early in the twentieth century canning became a possibility and by 1915 the Bay City Packing Company was shipping canned shrimp to northern markets. Bay City and other firms also dealt in fresh shrimp. Night shrimping began when it was discovered that pink and brown shrimp were nocturnal and soon the industry matched the importance of oystering in the local economy.

Although never a regular business, the sale of sturgeon brought in occasional money for men such as Captain Charles Anderson. The large fish was in demand for eating and even more so for its caviar. In dollars and cents, seafood was vital to Apalachicola's world, while, on a different scale, the presence of water shaped the culture of the region. Apalachicola Bay, the

Apalachicola River, the Ochlockonee River, smaller streams and rivers, the barrier islands, and the swamps attracted a myriad of birds and animals and made the area bountiful in fowl and animal life. The long summer heat was oppressive and hurricanes were inevitable and destructive. A living from the sea was a hard one but all of that was accepted and all of that was offset by a unique and beautiful world, a fact that was realized and appreciated by the people who lived there.

Early in the 20th century canning became a possibility and by 1915 the Bay City Packing Company was shipping canned as well as fresh shrimp to northern markets. Courtesy of the Florida State Archives.

The sale of sturgeon brought in occasional money for men such as Captain Charles Anderson. The large fish was in demand for eating and even more so for its caviar. Courtesy of the Florida State Archives.

At the turn of the century citizens used St. George Island as though it were public domain and picnics were uncountable. Courtesy of the Florida State Archives.

Seven

Advance and Retreat: Uncertain Decades and a New Century

IN THE 1880s LARGE PARTS OF ST. GEORGE Island became the property of the Humphries family who gave, sold, and exchanged acreage to themselves and to others. Among the others were Samuel E. and Emmalee Rice and C. H. and Mary F. Smith. Not that many people wanted the island but it had timber, especially slash pine valuable for lumber and naval stores. Then in 1889 one Horace H., one of the numerous Humphries, arranged with William H. Neel for the latter to put one hundred head of stock cattle on the island. Neel received one half of the island and Humphries got half of the cattle. The island had timber, turpentine, cattle (and wild hogs and a scattering of goats), and potential as part of the expanding seafood industry. Besides its value for recreational excursions, there was the possibility of building permanent vacation cottages. In the 1890s the Humphries recouped most of the island by several negotiations, especially with the expedient of a mortgage.

All of that was of little moment to most Franklin countians who shared the general economic grief of the state and country in the first half of the 1890s. A crippling economic depression was reflected in local foreclosures and bankruptcies. Adding to the misery was a series of hurricanes and freezes that damaged the shellfish industry, already suffering from overharvested oyster bars. The Humphries family was among the victims. Unable to pay their note, they saw St. George sold at public auction to Daniel O. Neel. He and his wife kept the property until 1900 when they sold it to Paul S. King and F. R. King of Colbert County, Alabama, who had bought and sold Franklin County land since the 1880s.

Meantime, citizens used the island as though it were public domain. Picnics were uncountable, as Captain

Captain Andy Wing's Crescent City *carried excursionists to St. George twice a week. Courtesy of the Florida State Archives.*

Andy Wing's *Crescent City* (a steamer owned by the Cypress Lumber Company) carried excursionists twice a week to the island. Each spring Wing had a work crew refurbish a wharf on the bayside. Swimming and fishing (a favored method was for wading parties armed with nail–pointed sticks and lanterns to catch flounders buried in the sand close to shore) attracted both sexes of all ages. People searched for eggs hidden in the sand dunes by giant sea turtles. They found them in abundance at places such as Nick's Hole where rattlesnakes, the co–tenants, resented the intrusions. Serious adventurers came with tents and spent several days exploring. In 1902 Captain Andy's men laid a boardwalk all the way across the island. To the trespassers delight, the Kings welcomed the activity.

The Porter name was significant in the region. Edward G. Porter, son of Richard Gibbs and Mary

People searched St. George for eggs hidden in the sand dunes by giant sea turtles and found them in abundance at places such as Nick's Hole. Courtesy of the Florida State Archives.

Tibbitt Salter Porter, became identified with Little St. George Island. Transferred there from the lighthouse at Cape San Blas, Porter became so fond of his keeper job that he bought 1,515.85 acres of land on the island in 1894. He soon built a cottage and a storm house and hired Miss Ola Rhodes to teach a school. The school's eleven students were six members of his own family and five from the family of his assistant keeper. Porter grazed as many as two hundred fifty head of cattle and two hundred hogs and maintained a large vegetable garden. He and the assistant made extra money by butchering meat and carrying it to the mainland for sale. The entire Porter family loved the island but none more than Pearl, the dexterous tomboy daughter, who ate berries and wild grapes, became self–appointed assistant to her father, and considered everything an adventure. Pearl loved the storms that blew across the island and the accompanying excitement that followed when the family took hurried refuge in the storm house. Porter's death in 1913 cut short his plans to build vacation cottages on Little St. George. Still, the one cottage he completed had a bayside dock and from spring to fall the house was constantly rented. Porter's efforts marked him as the first person to utilize the island commercially.

By 1902 Paul King and his wife Imogene King gained exclusive ownership of St. George Island and soon they and three sons moved from Alabama with intentions of settling permanently in Apalachicola.

Edward G. Porter became the lighthouse keeper on Little St. George Island, and was so fond of his job that he bought acreage on the island, built a cottage and storm house and hired Miss Ola Rhodes to teach school for the eleven children in his and his assistant's families. Courtesy of the Florida State Archives.

The Porter family on the porch of their home. L-R: Barnard, Josephine, Ethel, Eleanor, Jo holding Pearl and Edward G. Porter. Courtesy of the Florida State Archives.

Apalachicola and Franklin County, having survived Reconstruction and the following decades, bid farewell to the nineteenth century.

The new century itself was cause for hope in Franklin County and there were less abstract reasons for optimism: James N. Coombs's several lumber mills were profitable and so were the northern–owned Cypress Lumber Company, the Loxley Lumber Company, the Carrabelle Land and Lumber Company, and other smaller operations. Billions of feet of timber came from longleaf yellow pine, cypress, ash, cottonwood, sweet

The Cypress Lumber Company mill was northern owned. Courtesy of the Florida State Archives.

The James N. Coombs, owned by George H. Marshall, was piloted by Harry Porter on a regular run from Apalachicola to Pensacola. Courtesy of the Florida State Archives.

At the turn of the century James N. Coombs owned several profitable lumber mills. Courtesy of the Florida State Archives.

The Tarpon served Apalachicola and Carrabelle. Courtesy of the Florida State Archives.

gum, poplar, and tupelo gum. Lumber revitalized traffic on the Apalachicola River, increasing the volume of activity by almost 70 percent between 1898 and 1903. Captain W. G. Barrow's popular steamer, the *Philadelphia*, made weekly trips between Apalachicola, Pensacola, and Mobile. Despite limited federal expenditures on the harbor, many vessels cleared port.

Nothing was more exciting than the coming of the railroad. Former frustrations—failed editorials, unproductive public meetings, unanswered appeals—were forgotten in 1903 when Charles R. Duff and his associates began and in 1907 completed the Apalachicola Northern Railroad. Apalachicola celebrated on April 30, 1907 when the first engine steamed into town. The Northern's seventy miles of track extended from River Junction in Gadsden County. There it linked up with east–west Florida lines. Further north, at Climax, Georgia, it connected with the Atlantic Coast Line. In 1909–1910 a branch line from Apalachicola to St. Andrew Bay resulted in the founding of Port St. Joe at the site of long-vanished St. Joseph. The reborn port bustled with shipments of lumber and naval stores. The

Despite limited federal expenditures on the harbor, many vessels cleared port including the Naiad whose home port was Apalachicola and was reputed to have made more trips on the Chattahoochee-Apalachicola rivers in her twenty years than any other ship. Courtesy of the Florida State Archives.

Transporting supplies for construction of the Apalachicola Northern Railroad, begun by Charles R. Duff and his associates in 1903. Courtesy of the Florida State Archives.

The Franklin Hotel was built in 1907 by South Carolinian, James Fulton Buck. Courtesy of the Florida State Archives.

The first train to cross the bridge. Section foreman Thomas J. Nesmith is standing at right with his coat on his arm. Courtesy of the Florida State Archives.

An early interior view of the Franklin Hotel. Courtesy of the Florida State Archives.

new town soon boasted doctors, blacksmiths, hotels, and numerous stores. A ferry connection with Carrabelle gave Apalachicola access to the Georgia, Florida, and Alabama railroad with its rail service to Bainbridge and Tallahassee.

Boastful Apalachicolans pointed to their three barbers as evidence of sophistication and growth. Besides, there were two banks, a municipal waterworks, and two real estate companies, all by 1907. Social life for blacks and whites expanded: a popular black brass band, the Colored Odd Fellows, and various social activities (as reported weekly in the black news column of the

The town celebrated the completion of the Apalachicola Northern Railroad when the first train arrived on April 30, 1907. Courtesy of the Florida State Archives.

Mrs. M. Brash, Sr.'s hat shop was evidence of the sophistication and growth of Apalachicola. Courtesy of the Florida State Archives.

Social life included fraternal organizations such as the Masons. Courtesy of the Florida State Archives.

By 1907 there was a popular black brass band, the Colored Odd Fellows, and various social activities. Courtesy of the Florida State Archives.

Apalachicola *Times*) were complemented by the whites' City Cornet Band, a hunt club, and the Philaco Club (a diverse woman's group begun as a reading club in the 1890s). Dramatic evidence of a new century about to unfold came on August 22, 1900 when the Electric Light Company threw its switches and bathed the town with light.

The oyster industry expanded from a few dealers to one that included small, locally owned entrepreneurial ventures. The men who made it possible formed the Oystermen's Protective Association, a kind of uncoordinated labor union. Although its members never achieved uniform rates and fair prices, the shellfish industry recovered from the depression and prospered despite destructive hurricanes in 1898 and 1899. The gale of 1899 wrecked schooners off St. George Island while at Carrabelle it killed five people, drove thirteen ships ashore, and blew a train from its track. A freeze in 1899 sent temperatures plunging to ten degrees Fahrenheit.

Yet, for every negative there was a positive. In 1898 citizens turned out for Apalachicola's first "public school" graduation. Miss Steppie Rice's small group and the audience gloried in the occasion, even if student Farley Warren refused to participate because girls were in the graduation. The ceremonies ended with a well attended dance at the armory. In 1899, thanks to private and corporate donations, a statue was dedicated to Dr. John Gorrie, the town's leading historical figure.

Natural disasters were matched by the Great Fire of 1900. At noon on May 25, Mrs. George Broughton's

The hurricane of 1899 wrecked these ships on Dog Island. The dismasted vessel on extreme left is unidentified, the Norwegian bark Vale, *American schooner* James A. Garfield, *Norwegian bark* Jafnhar, *American schooner* Mary E. Morse, *Russian bark* Latava, *and the American barkentine* Vivette. *Courtesy of the Florida State Archives.*

View of the Apalachicola bayfront after the August 1, 1899 hurricane. Courtesy of the Florida State Archives.

Citizens turned out for Apalachicola's first "public school" graduation at Chapman High in 1898, except for student Farley Warren who refused to participate because girls were included. Courtesy of the Florida State Archives.

wood cookstove sent sparks into her kitchen and started a fire that spread to the nearby Methodist church. From there wind–fanned flames swept through Apalachicola, burning most of the business section (seventy one buildings) and causing damages of over a quarter of a million dollars. The town's new fire engine became an ironic victim to the flames before it could be put into service. The fire finally burned itself out at the river. Certain that the new century had to be an improvement, the people began rebuilding.

Meanwhile, the financially strapped Kings had to lease St. George to George W. McCormack who planned

The first graduation ceremony was followed by a well attended dance at the Armory. Courtesy of the Florida State Archives.

On April 30, 1900, thanks to private and corporate donations, a monument was dedicated to Dr. John Gorrie, the town's leading historical figure. Courtesy of the Florida State Archives.

At noon on May 25, 1900, Mrs. George Broughton's wood cookstove sent sparks into her kitchen and started a fire that spread to the nearby Methodist church. From there wind-fanned flames swept through Apalachicola, burning most of the business section (seventy-one buildings). Courtesy of the Florida State Archives.

Before it burned itself out at the river the fire caused damages of over $250,000, including the town's new fire engine. Courtesy of the Apalachicola State Bank.

to stock it with hogs and cattle and engage in fishing and oyster–planting enterprises. Still pressed for funds, the Kings finally sold the island in 1905 to W. F. Farley and W. E. Montgomery, two Franklin County businessmen. Pocketing $3,500, the Kings gladly retired from the island business. Farley and Montgomery further secured their property in 1910 by paying members of the Humphries family nominal sums for their remaining claims to St. George. The new owners expected to use their property in the shellfish industry and establish a regularly scheduled boatline for excursionists.

During this period George Washington Saxon of Tallahassee saw Franklin County as a land of economic promise. Born in 1848 in Leon County and limited in formal education to grade school, Saxon had remarkable natural ability. He lived briefly in Apalachicola before returning to Tallahassee and opening a successful grocery store. Saxon expanded his business into a dry goods store that serviced the city and farmers in Leon and surrounding counties. Successful as a commission merchant, the rising businessman became a private banker. From there he incorporated the Capital City Bank in 1895. He opened an Apalachicola branch and persuaded a New Yorker, T. F. Porter and Samuel E. Teague, a native son of Franklin County, to serve respectively as manager and cashier. Saxon's state bank operated until 1906 when local businessmen bought it out and Porter became its president. It was all done amicably and Saxon soon devoted himself to other interests in Franklin County.

He bought the bankrupt Kimball Lumber Company in 1904, a purchase that included sawmill equipment, eight thousand acres of land, and wharf and city lots in Apalachicola. Aided by an able wife, Sarah Ball Saxon, he acquired the Carrabelle Ice Company and holdings at Lanark Village (also known as Lanark Springs and Lanark on the Gulf). Six miles east of Carrabelle, the Lanark Village community was owned by the Georgia, Florida, and Alabama Railroad. The line built a fashionable resort there that attracted people from Florida and Georgia. Several bought lots nearby and built summer cottages. Astute businessman Saxon noted the success of Lanark Village, as well as St. Teresa, a well established enclave on nearby St. James Island that was settled in 1875 by people from Tallahassee; Panacea Springs, east of St. Teresa where the Ochlockonee River flowed into an arm of Apalachee Bay, and where a hotel opened in 1898 exploited numerous "curative" sulphur springs; and of Edward G. Porter's popular rental property on Little St. George. Such enterprises convinced him that St. George Island could be made into a profitable recreational center.

An outing on St. George Island in 1915. Standing L-R: A. E. Martin, Dan and Fred Jenkins. Middle: Edna Jenkins. Sitting: Mercedes Holland, Harry Jenkins, Sadie Jenkins and Sadie Hunter. Courtesy of the Florida State Archives.

Primitive Apalachicola transportation in the early 1900s. Courtesy of the Florida State Archives.

Six miles east of Carrabelle, the Georgia, Florida, and Alabama Railroad built a fashionable resort, including the Lanark Inn, that attracted people from Florida and Georgia. Courtesy of the Florida State Archives.

The Dreamland Theatre was built on the corner of Market Street and Avenue D, before 1900. Courtesy of the Florida State Archives.

A thatched fisherman's hut on St. Vincent Island, about 1909. Courtesy of the Florida State Archives.

Visitors to Edward G. Porter's popular rental property on Little St. George Island used this pier. Courtesy of the Florida State Archives.

In 1910 Saxon persuaded area residents and others from Georgia to invest in his St. George Island Company. Meanwhile, he signed a mortgage purchasing the island from Montgomery and Farley. Then as trustee for the corporation, Saxon executed a trustee's deed and turned the property over to the company which mortgaged the island to secure its indebtedness ($19,600) to Montgomery and Farley. The deal was all inclusive and helped by local officers (most of them former bank associates such as Teague and the Porters), he made plans to build cottages, an island hotel, and engage in the myriad activities associated with a resort area.

Activity on St. George Island infused Apalachicola and the area with confidence. The successful New Pace Vaudeville theatre, begun in 1909, was succeeded by the even more popular Dreamland, the town's first movie house, which opened in 1910. Back on St. George building preparations were aided by S. J. Ruff and his "Ruff's Survey." It made possible lot divisions

(99 year leases had restrictions limiting lot transfers to Caucasians). Leasing the land carried automatic membership in the St. George Island Club. In 1911 streets were laid out but not built, a bayside wharf was constructed and so was a small building fronting the Gulf. Known as the Club House, it was opened and served meals during the warm months and occasionally housed visiting parties. The personnel rented bathing suits and boats to guests but the Club House was never a true hotel. In 1912 H. L. Oliver of Apalachicola leased the

The City of Carrabelle, a steam tug, docked on the east side of the Carrabelle River at the foot of Coombs Hill, on Marine Street. Captain James C. Storrs seated at right. Courtesy of the Florida State Archives.

About 1911 the Club House opened on St. George Island. The personnel served meals and rented bathing suits and boats to guests. Courtesy of the Florida State Archives.

island's growing timber, obtaining exclusive rights to "turpentine" it for six years. Then in 1915 George M. Counts, Sr., a local businessman, joined forces with Oliver and until 1918 spent much time in quarters at Nick's Hole directing a black work force in the naval stores operations.

Saxon tightened his managerial control over the corporation but never realized the influx of people he expected. At $250 a lot, the cost was not prohibitive but before World War I, no more than three cottages were constructed. Even so, the Club House remained popular and the island was host to many visitors, fishermen, and hunters. As automobiles became more visible, it became fashionable to ferry a car across to St. George and drive up and down its wide beaches. Apalachicolans gave little thought to the war in Europe but much thought to the newly organized Chamber of Commerce and the concerts of the new Citizens's Band in recently established Battery Park. Everyone went to see and hear Allen's Negro Minstrels when they came to town. The renovated Dreamland theatre added a cornet player and traps drummer to its orchestra but was supplanted as an entertainment center by Alexander Fortunas's Dixie Theatre.

G. M. Counts's 1915 Mardi Gras parade entry won first prize in the commercial category. Courtesy of the Apalachicola State Bank.

The Dixie Theatre opened in April 1913 to great fanfare. There was much to recommend it—the front, glowing with a hundred colored electric lights, the conical ticket office with glass windows, the main hall with 360 folding opera chairs, the horseshoe–shaped balcony with private boxes, the sunken orchestra pit, and the heavily curtained stage. There were noiseless rubber carpets and fourteen oscillating fans. From Tampa to Pensacola the Dixie Theatre had no rival.

In 1914 Apalachicola followed America's Progressive trends in local government by adopting the city commission form of government. The town celebrated itself by establishing a Mardi Gras festival in February and an Oyster Day in September. King Retsyo I ("oyster" spelled backwards) presided over a winter Mardi Gras in 1915 that featured exhibition flights by W. S. Luckey in his Curtis aeroplane. The area's economic success did not extend to St. George Island. Saxon, who liked the island and had successfully "quieted the title" to it with drawn–out legal action, decided to abandon the unprofitable investment. To do so he would deal with William Lee Popham, who was not the type of businessman Saxon usually encountered. As early as July 1916 Popham had visited and inspected Apalachicola and St. George Island. Within

In 1915 Apalachicola established a February Mardi Gras festival. Band members from the Original Broadcasting Band of 1915 were left to right: Frank Holley, W. M. Pooser, Raymond Weatherspoon, unknown boy, Reaver Cummings, Bud Nedley, Reverend Sheridan, L. A. Rocco, V. M. Hoffman, Leon A. Rocco, Charlie Robinson, Fred Myhoff and Allen Murray. Courtesy of the Florida State Archives.

King Retsyo (oyster spelled backwards) presided over the winter festival, and is shown here mounting his float for the parade. Courtesy of the Florida State Archives.

Part of the Mardi Gras parade during the three day celebration in 1915. Courtesy of the Florida State Archives.

Local tranquility was marred when movie footage of the Great War in Europe joined newspaper headlines to declare American participation. Apalachicola's Company "L", First Florida Infantry included: 1. Mr. Rodgers, 2. Mr. Edwards, 3. Lonnie Meyer, 4. Mike Nedley, 5. Mr. Edwards, 6. Peter Hill, 7. "Gip" Gibson, 8. Charlie Hobart, 9. Ramsey Summerford, 10. Mr. Floyd. 11. Veto G. Sangaree, 12. Frank Martina, 13. Walter Yearty, 14. Charles McClay, 15. John McClay, 16. Fred Maddox, 17. Son Montgomery, 18. George Yearty, 19. John Houston, 20. Mr. Rodgers, 21. Jimmie DeCosmo. Courtesy of the Florida State Archives.

Girls enjoying life on Little St. George, about 1916: Josephine Porter, Hazel Nickmire, Pearl Porter, Eleanor Porter, and Rosa V. Montgomery. Courtesy of the Florida State Archives.

a month he brought a group of potential investors from Montgomery, Alabama to do the same.

Even before Popham arrived, his front man, William Roat, an architect–contractor, moved to St. George and assumed the name of "Island Man." As Popham's employee (with neither approval nor disapproval from Saxon), Roat declared himself resident agent. He wrote numerous letters to the Apalachicola *Times* promoting the island. Then in 1917 Popham took center stage. Some locals had heard of him as a Baptist preacher, Chautauqua lecturer, and author. They soon learned that he was also president of the St. George Island Development Company. Rumors became believable in 1917 when Popham appeared publicly in Apalachicola to deliver an invited sermon at the Methodist church. He impressed a large audience and was asked to return soon.

Unexpectedly, local tranquility was marred when the Pathé Daily clips at Dreamland took on new meaning. Footage of the Great War that had shown a distant European conflict now joined newspaper headlines to declare American participation. In 1917 the United States went to war on the side of France, Great Britain and their allies against Germany and Austria and the powers aligned with them. Changes in American life and that of Apalachicola and Franklin County seemed inevitable.

An Apalachicola waterfront view in the 1910s included a steamship, shrimp, fishing and oyster boats. Courtesy of the Florida State Archives.

The Owl Cafe was on the corner of Avenue D and Commerce Street, with the Masonic Hall and Post Office on the left. Courtesy of the Florida State Archives.

Doughboys from Franklin County went overseas to fight in France. Volunteering for various branches of the military were 248 men (174 whites and 74 blacks). Courtesy of the Florida State Archives.

Eight

Popham and the Early 1920s

WILLIAM LEE POPHAM (APRIL 14, 1885—August 22, 1953) was an extraordinary man. Born in Hardin County, Kentucky (sixty miles from Louisville), he came from the Pophams who settled in Virginia in 1708. After the American Revolution the family scattered north and south with one branch going to Kentucky. Virgil Popham, William Lee's father, was a small but successful nurseryman–farmer near Big Clitty. He was also a merchant and schoolteacher. William Lee inherited his literary and oratorical talents from his mother Clara and her family. Clara Popham's life was that of a mother and housewife devoted to her family. William Lee had a brother and two sisters. Another brother died at birth.

The future author, minister, public speaker, developer of St. George Island, and oyster monarch received a common school education and briefly attended a small college. In 1897 he persuaded his family to move to Louisville where he had private teachers and attended night school at the Southern Baptist Theological Seminary (during the day he was a special delivery messenger for the post office). He was an incurable romantic, an unfailing optimist, a man with a vivid imagination. He was always making plans and revising them, always driven by an insatiable curiosity and consuming ambition. William Lee was a voracious reader, had intellectual confidence, and, despite his drive, was a gentle and kind man who believed his every scheme, no matter how outlandish, was destined to succeed.

Profoundly moral, Popham was affected by the natural setting of his rural background. As a boy he combined poetry writing with rests between plowing and tending sheep. The future Oyster King had few intimate friends although he was extremely close to his mother and his wife Maude Miller Estes. By the time he was eleven, Popham was a published poet, although not a good one, and once he learned how to rhyme words, he progressed no further. Even so, the sheer amount of writing he accomplished and its variety (one effort, "Consider The Oyster," was a subject few others considered poetically) were impressive. He later extended his status as a poet to that of author, although his numerous books were as bad as his poems. Yet once again the bewildering diversity of his prose and its volume commanded respect.

At the age of seventeen Popham became a successful evangelist, as well as a popular lecturer on the Chautauqua circuit. The slim, black–haired, blue–eyed young man (in maturity he was stocky and semi–bald, although he never lost his intense, dramatic look), galvanized audiences with his sonorous voice and utter sincerity. The talk–circuit took him many places, especially the South. He had no less than thirty–four topics in his repertoire, including "Men and Swine, Women and Wine," and "Fools, Follies, Fibs, and Fancies." His brief editorship of a magazine, the Louisville *Happy Home and Fireside*, provided him the impetus to publish his sermons, homilies, and speeches as books and to do the same for his poems and fiction. Two small publishers in which he probably had a financial interest, began bringing out his works, all copyrighted in Popham's own name. His confidently titled *The Road to Success: The Best Book in the World* appeared in 1905, sold for fifty cents, and was a quintessential example of the "positive thinking" genre. In earnest prose it proclaimed simple piety reinforced with character building admonitions. Popham, who believed every word he wrote, also believed every word he spoke and his ora-

Shrimp boats line the docks of Apalachicola's Water Street. Shrimping has been traditionally the most important form of commercial fishing in Franklin County.

tory was better than his prose. He mesmerized his audiences, especially those in the South who prized oratory above all else.

Popham's brief works of fiction—*Love's Rainbow Dream, The Village by the Sea* were good examples—had simplistic plots that never varied; a young man and a young woman became attracted to each other, faced conflict, overcame it and lived out their days in serene bliss. True love always triumphed. Popham also wrote a number of books combining light romance and travel. The collection was known as the "Seven Wonders of the World Series (American)." *Yosemite Valley Romance, Garden of the Gods Romance,* and *Mammoth Cave Romance,* like the four others, featured an accidental meeting of the main characters at one of the scenic places, followed by the usual romance, conflict, and resolution. All of the writing gave Popham the skills to draft future contracts and agreements relating to St. George Island and Franklin County. His witty and imaginative style livened up the prose of what would have been dull, legalistic documents.

The judge of the ordinary court for Henry County married William Lee and Maude on May 11, 1912. Performed at the courthouse in McDonough, Georgia, the ceremony came during one of Popham's lecture–revival meetings in the Atlanta area. From there the couple honeymooned in Florida and were so impressed that Popham bought a hundred–acre farm on the Alafia River near Tampa. He paid for the land and subsequent improvements with money saved from his lectures and book sales. Soon he was buying and selling property in the Tampa area where he met James J. Abbott, who later became his partner in St. George Island activities. In 1916 Popham heard about St. George Island and he and Maude paid a visit to the island and Apalachicola. He was so impressed that he went immediately to Tallahassee where he located George W. Saxon and offered to buy the island. The Tallahassee banker, discouraged with sales on his Franklin County enterprise, was happy to oblige.

The present day First United Methodist Church in Apalachicola was constructed in 1901. The original church building was destroyed in 1900 after a devastating fire destroyed not only the church but more than 70 other buildings in Apalachicola.

The historic Gibson Inn was originally built in 1907. Previously called the Franklin Hotel, the Gibson was built by a native of South Carolina, James Fulton "Jeff" Buck. Owner of a turpentine business in Apalachicola, Buck was said to have handpicked the inn's cypress woodwork from his own trees, located in the east Bay area.

The Fry-Conter house was built in the 1840s. It is located at Fifth Street and Avenue F and is currently being restored under the direction of Willoughby Marshall.

Saxon accepted as part of the purchase price of $30,000 the copyrights to all of Popham's books, though it is doubtful that he had read any of them. In return Popham was authorized to sell lots on the island, provided 75 percent of the purchase price was placed in the Capital City Bank. Once the debt was paid (Popham was authorized to stake off lots, send out literature, and promote the island), the multi–talented Kentuckian would assume total ownership. Meanwhile, in February 1917, Popham sold a thousand acres of St. George to Sidney E. Trumbull and the Florida–Canadian Farms Company of Lakeland, Florida, which later became the Saint George Company. He received a substantial down payment. The next month a similar deal with a Tampa physician began well but quickly fell through. Still, the Saint George Company moved forward under Helen Brooks Smith of Lakeland and John Malcolmson, a Canadian who had experience running hotels. "Island Man" Roat repaired the small hotel which Smith renamed The Breakers (the same name she gave a sixteen–passenger boat that was to haul guests over from the mainland). With Helen Smith and Malcolmson, as manager of The Breakers, it was hoped that prosperity would follow in the form of hotel guests and people who would buy lots and construct cottages.

Popham created his own company, appropriating Saxon's old title The St. George Island Company. He made sales in Tallahassee among state officials and employees and in Jacksonville, but even though people had money, the idea of a resort hotel did not fit the patriotic spirit of the times. Stalled by World War I, Popham admitted temporary defeat and to his credit, repaid those who had invested with him. Even Roat went to work for the government. The Lakeland investors in the Saint George Company met a similar fate of economic failure.

World War I which came in April 1917 meant that the Apalachicola *Times* began mixing stories about worldwide events with local news. Doughboys from Franklin County went overseas to fight in France and everybody was concerned somehow with the war effort. Although President Woodrow Wilson called for patriotism, he backed his plea with a military conscription law. It was not needed in Franklin County which had thirteen hundred men of draft age. Volunteering for various branches of the military were two hundred forty-eight men (one hundred seventy-four whites and seventy-four blacks). Franklin was one of three counties nationwide where volunteer enlistments exceeded the quota in the first two drafts. Civilian dedication was no less manifest, as the county easily topped its assigned total in a Liberty Loan drive.

Spanish influenza in Apalachicola, Carrabelle, and St. Marks spread into the county but people kept their spirit. All were saddened by the death of popular Lieutenant Willoughby C. Marks, killed in action in France, and the ultimate deaths of eleven other county residents. Yet the citizens agreed with the Apalachicola *Times* editorial of August 31, 1918: "The main business of this country is to lick the Kaiser and it is your duty to get busy."

People got away from the war with brief visits to St. George Island. Popham moved to Jacksonville where he worked at various jobs for the booming St. Johns Shipyard before becoming the editor of the company's *Hun Hammer*. His widely read editorials urged greater production, the sale of Liberty bonds, and patriotic resolution. On Christmas Eve, Maude gave birth to William Lee, Jr., their first and only child. Throughout 1918 Popham took prospective buyers to St. George and remained Saxon's number one possibility to buy the island.

Finally Popham hit on a scheme which he called the St. George Co-Operative Colony, Unincorporated.

The restored J. E. Grady & Company Hardware store and ship chandlery was originally built in 1884. The brick building was home to a family-owned business whose specialty was supplying steamship and cargo ships that tied up at the Water Street docks in front of the store. The destructive fire of May 25, 1900, destroyed much of downtown Apalachicola, including the Grady Building. Reconstructed in November 1900, the building was reopened for business and remained in operation until the mid-1930s. The building was restored in 1998 by Herbert Duggar Construction Co. and now houses retail space downstairs and rental suites upstairs.

The courthouse, seat of Franklin County's government, was built during the Great Depression. Completed in 1940, it was a symbol of the county's emergence from the harsh economic decade of the thirties.

The Dixie Theatre was opened in April 1913. With its lush appointments the picture show had no rival for entertainment between Pensacola and Tampa. It was reconstructed by Rex and Cleo Partington in 1998, and now serves as a local playhouse.

The Chestnut Street Cemetery was established in 1831. In it are buried locals and many others who came to Apalachicola in connection with shipping, timber, and seafood. There are also a number of Confederate and Union soldiers interred there.

Carrabelle flourishes as a sportfishing center offering anglers easy access to the deep waters of the Gulf of Mexico.

Apalachicola State Bank was established in 1897. The original building was an impressive two-story structure with towering columns and enormous cathedral-like windows. Apalachicola State Bank has four offices throughout Franklin County in Apalachicola, Carrabelle, Eastpoint, and St. George Island. It is one of the oldest independent banks in the State of Florida.

A shoreline scene looking back north from Saint George Island to Eastpoint. In the background the new Bryant Patton Bridge stretches toward the mainland..

Little Saint George Lighthouse is located at Cape Saint George off the coast of Franklin County. A precarious sentinel, the lighthouse has stood since the mid-1800s. The structure is, through the attrition of time and the weather, now in the water. Local efforts, spearheaded by John Lee and others, have managed to stabilize the grand historical monument.

The Crooked River Lighthouse (not really located on the Crooked River) was constructed in 1895 after a hurricane in 1873 toppled the lighthouse on Dog Island. The new lighthouse, located about four miles west of Carrabelle, served as a beacon to the lumber shipping steamers that traversed the waterways in the late 1800s.

The Raney House, located in downtown Apalachicola, was built in 1838 and has stood since the City's very beginning. The structure was placed on the National Register of Historic Homes in 1972 and was purchased by the City of Apalachicola in 1973. David Greenway Raney built the house which narrowly escaped destruction during the Civil War.

An early morning fisherman prepares to test the waters of the Carrabelle River. The privately owned Carrabelle marina The Moorings is in the background.

Pristine coastlines such as this are familiar to the residents and visitors to Franklin County.

This stately red brick church is home of Apalachicola's African Methodist Episcopal Church (AME). The structure was built in the early 1900s and it is said that this church once had one of the largest AME congregations in Florida.

St. Patrick's Roman Catholic Church was constructed in 1929. The congregation was organized in 1845 by the Rev. Timothy Birmingham. The original structure, which served a number of Irish, Italian, and other families, was an ornate wooden structure with elaborate interior stencil work.

It was an industrial colony based on a mutual sharing of investments and profits by its members who would constitute a classless society. Popham would make money as a promoter but others would profit as well. Two hundred members were to pay $200 cash and receive four lots in a city to be established on the island and a small interest in the colony's holdings and operations. All profits from the ventures would be shared. Colony members would build the city themselves and be paid $5 a day for their labors.

Prospective members held meetings in Jacksonville, where W. W. Anderson was elected president and Charles N. Hampton became secretary (like J. J. Abbott, Hampton was a future close associate of Popham's). An elected board of directors, which included Popham as the featured speaker, met informally until after the war. Popham got the St. George Co-Operative Colony, Unincorporated to agree to pay him $65,000 for the island (although Saxon had upped the price to $35,000, Popham would still make a profit of $30,000). All went well with sales in Jacksonville and Tampa until Colony officials discovered the monetary details. They hastily decided to buy the island from Saxon. Popham was reduced to becoming a Colony employee with a salary of $30 a week and accepted $13,000 for his previous work.

In his new role Popham worked successfully to recruit the desired number of members. He and Anderson made a down payment to Saxon and in February 1919 the Tallahassee banker sold the island to the St. George Co-Operative Company, Unincorporated for $30,000. Monthly payments were to complete the transaction but if they failed to be made, the contract would be forfeited. Meanwhile, Popham maneuvered successfully to gain control of the Colony's board of control. With the aid of Abbott, Hampton, and a new confidant, William H. Collier, a young navy veteran, Popham got Abbott elected president and Collier chosen as secretary. The evangelist-poet's Byzantine exploits gained him newspaper attention. An interview in the Atlanta *Journal* of July 13, 1919, yielded conversation that was vintage Popham: truths, half-truths, and

The history of Apalachicola and the history of Trinity Episcopal Church are closely woven together. The white pine building is believed to be Florida's first pre-fabricated structure. It was shipped in sections from White Plains, New York to Apalachicola and completed in 1838. Early active members of the church included inventor Dr. John Gorrie and botanist Dr. Alvan Chapman. The ornately stenciled ceiling has never been repainted. The original bell was melted for a cannon during the Civil War, and the cushions and rugs were used for blankets and clothing. The church is on the National Register of Historic Places.

Scipio Creek, which empties into the Apalachicola River, accommodates a variety of commercial fishing boats.

falsehoods all delivered with compassion, imagination and showmanship. Popham told of building a cottage on the island and living there for seven years (two back-to-back untruths), explained how the Colony would operate with the various members working at several trades for $5 a day, especially fishing, and how the money would go into a common fund and be divided equally.

Elaborating, Popham explained that members would escape boredom by periodic transfers of jobs. Oysters, shrimp, fish, and other seafoods would be processed in factories and bring in money, as would porpoises whose hides would be used to manufacture shoestrings and whose previously inedible meat would now be eaten. Fresh water fish, he declared, were also abundant in St. George's six lakes. In truth, there were no lakes on the island. No government-built bridge connected St. George with the mainland at Eastpoint, although Popham said one did (a bridge was built forty-six years later in 1965). The promoter spoke of future racecourses for cars and rails for streetcars. Leisure would come from racing, boating, hunting, and fishing. Picture shows and theatres were planned but no vampire movies or sex plays would be presented. The only rule would be the Golden Rule, which was just as well because there would be no police force or jail and for that matter, no bill collectors. Members agreed that if they broke the peace they would be expelled. Children could not be forced to work and would be educated from grammar school through college by the island's educational system. The Atlanta reporter left the interview hypnotized and enraptured.

Along the way, Popham enticed the redoubtable Roat to return to the island and after some resistance, absorbed the St. George Co-Operative Company into the St. George Co-Operative Colony, Unincorporated. The latter company soon spruced up the island, repaired the boardwalk and the hotel, and purchased an island cruise boat as well as various craft for shrimping enterprises. Under Popham's direction an office was opened in Apalachicola and fish and oysterhouses were established on the mainland and on St. George. Roat's primary contribution was to survey the island in 1919. Some prospective colonists arrived in Apalachicola and activated the rental market. Apalachicolans marveled at it all.

In truth, the Colony's officials did not keep good books and there were internal problems. Finally, the Colony went into receivership but not before it paid Popham a considerable amount of money. After that it was reformed under the leadership of Hampton, Collier, and Abbott as the St. George Co-Operative Colony, Incorporated (incorporation was in Delaware). All of the reshaping was an expansion on a much wider scale, of the old unincorporated company. Actually, Popham was in control of the island and he sold it in 1920 to the new corporation for $27,000. Plans now reached a grandiose scale. The new company would deal in real estate, create a town on the island, operate fisheries, open fertilizer factories, own surface and water vehicles, have livestock and poultry, and engage in agriculture. Although not officially connected with the company, Popham made its operations possible. He became the best known and most admired citizen of Apalachicola and the columns of the *Times* were filled with articles about him and poems that he wrote himself.

Popham loaned the company money and even made some of its payments to Saxon out of his own pocket but the corporation could not meet its payments to the Tallahassee banker on a regular basis. The contract lapsed and Saxon repossessed the island. Biding his time, Popham stayed creative by publishing more poems in the *Times*. Soon he and his wife formed the Oyster Growers' Co-Operative Association and tied its future to his gaining outright possession of St. George. The association enlisted members across the United States who bought shares with the expectation of taking profits two years later and in perpetuity from the sale of oysters whose beds Popham was busily planting. Popham soon had enough money and, using the St. George Co-Operative Colony, Inc. as his agency, paid $5,000 down and followed it with a final check for $22,224.50. He took *de jure* as well as *de facto* possession of St. George Island. By combining the island's real estate possibilities with oyster production, Popham fully expected future prosperity for himself and the entire area.

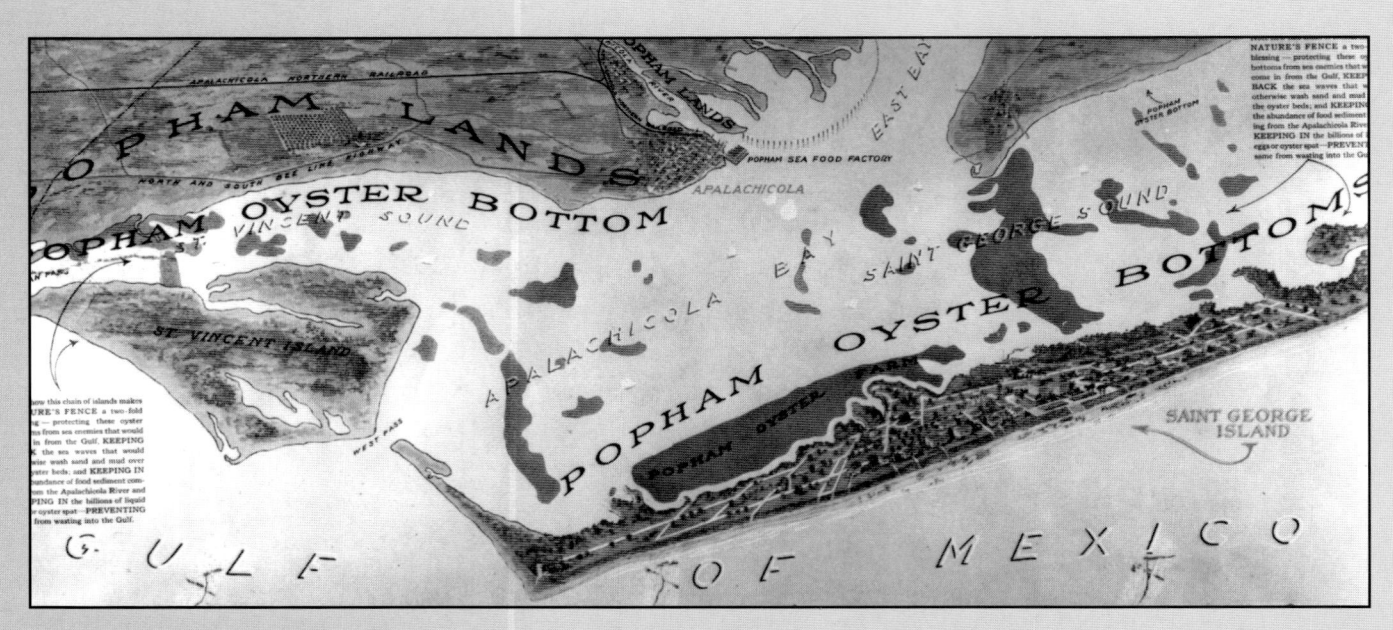

William Lee Popham, Baptist preacher, Chautauqua lecturer, and author, formed, among other organizations involving islands, St. George Co-Operative Colony and the Oyster Growers' Co-Operative Association. Courtesy of the Florida State Archives.

Nine

The Triumph, Decline and Fall of the Oyster King

*I*N THE 1920s POPHAM'S ACTIVITIES HAD A positive effect on Apalachicola's economy. Rich natural oyster beds and abundant shrimp meant prosperity, as did the sawmills that received, fashioned, and shipped the logs towed by tugs and steamers. Various factories made wooden sashes, doors, and blinds. The Dixie Theatre played to large crowds and people ignored, praised, denounced, and violated the Eighteenth Amendment. Popham bought a strip of land five miles long in the Apalachicola River across from the town's waterfront, named it Venice, and planned to sell lots on it and develop a small city. But Venice was a pseudo island that disappeared entirely at high tide. Popham turned instead to the Florida Co-Operative Colony which he organized in April 1920. It was similar to the previous colonies and with his usual associates—Abbott and Collier—and some outsiders, Popham proposed to sell investors water bottoms of twenty acres. He would then use the acreage to plant, harvest, and market shellfish for them. He sent out imaginatively written pamphlets and brochures (sprinkled liberally with his poems) soliciting members. Agent Popham's Venice Island venture, later denounced by the federal government as a scheme to steal, was taken over by the new Colony.

An investor put up a total of $135 to pay for forty small lots on Venice Island, one of which fronted the Apalachicola River. The investment included payment for twenty acres of oyster-covered water bottoms leased from the state and managed by Popham. Within five years, Popham claimed, the investor would have land worth $8,000 and income from the oyster farm would be $1,300 a month. His salesmanship convinced 912 investors from all over the country to sign up. The

Young boys were employed on Apalachicola oyster boats to shuck oysters. The boats went out at 4 A.M. and the boys received a share of the proceeds. Courtesy of the Florida State Archives.

Oyster shuckers at Apalachicola, about 1909. Courtesy of the Florida State Archives.

Spartan Jenkins, owner of the Sadie J (the first boat on Apalachicola Bay with an engine) rented her to Popham's Cultivated Oyster Farms for $20.00 a month, in 1933. Courtesy of the Florida State Archives.

Apalachicola and Carrabelle sawmills received, fashioned, and shipped out the logs harvested in Franklin County forests and swamps. Courtesy of the Florida State Archives.

William L. Popham sent out imaginatively written pamphlets and brochures touting his latest land scheme and sprinkled liberally with his poems. Courtesy of the Florida State Archives.

112
At the Water's Edge

irresistible plan required no work and an investor was free to come down, watch the money flow in, and enjoy a Florida vacation at the same time. Or better still, an investor could move permanently to Franklin County. Popham called the Florida Co-Operative Colony "a liquid gold mine."

Ever the innovator, Popham increased the payment terms, once he acquired St. George, and threw in a small lot on the island for a residence. If a member wished, he could also invest in the Colony's packing house. Members Abbott and Collier sought greater profits for themselves in 1921 by breaking with Popham and forming their own organization, the Apalachicola Land and Development Company. They proposed a plan similar to Popham's and made the extravagant and false claim that the area's oyster bottoms belonged to the abutting property owners, not to the state or to the federal government. Their company, they claimed, had control over submerged lands and riparian rights. Inspired by Popham, the men promised large profits from real estate and the oyster and shrimp business.

Angry at first by the apostasy of his former colleagues, Popham soon endorsed them as honorable men, resigned as president of the Florida Co-Operative Colony, and permitted his members to transfer their interests to the Apalachicola Land and Development Company. In turn Popham formed a new company: the Oyster Growers' Co-Operative Association with himself as president. Perhaps Popham figured that the new company would lose its legal case, as it did in 1923, when the Florida State Supreme Court ruled that the Indian-Spanish grants did not include submerged lands or tide lands. Even so, Collier and Abbott claimed credit for the Butler-Lindsay Riparian Act which said that property owners owned the oyster bottoms that their land abutted. The act was negated by Popham's lobbying efforts in Tallahassee. He received assurances from Commissioner of Agriculture William A. MacRae that he could lease five hundred acres of oyster bottoms in the bay. He got his old friend Roat to obtain the necessary permit and to begin planting oysters for them both. His new Oyster Growers' Co-Operative Association quickly sold shares to one thousand customers, while Abbott and Collier's company, which had not leased even an acre from the state, collapsed. By January 1922, Popham took over the Colony with a payment of $10 and agreed to pay off its mortgage. The Colony disappeared as completely as Venice Island at high tide. Popham allowed Abbott and Collier to rejoin his new company, whose purpose was to develop St. George Island and expand his oyster kingdom. When newspapers mentioned the actions of the Oyster King, Popham was the name that came to mind.

For the next four years Popham and his confederates Abbott and Collier used their extraordinary talents to promote sales for the Oyster Growers Co-Operative Association and later in the Million Dollar Bond Plan. Popham's *Oyster Farm News* (he was sole owner and editor) kept investors informed and recruited new ones. The Association was widely advertised in Florida and Georgia newspapers. Besides using oyster shells for road construction on the island, Popham planted them on the leased underwater bottoms. Wire mesh was placed on the bottoms to prevent the shells from sinking or floating off with the current. By 1921 he had planted one hundred thousand barrels of live oysters and shells. In many statewide speaking engagements, Popham informed the public of plans to build three oyster factories in the bay area. Popham soon was opposed by John G. Ruge, the prominent Apalachicola civic leader and oysterman, who saw the Kentuckian as an economic threat. The two men became rivals and enemies.

Apalachicolans admired Popham's dash and confidence. He purchased and refurbished inside and outside the old home of botanist Alvan W. Chapman. Following the death of her husband in 1922, Popham's mother Clara moved into Chapman house, and so did "Silent Jim" Estes, Maude's mentally retarded but harmless brother. Besides Popham's house, locals admired his bright red, four-door, seven-passenger Willys-Knight automobile—more elegant than Ruge's Studebaker. Popham drove his family around town in style and when he carried William Lee, Jr., to school in the morning, permitted other children to ride with them.

Meantime, Popham purchased wharf lots in Apalachicola and other lots and tracts of land as well. Appropriately enough, when William Jennings Bryan visited Apalachicola in 1923, the Pophams entertained him in their home and William Lee introduced him when he spoke at the Dixie Theatre. Bryan, no slacker at public discourse, said it was difficult for him "to come

The Manteo at Carrabelle about 1918. Courtesy of the Florida State Archives.

Popham purchased and refurbished inside and outside the old home of botanist Alvan W. Chapman. Courtesy of the Florida State Archives.

down to earth after such a flowery introduction." Popham launched new ventures and dreamed of others—selling land for people through a real estate department attached to the Oyster Growers' Co-Operative Association (accomplished), establishing the Florida Wholesale Land Company, Inc. to develop forty thousand acres in Franklin and Liberty counties (accomplished), laying plans for the large scale planting of satsuma oranges (never accomplished), promoting economic ventures in Brazil (never accomplished). He continued to acquire "almost islands" and oystering rights to other bottom lands. Apalachicolans Francis Lovett, Harry Cummings, and Homer Marks would recall many years later how the local post office was deluged with mail addressed to the Oyster Growers' Co-Operative Association.

Sales on St. George Island increased rapidly and led to a resurvey of the island, this time by C. M. Dechant, and yet another Popham scheme: the New and Enlarged Plan, or the Million Dollar Bond Plan. In essence, the plan enlarged the Association (the members approved) and involved the American Exchange Bank at Apalachicola and the construction of a mammoth oyster packinghouse and factory in Apalachicola. Amendments were added later and by 1924 the four thousand members from every state in the union looked forward to having a homesite and a lifetime cash income from oysters and other seafood. The conservatively dressed Popham and his staff, led by Abbott and Collier, oper-

Partial View of Dock, Apalachicola, Fla.

A partial view of the Apalachicola waterfront. Courtesy of the Florida State Archives.

The conservatively dressed Popham and his staff operated from a building on Market Street with state of the art equipment, including a dictaphone and "Addressograph." Courtesy of the Florida State Archives.

ated from a building on Market Street. It had state of the art equipment—the town's only dictaphone and an "Addressograph." Popham eliminated almost all organization and standard contractual and bookkeeping methods from his operations, justifying his unorthodox methods as eliminating expenses. Besides, he said, "All promises, like pie crusts, are easily broken."

St. George's natural beauty was increased by physical improvements on the island and Popham's vision exceeded temporary inconveniences. He spoke of a thousand-room, rainbow-hued, million dollar hotel, of attractive cottages, of a ten thousand acre game preserve, of broad paved avenues—and he had it all illustrated in his advertising literature, noting without emphasis that certain features were in the planning stage. As for the oyster industry, Popham borrowed effectively from the ancient Japanese practice of binding scrub oak branches with wire and anchoring them at intervals on the bay bottom. They became ideal places for the spat to mature into oysters. His oyster ventures brought him and other Florida shellfishermen into conflict with the colorful Shellfish Commissioner of Florida, T. R. Hodges.

The Shellfish Commissioner acted in an imperial manner carrying out his duties of enforcing laws, collecting license fees, planting and protecting oysters,

T. R. Hodges, Shell Fish Commissioner of Florida, antagonized neo-Populist governor William J. Catts (center of photo sitting in front of the standing man in a white suit) who removed him from office, but in 1921 he was reinstated by governor Cary Augustus Hardee (seated to the right of middle, front row). Courtesy of the Florida State Archives.

and supervising the fishing industry. Hodges had antagonized neo-Populist governor William J. Catts (1916–1920), who had removed him from office but in 1921 he was reinstated by governor Cary Augustus Hardee. Hodges questioned Popham's oystering methods, although they worked, and the state itself soon copied his pioneering techniques. Besides, Popham offered employment to a number of Franklin County's young men. He remained popular and was easily Apalachicola's best known and most admired man. He spoke frequently at the Calvary Baptist church where he was superintendent of the Sunday School. He was president of the Apalachicola Chamber of Commerce and headed the Franklin County branch of the Automobile Association of America (AAA). With Rudolph Marshall driving, his *Lady Popham* boat made Fourth of July races a popular event and his business success led to the opening of a sales office in Tallahassee. He had a fleet of trucks, as well as vessels, barges, skiffs, and a power dredge boat. Popham's money was deposited in several banks. His two-story oysterpacking factory on the waterfront, completed in 1923, was his most visible accomplishment. Spelled out in oyster shells across the front was the statement "POPHAM OYSTER FACTORY NO. I." Local oystermen despised Hodges and joined other citizens in their high regard for Popham. They saw Apalachicola as Miami, Franklin County as Dade County, and St. George Island as Miami Beach—only better. Boom and prosperity rivaling that of South Florida would surely be theirs.

Oyster packing houses and acres of oyster shells on the Apalachicola waterfront. Courtesy of the Florida State Archives.

In 1922 Popham ran for the Democratic nomination to the Florida House of Representatives from Franklin County. In a one-party state such as Florida nomination in the primary guaranteed victory in the fall general election. His opponents were W. A. Register of Apalachicola and S. J. Giles of Carrabelle. The usual pattern of exchanging the seat every two years between Carrabelle and Apalachicola was abandoned in 1922 and the campaign was wide open. All three men ran on conservative tickets, with Giles attacking Popham as a carpetbagger, an outsider, and praising himself as a native man. Register, who lived in Apalachicola, was a former judge in Wakulla County and a respected man. Popham did not campaign much, and when he did, complimented his opponents' abilities. The Oyster King's main plank was his promise to get Shellfish Commissioner Hodges removed from office. Popham carried Apalachicola but split the vote with Register. The victorious Giles took Carrabelle by a wide margin and prepared to go to Tallahassee.

Popham, who had run mostly as an afterthought, was not disturbed by his defeat but he was upset by a mounting number of difficulties. He argued orally and in print with Ruge, narrowly avoided a fistfight with another critic, and actually exchanged blows with two local seafood men. According to Popham in 1922 Ruge and Shellfish Commissioner Hodges brought charges that he had violated a federal law by using the United States mail to obtain money by false and fraudulent advertising. They claimed further that by leasing oyster bottoms to nonresidents of Florida, Popham had violated a state law. A federal grand jury at Tallahassee returned two indictments against William Lee and Maude, as well as Collier and Abbott. Popham maintained an outward air of confidence and support for him in Apalachicola was widespread, especially from members of the Association; Henry W. Johnston, editor of the local *Times*; and Dr. J. P. H. Feldman, pastor, and his congregation at the Calvary Baptist church.

Apalachicola Fish and Oyster houses including, top left, William L. Popham's Cultivated Oyster Farm Corporation's packing house. Courtesy of the Florida State Archives.

To Popham's disappointment, legal problems delayed the trial. He was accused by the Bureau of Internal Revenue of the Treasury Department of owing a large sum of money in unpaid income taxes. Tax liens were filed against him and all properties of the Oyster Growers' Co-Operative Association were placed under attachment. In addition, in 1923 the four accused people were indicted again by a federal grand jury in Pensacola for fraudulent use of the mail in advertising St. George Island. A lesser man would have despaired, but Popham simply quoted Matthew's New Testament statement: "Blessed are ye when men revile you." A thousand Apalachicolans signed a petition demanding that the governor oust Hodges. Popham even went to Tallahassee and campaigned there in the press and to legislators and the public against Hodges.

In 1923 Popham was able to continue making lot sales on St. George Island but he and Hodges were summoned to Washington to testify before Post Office Department officials in closed hearings. No resolution followed but in November Popham was triumphantly elected mayor of Apalachicola—his opponent got two votes. Yet the government, led by Assistant District Attorney Earl Hoffman, was building its case. An order fatal, if permanent, to Popham was issued to hold his mail. He gave his investors a moratorium on their payments pending dismissal of the charges. He placed a paid advertisement in the Tallahassee *Democrat* excoriating Hodges and Ruge and after his signature placed the words: "The Persecuted."

During all of his troubles Popham remained indomitable. The trial was finally set for Tallahassee in late January 1924 but before it began new indictments involving the Million Dollar Bond Plan were issued. The opponents were: for the defense Philip Beall of Pensacola, John P. Stokes of Miami, State Senator W. C. Hodges, and Fred H. David and E. T. David of Tallahassee; for the prosecution District Attorney Fred C. Cubberly and Assistant District Attorney Earl Hoffman. The courtroom was packed with spectators, many of them from Apalachicola. The defense started well by getting Judge William B. Sheppard to throw out the most recent indictments. Charges against Maude had already been dropped. The move prompted Hoffman to ask for a continuance and get it despite the defense's protest. Still, Judge Sheppard threw out the original indictments except one because they were not prosecuted soon enough. He announced that he would try it—fraudulent use of the mails—in February.

Popham returned to Apalachicola and wrote his investors (he could send mail but could not receive it) predicting total victory and declaring that the govern-

Even after a federal grand jury returned two indictments against William Lee and Maude Popham there was widespread support for them in Apalachicola, including Dr. J. P. H. Feldman, pastor, and his congregation at the Calvary Baptist Church. Courtesy of the Florida State Archives.

ment had no case. Even so, with Popham's blessing, a suit was brought by Mabel L. Osborne, an investor, and the Association was put in receivership. Circuit court judge E. C. Love appointed R. G. Porter as the trustee and S. E. Rice, Jr., as the receiver of what became the Popham Trust Estate. The great promoter was reeling from the legal blows.

Preoccupied with his legal and financial troubles, Popham went through a listless political campaign in 1924 seeking election to the State House of Representatives. He lost in the Democratic primary to former representative E. R. L. Moore of Carrabelle by a vote of 417 to 391. A pleasant interlude came when William Jennings Bryan, successfully seeking election as a delegate-at-large to the Democratic national convention, came to Apalachicola. Popham entertained the Great Commoner, and, as mayor, introduced and endorsed him when he spoke to the citizens. Popham attempted to sell land in Franklin and Liberty counties and elsewhere in Florida through his Florida Wholesale Land Company, Inc. but had to defer his plans. At least he came up with a catchy slogan: "The Best Investment On Earth, Is The Earth Itself." With his Oyster Growers'

Co-Operative Association in receivership, Popham had to shelve plans to enlarge it.

Meanwhile, Earl Hoffman got the previous government charges consolidated, and a grand jury in Pensacola indicted Popham, Abbott, and Collier again and added Charles N. Hampton and Jefferson D. Kenney. There were seven counts for using the mail to defraud and one for conspiracy (it affected Kenney and Popham's relationship). The new charges led to an abortive attempt by some Apalachicola citizens to remove Popham as mayor because he was giving the town a bad name. The defense got a change of venue and the trial was shifted to Tallahassee. It began in January 1924, with W. I. Grubb, judge of the U. S. District Court for the Northern District of Alabama, presiding under special designation. The defense team of Beall, Hodges, and Davis added Jonathan P. Stokes and John M. Coe to their forces. U.S. District Attorney Cubberly headed the government's case with the assistance of Hoffman and Special Assistant Attorney General Arthur N. Sager. The trial lasted from January 12 to January 21, and in those eleven days the jury heard eighty-one witnesses (there were 1,187 pages of testimony and 600 exhibits). For reasons still unknown,

State Senator William C. Hodges, of Tallahassee, was one of five defense attorneys employed by W. L. Popham. Courtesy of the Florida State Archives.

This view of St. George Island, from the lighthouse, attests to the statement by Popham that "The best investment on earth, is the earth itself." Courtesy of the Florida State Archives.

Hampton was the only defendant to take the stand. Where was Popham? The disappointed crowd wondered why the eloquent Oyster King did not defend himself. Their questions have never been answered.

Popham's opponents, especially Ruge and Hodges, leveled devastating charges against him. Judge Grubb saved the jury some trouble by throwing out the conspiracy indictment against Kenney but the members still deliberated unsuccessfully for ten hours. Locked up for the night, they reached a decision at 9:30 the next morning. Abbott, Collier, and Hampton were declared innocent of all charges. Declared guilty on all seven counts, Popham was sentenced to four years' imprisonment at the federal penitentiary in Atlanta. His lawyers appealed the decision, and, although denied, were issued a writ of error and given ninety days to prepare. Meanwhile Popham did not seek reelection as mayor of Apalachicola. Both sides filled their briefs, and the court of appeals sitting in New Orleans upheld the lower court's decision on March 17, 1926. Even so, Popham's lawyers brought out evidence that the jury had been tampered with and were given until September to file for a new trial.

During this time Abbott broke with Popham stating that he was guilty as charged. Undiscouraged, Popham correctly anticipated that his motion would be turned down and his attorneys made a final effort to get the United States Supreme Court to grant a new trial. Popham seemed strangely undisturbed and resigned his fate to the will of God. He said, "I am not at all discouraged," adding that "if I am guilty of any dishonesty, I am fully certain that the high court will commit me to prison—where dishonest wrongdoers belong."

In November the Supreme Court refused to review his conviction and some last minute maneuvering by the defense came to nothing. Later that month Popham joined some other prisoners at Tallahassee and was taken to Atlanta. Popham was now a prisoner but he took with him a suitcase full of his books which he donated to the prison library whose officials were glad to get them.

Before there were "supermarkets" most of the women in town churned their own butter. Courtesy of the Florida State Archives.

Ten

The Great Depression

SOUTH FLORIDA'S LAND BOOM COLLAPSED in 1925. Paper fortunes were wiped out and speculators and promoters suddenly became fleeing predators, while investors, large and small, lost everything. Accompanying the land debacle were bank failures, especially state banks, although national banks closed as well. Tourism and the construction industry were hurt by a strike on the Atlantic Coast Line Railroad in 1925. During the decade Florida was crippled by a devastating hurricane in 1926 (four hundred people were killed, sixty-three hundred injured, and fifty thousand left homeless) and another one in 1928 cost an estimated two thousand lives. The Mediterranean fruit fly struck in 1929 and temporarily devastated the citrus industry. With raging "Medflys," hurricanes, strikes, and bank failures, the Sunshine State had its own depression before the more general one of 1929. The Great Depression began for the rest of the country with the stock market crash on Wall Street in October.

At Apalachicola the Popham Trust Estate remained in receivership. Gambits toward purchasing it came from several sources but none materialized. In 1928 the court appointed Greene S. Johnston, Jr., of Tallahassee as trustee. Most of the investors had not paid their taxes and their lots were put up for public sale. Not many were taken at any price because Franklin County and its people were suffering financial hardships. Little St. George Island was not part of the Popham Estate. The family sold it in 1929 and so the Porters and Popham no longer controlled the island.

Apalachicolans and Floridians girded themselves against adversity. Local citizens listened in 1927 to the second boxing match between Jack Dempsey and Gene Tunney by special arrangement with Jacksonville's radio station WJAX. Some of the younger generation helped greet the nation's leading crooner Gene Austin who docked his yacht for a brief stay in 1928. Miniature golf swept the nation and became a local craze. Hard times could not deter those who went to the remodeled Dixie Theatre in September 1929 to see "The Broadway Melody." It was the town's first talking picture. Even so, the Great Depression represented bitter poverty at its worst and, as if the people needed a reminder of nature's potential for punishment, a hurricane hit the region in 1929. Still, there were exceptions to despair, one being the opening in 1930 of the Intracoastal Waterway.

The 1932 baseball team roster included, back row: Red Porter, Richard Porter, Fred Richards, Joe Hiles, Bill Owens, J. J. Teague, George Hiles, J. Johnston and Dick Porter. Front row: George Core, George Suber, Willie F. Randolph, Carl Morton, B. Frances Bloodworth, Ivan Truman, Ed Hiles and Rex Buzzett. Courtesy of the Apalachicola State Bank.

The 1930–1931 oyster season was one of the worst on record for the quality of the mollusks, the demand, and the prices received. All the same, the seafood industry remained the chief means of livelihood. The state Shell Fish Department planted shells in key areas. St. George Island was inhabited mainly by cattle, goats, and hogs, although the turpentine lessee made his rounds. Duck hunting season saw an invasion of men and boys and there were always Sunday excursionists. Apalachicola seemed cut off from the world as efforts to build a bridge across the bay failed for lack of money. The Wing ferry line remained in operation and citizens did not give up hope.

Efforts to build a bridge across the bay failed for lack of money and except for the Wing ferry line Apalachicola remained cut off from the world. Courtesy of the Florida State Archives.

Duck hunting season saw the invasion of St. George Island by men and boys out for their daily limit. Shown here after a successful goose hunt are Rodman Porter, Jr., Buster Porter, Chester Kerns, Joe Hickey and Rodman Porter, Sr. Courtesy of the Florida State Archives.

In 1923 sisters Annie Gibson Hayes and Mary Ellen "Sunshine" Gibson bought the Franklin Hotel and changed the name to the Gibson Inn. Courtesy of the Florida State Archives.

The Popham Trust Estate floundered along. Finally in 1932, it sold for $10,000 to a combination of Apalachicola oyster men. Three months later they sold it to the Cultivated Oyster Farms Corporation, a firm with a name worthy of William Lee Popham. People were too concerned with personal survival to care much but once they learned that it was Popham's company, they paid attention.

Apalachicolans knew about his imprisonment in 1926 and early release after serving only two of his four years' sentence. Many had been among those who welcomed him home in 1928. Some even knew that while in Atlanta he had been prison librarian and had pub-lished yet another book entitled *Prison Poems*. It had circulated in Apalachicola but even at the price of ten cents, attracted few buyers among the cash shy citizens. In his absence Maude, William Lee, Jr., Clara, and Jim Estes had remained at home and been well treated by the townspeople.

Moving against the tide was nothing new to the former Oyster King who promptly produced another book, *Heart Poems*, got his mother to mortgage property that he had transferred to her, bought St. George Island, and prepared for a comeback. His poetry did not sell but he at least got his mailing privileges restored. Now in the early thirties Popham used his Cultivated Oyster Farms Corporation (a product of similar companies he had

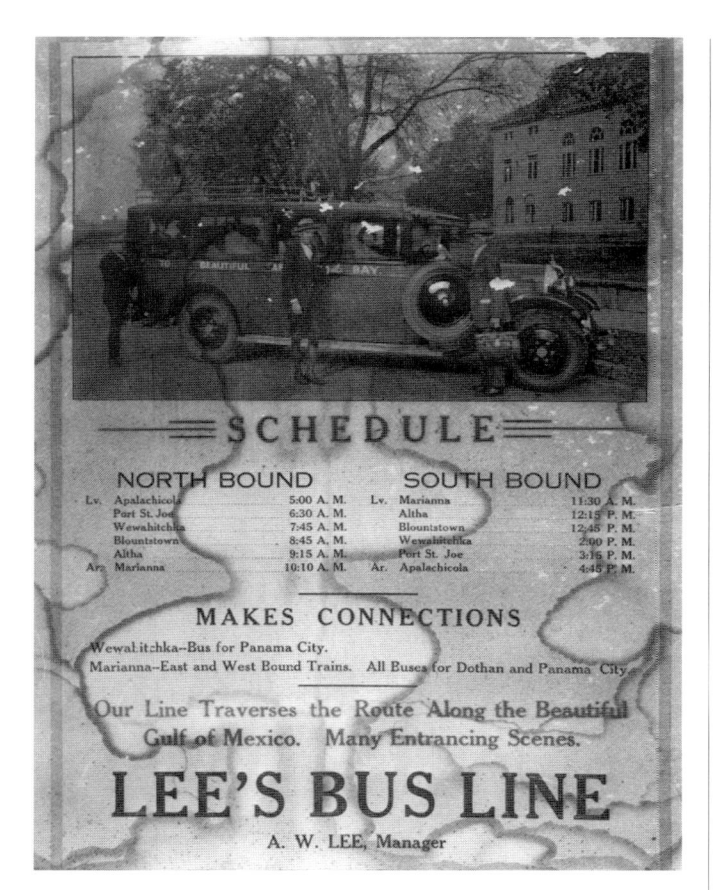

Lee's Bus Line provided overland transportation from Apalachicola to Marianna, via Port St. Joe, Wewahitchka, Blountstown and Altha, beginning in 1928. Courtesy of the Florida State Archives.

After serving two years of a four year sentence, William L. Popham got his mother to mortgage property that he had transferred to her, bought St. George Island again and started the Cultivated Oyster Farms Corporation. Courtesy of the Florida State Archives.

formed) to lease five hundred acres of water bottoms in Apalachicola Bay and to undertake oyster farming. Former state commissioner of agriculture William A. McRae was one of his associates.

A sense of déjà vu affected those who read his promotional literature: investing in his corporation meant personal wealth for them. Here was the Oyster King once more. He promised, without saying how, to utilize St. George Island. Some leases were signed and Popham proposed consolidating all of the oyster and seafood factories in the area.

Over the years Popham's imagination had actually become more fertile. In 1934 he formed two new companies: World-Wyde Products, Incorporated and Florida Oyster Farms, Incorporated. He planned to build three thousand Oyster Huts and Seafood Restaurants to handle his corporation's products. It was one of the first fast food concepts in the country. He also devised World-Wyde Oyster Puree which could be packaged in pow-

dered form and as cubes and tablets. Next, the inventive Popham developed a nutritional nickel drink called Oyster Nip that could be consumed hot or cold. Here were pioneering steps in America's future multi-billion dollar business in instant foods and liquid health products.

The Great Depression thwarted Popham's plans. In 1935 he attempted to expand with his Florida Sunland Farms, combining the sale of small acre farms in DeSoto County with the Cultivated Oyster Farms Corporation. He put his headquarters in Jacksonville and set up branch offices in other Florida cities. Taking his message into Georgia and the Carolinas, Popham produced a talking movie to illustrate his projects. As part of his pitch, he played gramophone records over loudspeakers. The audiences were respectful and polite but few people invested.

William Lee, like others in depression Apalachicola, could not depend on the local economy and for the first

Children boarding a Franklin County school bus in the 1930s. Courtesy of the Florida State Archives.

View looking toward the post office and Gibson Hotel, just as the Depression was about to hit, October 1929. Courtesy of the Florida State Archives.

years of the thirties there was not enough commitment by the state to offer substantial relief. Yet, following the victory of Franklin D. Roosevelt over Herbert Hoover for president in 1932, a new approach to government at the federal level was launched. Americans had never seen anything like the New Deal. The Democrats enacted major programs affecting the economic and social life of all Americans.

The national government switched from its traditional role as umpire of events to that of being a major participant and regulator. FDR, as Americans called him, became a folk hero to many people in Franklin County and throughout the country. Bank windows showing membership in the Federal Deposit Insurance Corporation reassured people that their funds, however small, were safe. At Carrabelle a mattress factory was opened with money from the Federal Emergency Relief Administration (FERA). In Apalachicola the Rice Brothers Packing Plant became a beef-canning factory and eased the unemployment problem. Other FERA funds were used to build an airport for Apalachicola in 1934. New Deal agencies such as the Public Works Administration (PWA) and the Works Progress Administration (WPA) boosted the local economy. The Home Owners Loan Corporation (HOLC) enabled citizens to hold on to their homes. Construction of the new courthouse, opened in 1940, was made possible with federal funds.

Young men from Franklin County enrolled in the "Tree Army," the Civilian Conservation Corps (CCC). In 1938 over four hundred Franklin countians were working part or full time on government projects. The most symbolic incident came in November 1935: the John Gorrie Bridge was opened and linked Apalachicola with Eastpoint and places beyond. It was six and a half miles of concrete ribbon that stood for hope and people by the thousands celebrated its grand opening.

Yet the Great Depression was far from over. The dry spell that caused the Dust Bowl on the American plains created a shortage of fresh water in the Apalachicola River valley. Oyster leaches flourished because of the bay's increased salinity and decimated the beds. The 1935 oyster season was ruined and it was the late 1930s before remedial action finally returned production to normal.

The difficulties adversely affected Popham who was working hard to regain lost credibility. As his income declined he used bravado to keep up a front and increased his sales efforts across Florida. Popham's family lived at home under greatly reduced circumstances but they were able to send William Lee, Jr., to the University of Florida at Gainesville. Popham barely paid

After the bank failures of the late 1920s, bank windows showed membership in the Federal Deposit Insurance Corporation to reassure people that their funds, however small, were safe. Courtesy of the Florida State Archives.

New Deal agencies such as the Public Works Administration and the Works Progress Administration boosted the local economy. The new courthouse, made possible with federal funds, opened in 1940. Courtesy of the Florida State Archives.

In November 1935 the John Gorrie Bridge opened linking Apalachicola with Eastpoint and places beyond. It was a six-and-three-quarter-mile concrete ribbon that stood for hope, and people by the thousands celebrated the grand opening. Courtesy of the Florida State Archives.

his bills (light, water, rent). Deeply in debt, he attempted to use St. George Island to meet his obligations. He formed a new company (the Florida Goat, Sheep, and Turkey Farms), borrowed $5,000 from his old friend George M. Counts, and leased turpentine rights on the island to Clifford C. Land. He permitted Land to put cattle there. William Lee's struggles were interrupted by news that had a catastrophic impact.

On September 5, 1936, a federal grand jury indicted William Lee, Maude, and William A. McRae for violating Section 215 of the U.S. Penal Code. The familiar charge was fraudulent use of the mail. Claiming that he had been "framed by business competitors" and "railroaded by government agents," Popham was arrested and brought to Jacksonville where he and Maude were arraigned. Because of illness McRae was excused from appearing before Judge Louis W. Strum in the U.S. District Court for the Southern District of Florida. McRae raised his bond money and Popham obtained funds for Maude's release. Unable to raise money for himself, Popham remained in jail for two months before he got it lowered.

In January 1937, Judge Strum presided over a trial that heard ninety witnesses from across the country. William Lee and Maude had no money but subsisted on fifteen dollars a week given them by Popham's brother. Popham still had St. George Island and its value enabled him to hire a outstanding defense team of lawyers: State Senator Edgar W. Waybright and his son, Roger J. Waybright of Jacksonville; and State Senator William C. Hodges and Clyde A. Atkinson of Tallahassee. When they visited Popham in jail the lawyers found him confident of an innocent verdict. McRae had his own lawyers. The prosecutors were Damon O. Yerkes, William A. Paisley, two assistant district attorneys, and U.S. District Attorney Herbert S. Phillips.

Basically, the case against Popham was that he had deliberately misrepresented the facts of his venture to his customers. The government lawyers used confusing charts and arcane arguments to trace Popham's Byzantine machinations. The defense lawyers merely read letters from individuals, including former governor Doyle E. Connor, declaring Popham a man of good

Franklin Countians depended even more on fishing when increased salinity and oyster leaches decimated the local beds. Shown here are Thomas Jefferson Nesmith and wife Milton, with Ed Black mending a three hundred yard gill net at their place eleven miles west of Apalachicola. Courtesy of the Apalachicola State Bank.

William C. Roberts, son of the lighthouse keeper, in his goat cart on St. George Island, about 1930. Courtesy of the Florida State Archives.

character. They relied primarily on Popham who testified in his own behalf. Avoiding the first trial's basic mistake, William Lee was brilliant in two days of direct and cross-examination. He was eloquent, performing with evangelistic energy and persuasiveness. A mesmerized judge, set of lawyers, and spectators watched and listened to the performance.

The trial ended on January 15. Judge Strum directed the jury to find Maude Popham not guilty because she played no role in any of the promotions. While the jury was deliberating Popham told his lawyer Clyde Atkinson conviction would be acceptable since he needed a chance to rest and write. After three and a half hours, Foreman W. A. Evans and the other jurors returned to the courtroom. Evans read their decision: the defendants were not guilty on all counts. Popham was vindicated.

The problem remained of paying his defense lawyers and Popham mortgaged St. George Island to them. He borrowed money from Alphonse Pichard of Tallahassee by issuing him a second mortgage to the island. He hoped to revitalize the Florida Goat, Sheep, and Turkey Farms, Incorporated, but nothing worked. In March 1938, after Popham was unable to make his mortgage payments, the circuit court awarded the island to his defense lawyers. Counts also held a mortgage of St. George but he made a financial deal with William H. Wilson, brother-in-law of William C. Hodges. Tallahassee businessman Wilson and Atkinson became key figures in shaping the island's future. By April 1940, Wilson obtained possession of the other owners' claims to St. George and became the exclusive owner.

In the meantime Popham and his family had no incentive to remain in Apalachicola and Franklin County. Conditions were still bad there economically, although the area was improving, especially the seafood industry. The shrimp and crabmeat industries, as well as the oyster factories, increased in number and importance. Shrimp boats and others seeking deepwater fish stood to gain if Congress appropriated money creating a permanent cut through St. George Island. Deepening the

The shrimp and crabmeat industries, as well as the oyster factories, began to increase in number about 1940 and the Jessie Mae *was busy carrying mail, freight and passengers between Apalachicola and Carrabelle. Courtesy of the Florida State Archives.*

channel at Carrabelle helped revive the old and profitable lumber industry. The L. B. Buck Lumber Company and others were able to increase their earnings. In 1940, World War II moved closer to American shores. That was seen locally when a Carrabelle lumber company entered an agreement with the British government that skirted the edges of American neutrality policy. In the summer of 1940, the combat readiness of Company E of the 106th Engineers, Apalachicola's National Guard unit, became a matter of concern and new members were recruited. It was an anxious and dramatic time.

William Lee Popham's mother Clara died shortly after the trial. He and his family left Florida—he probably agreed with the suggestion from the *Times* of making St. George Island a state park. He and his family moved around, never able to regain a substantial living. Yet, he never gave up hope of making a comeback. Finally settling in Los Angeles, William Lee became a realtor. William Lee, Jr., also lived in California where he married and raised a family. Popham was sixty-eight when he died of uremia in Los Angeles on August 21, 1953. Maude died there in 1980 at the age of ninety-three. The Oyster King never forgot Apalachicola or St. George Island. A man far in advance of his time, the remarkable Popham left a legacy that, in many ways, is still felt throughout Franklin County. The decade of the 1940s would be far different from the one that preceded it.

By 1940 the Gorrie Bridge across Apalachicola Bay was opening up Florida to Apalachicola more than ever. Courtesy of the Florida State Archives.

Eleven

World War II

AS THE THIRTIES ENDED ECONOMIC hardship was still a mainstay in the United States. Apalachicola and Franklin County were no exceptions. Although the New Deal programs of Roosevelt's administration had stimulated the job market, the Great Depression lingered. As late as 1941 lands, including acreage on St. George Island, were being sold at public auction for taxes. Even so, there were good signs. The bridge across Apalachicola Bay was opening up Florida to Apalachicola more than ever. Connecting a former transportation mode with the present, the steamer *George W. Miller* made three trips a month to Columbus, Georgia, carrying freight and passengers from Apalachicola and Port St. Joe.

The seafood industry prospered and locals S. E. Rice and Willie Fred Randolph were involved in

Tonging for oysters in Apalachicola Bay. Courtesy of the Florida Department of Commerce.

Connecting a former transportation mode with the present, the steamer **George W. Miller** *made three trips a month to Columbus, Georgia carrying freight and passengers from Apalachicola and Port St. Joe. Courtesy of the Florida State Archives.*

Shucking freshly tonged oysters. Courtesy of the Florida Department of Commerce.

founding a union organized in Jacksonville and known as the Florida Commercial Fisheries Association. At least one hundred twenty-nine shrimp boats and twenty-nine snapper boats used West Pass—leading the Apalachicola "Jaycees" to push for congressional funds for harbor improvements. Unfortunately, the president vetoed all local maritime projects not directly connected to national defense. Shrimping and shrimp canning increased as the industry came to rival oysters in importance. Joe Taranto pioneered in shipping iced seafood by trucks to northern customers, and Belton Tarantino used the same swift means of marketing. Other firms relied on the railroad for transportation. Apalachicola's unique location seemed to promise an inexhaustible and self-perpetuating supply of seafood. Variety came with the establishment of a crabmeat factory in 1940 and by the end of the year Wallace M. Quinn was building a menhaden (a salt water fish used for making fertilizer and oil) factory. Local bragging was backed by statistical facts when it was revealed that 1940 set a record for the fishing industry: 112,089 pounds of seafood and 51,700 gallons of oysters.

The fact that it was 1940 meant the hard decade was behind and in the new transitional period there were signs of stability. The Philaco Club (the name was derived from the word "Apalachicola" without using any letter twice) founded in 1896 and originally known as the Women's Reading Club, was still going strong. Even more tangible and reassuring was the move of the

Shrimp and shrimp canning increased as the industry came to rival oysters in importance and Joe Taranto pioneered in shipping iced seafood by trucks to northern customers. Courtesy of the Florida Department of Commerce.

An addition to the shellfish industry was the establishment of a crabmeat factory in 1940. Courtesy of the Florida Department of Commerce.

county government in January to a new New Deal courthouse. Its Classical Greek architecture gave off a sense of strength. Circuit Judge E. C. Love of Quincy dedicated the built-to-last structure that was begun a year earlier, at a cost of $137,000, and was the result of efforts by the county and the federal government. Funding from the WPA and the PWA were crucial.

To speak of government meant speaking of politics and the people continued their interest in local, county, state, and national contests. In 1940 the Apalachicola *Times* described the national election as "quiet locally." Franklin County cast 1,400 votes for Franklin D.

Apalachicola's unique location seemed to promise an inexhaustible and self-perpetuating supply of seafood. Courtesy of the Florida Department of Commerce.

The Philaco Club, founded in 1896, was still going strong in the late 1930s. Back row left to right: Mrs. George Wefing, Mrs. A. N. Lefevre, Mrs. J. D. Rush, Mrs. John Wakefield, Mrs. Joe Messina, Mrs. Harry Marks, Miss Mattie Patton and Mrs. Brunson. Front row: Mrs. Willoughby Marks, Mrs. John Ruge, Mrs. W. H. Whiteside and Mrs. S. E. Rice. Courtesy of the Apalachicola Library.

Roosevelt but only 102 ballots were marked for Republican candidate Wendell L. Wilkie. FDR took 93.2 percent of Florida's popular vote. There would be no significant switch in 1944: Roosevelt defeated Republican Thomas E. Dewey by a vote margin of 1,176 to 102 (possibly the same 102 people who voted Republican in 1940). The popular Democrat's share of the statewide popular vote was 92 percent.

Despite the good signs, devastating wars in Europe and Asia were constant reminders that international conflict and hardships might be added to domestic woes before time improved conditions. It also became increasingly evident that America's attempts to isolate herself through neutrality legislation, passed by congress, were beginning to crumble. The country could ill afford to abandon trade with nations at war. Emotional and ethnic ties kept encroaching on objective resolves to stay out of conflict. Mixing economics with sympathy locally, Gex and Lenin Lumber Company of Carrabelle signed a "cash and carry" contract in 1940 with the British government. The company made a weekly shipment of pine and cypress poles for use in the barbed-wire entanglements on the French Maginot line.

Then on Sunday, December 7, 1941, devastating news hit America: Pearl Harbor had been bombed. Shortly afterwards the United States entered the Second World War. Don McLeod, local columnist for the Apalachicola *Times,* voiced the sentiments of Franklin County when he wrote on December 12, "Our country is at war. It has been treacherously and viciously assaulted....To its cause I dedicate every service or other thing it is in my power to give, together with my life and my home. I owe this for the privilege of being an American citizen...."

An unmistakable period of war had come to Franklin County more than a year before Pearl Harbor. The local National Guard, Company E, 106th Engineers, participated in extensive army maneuvers in Louisiana during the summer of 1940. A few months later the unit was called into active duty on November 25, 1940. Rapidly building to wartime strength, the 106th was commanded by Captain H. O. Marshall (James M. Henry and W. N. Creekmore, Jr. were second lieutenants) and had seventy-three men.

Prior to departing in full uniforms to the accompaniment of stirring patriotic music from the Chapman High School band, the men had been in training eight hours a day at the Armory. The unit was sent to Camp Blanding, supposedly for one year. A 27,000-acre preserve in Clay County near Starke and Jacksonville, the partly complete installation opened in 1939 as a summer camp for the Florida National Guard and by 1940 was growing rapidly.

The area's first draftees under the Selective Training and Service Act (the Burke-Wadsworth Act of September 1940) were also sent to Camp Blanding for physical examinations in August 1941. The first draftees were a black, Mose Langston, and three whites, Charles Huggins, James Hagans, and Edward Wilson. They received an oratorical and musical send off that was unmistakably Red, White, and Blue in its sentiment. Over two hundred citizens turned out for the departures of the national guard and the draftees. Throughout the war Camp Blanding was the initial destination of draftees. By the end of 1942, three hundred ninety-eight Franklin County citizens were active in the armed services. Another 1,978 were registered for the draft and still others volunteered.

Although Franklin County appeared to have no direct physical threat from Germany and Japan, the face of the area rapidly changed. Besides the young men and women who saw active service, civilians on the home front were affected by the long period of conflict. During World War II Florida had almost two hundred military installations and Apalachicola Army Air Field, two miles west of town, was one of them. The field had been built during the Depression with federal funds. Politics played a role in the base's selection. For months members of the Jaycees sought the facility. J. P. Coombs

Florida had almost two hundred military installations including the Apalachicola Army Air Field, two miles west of town. The field, which had been built during the Depression with federal funds, became a branch of Tyndall Air Field in Panama City and received the awkward formal name of Army Air Forces Flexible Gunnery School. Courtesy of the Florida State Archives.

Men in training at the gunnery school about 1943. Courtesy of the Florida State Archives.

added his influence, and Congressman Robert L. F. "The 'He' Coon," Sikes's aid was enlisted.

Ultimately, in September 1941, the War Department and the Civil Aeronautics Authority looked Apalachicola's way. The small facility became a branch of Tyndall Air Field in Panama City and served as a training center for aerial gunners. It was on suitable high ground, had good roads, and contained 1,090 acres. WPA funds were used to help build the field which had an awkward formal title: the Army Air Forces Flexible Gunnery School. The first commander was Major William P. Kevan, Jr. who graduated from West Point in 1940 and was assigned to the Army Air Corps in 1941. Major Kevan erected a series of targets on St. George Island near Nick's Hole. There was constant strafing training during daylight hours and the area was off limits to all boats and civilians.

Over the next four years the greatest impact would be that of American servicemen who were sent to a section of the coast along Franklin's southeastern border.

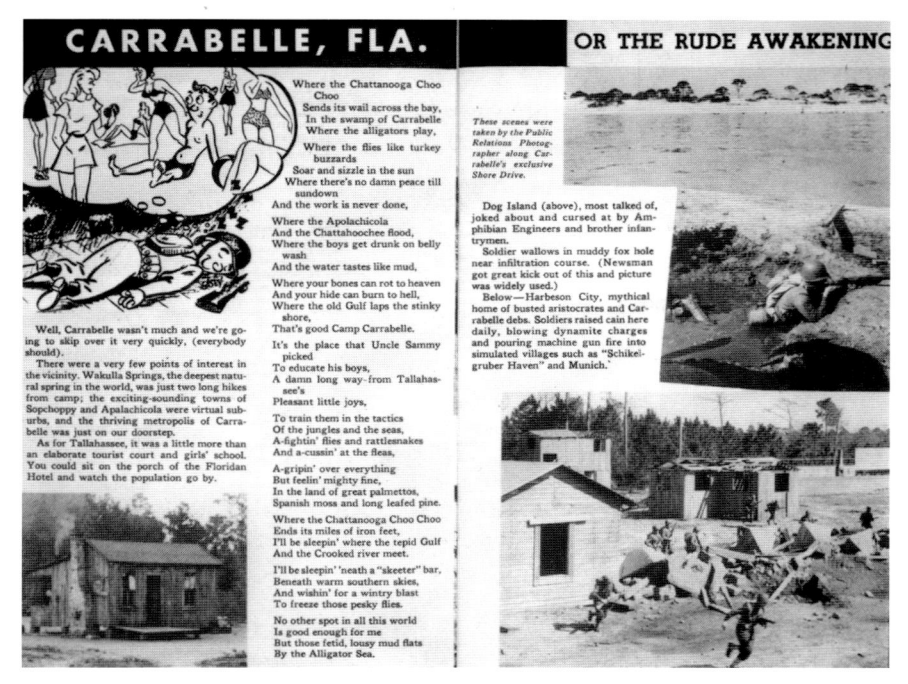

This poem about Camp Carrabelle, later named Camp Gordon Johnston, attests to the descriptive titles used by the servicemen sent there including "Hell by the sea", "Alcatraz of the Army" and other epithets in cruder Anglo-Saxon language. Courtesy of the Florida State Archives.

Their assignment was to a training base hastily constructed and named Camp Carrabelle. In May 1942, the Amphibious Training Center (ATC) had been established by the War Department. After its initial training at Camp Edwards, Massachusetts, the ATC saw its operations transferred to Florida's Gulf coast. Later, at the beginning of 1943, the name was changed to Camp Gordon Johnston. A native North Carolinian, veteran of the Spanish American War and the Philippine Insurrection, as well as World War I, Johnston died in an accident at Fort Sam Houston, Texas, in 1934. Among his military decorations was the Congressional Medal of Honor

The roughly 30,000 soldiers who were sometimes assigned to the installation (there was seldom less than a division) made it the second largest in Florida. Early on and later, the servicemen referred to their temporary North Florida home with titles descriptive of the raw and rigorous camp: "Hell By The Sea" and "Alcatraz Of the Army." Other epithets were expressed in cruder Anglo-Saxon language.

The first commander was Colonel Walter E. Smith and he was there for two years. Ultimately, the camp sprawled twenty miles along the coast between St. George Island, Carrabelle, and Alligator Point. It included the small, strung-out settlements of St. Teresa and Lanark. There were four separate camps—three for training and one for ATC headquarters, post headquarters (the Lanark Hotel served that function temporarily), a hospital, and various support facilities. Alligator Point was the eastern boundary for aerial gunnery. To the west Dog and St. George islands were used for airborne drops and amphibious landings. On September 10, 1942, Colonel Smith took formal command of the Amphibious Training Command Military Reservation. Within a month a newspaper, the *Amphibian*, was established and began publishing base news both official and anecdotal.

From 1941 on, economic activity increased in Apalachicola and Franklin County and brought prosperity. As early as April 1941, the Apalachicola *Times* boasted, "The sleepy old town is waking. Spring is here; fishing is better; tourists are coming through; boats are chugging away in the bay; workmen are rebuilding old buildings; industries are opening up; guests are signing on the hotel registers." In 1942 the citizens of Carrabelle approved a port authority by an overwhelming vote and bonds were issued for docks, warehouses, and other terminal facilities. In Apalachicola the Tent and Awning plant was a new industry completely related to defense and later to the war effort. Opened in 1941 and managed by Corey Henrikson, who moved with his family from Maryland, the plant manufactured tents for the army on a contract basis. The sixty-five workers provided a needed payroll for Apalachicola.

Only one industry suffered loses. The military presence practically put the seafood industry on hold for the duration. Fishing boats were restricted to operating during daylight hours and in designated areas. By the fall of 1943 the oyster industry was suffering from a lack of labor. Even though there were plenty of the mollusks available, access to them was not, and less than fifteen oyster houses operated in Apalachicola, Eastpoint, and Carrabelle. Despite the limitations, oysters were shipped commercially to five states. By the spring of 1944 the shrimp and oyster dealers and fishermen began to re-emerge as wholesale and retail sales increased. Still it was not until the fall of 1945 that the War Department lifted fishing restrictions from Port St. Joe to Carrabelle. That October the Franklin County Commercial Seafood Dealers Association was formed, and the organization began making plans for the postwar economy.

Owners of rental property experienced a bonanza. Base housing was always inadequate and shelter of almost any kind for servicemen and civilian workers was in heavy demand. In late 1942 Franklin and Gulf counties were designated the Apalachicola Defense Rental Agency. All landlords had to register with the agency, submit to rent inspection, and subscribe to a long list of regulations. In April 1942, the Federal Housing Agency approved construction of 288 houses and 102 apartments in Carrabelle. A construction company in Marianna, Florida, was given forty-five days to complete the job which represented a contract for over $700,000.

Mabel Osborne, chairman of housing for the Apalachicola Women's Auxiliary of the Chamber of Commerce, helped accommodate the large number of new people. Osborne and her committee placed three thousand people in housing between 1942 and 1943. From 1940 to 1943 Franklin County grew from 5,991 people to 7,555, an increase of 26.1 percent. Carrabelle's population more than doubled.

In 1996 Audrey Roux of Apalachicola remembered that as a teenager in the 1940s her father restricted her social activities, but she recalled that "the town was just booming with people. Mr. Alex Fortunas's Dixie Theatre was always full of customers. People who had houses rented them and those who had spare bedrooms rented them also." Living in a single room was

During the war years Apalachicola boomed with people and Mr. Alex Fortunas's Dixie Theatre was always full of customers. Courtesy of the Florida State Archives.

These women sewing on insignia at Camp Gordon Johnston were part of the civilian employees who earned $1.25 million dollars annually throughout the war. Annie Haddock Posey of Crawfordville, is third from left. Courtesy of the Florida State Archives.

no sacrifice for a soldier's wife who wanted to be with her husband before he was sent overseas. Audrey Roux related how a worker at the Apalachicola air base, in town only briefly, built a plywood shack and an outdoor privy on her father's land and lived in it with his wife and three children. One family lived in a small Boy Scout "Hut" in Battery Park. With the purpose of helping the servicemen, the city built restroom facilities in the park with showers on one side and toilets on the other. Battery Park was also opened to military families for their trailer homes. Housing space remained critical throughout the war.

Camp Gordon Johnston paid out approximately $1.25 million dollars annually to its civilian employees. Wives of military personnel were included in the monetary statistic and the impact was significant. According to a March 1943 report from the Florida Industrial Commission, Franklin County, along with the rest of the state, boasted one of the nation's lowest unemployment rates. Only one out of every six hundred Franklin countians was unemployed. Fifty years later resident Martha Norris McLeod recalled that despite the relief that job opportunities brought, a period of adjustment was necessary. That was because "the occupations of this area have always been of a man's making, allowing him to work or play at will. Such freedom is not to be enjoyed in government jobs." Still, a regular paycheck was involved and both women and men easily adapted to the requirements.

Even though there were no significant harbor improvements, Apalachicola hoped to gain in the future from a grant of over six million dollars by Congress. The 1941 legislation authorized the establishment of a series of locks and dams on the Apalachicola, Flint, and Chattahoochee River systems. The closest dam would be at Chattahoochee, Florida, at the confluence of the Flint and Chattahoochee rivers.

On July 8, 1942, ground clearing began for Camp Gordon Johnston. There was little time to waste in training the soldiers for ship to shore and shore to shore

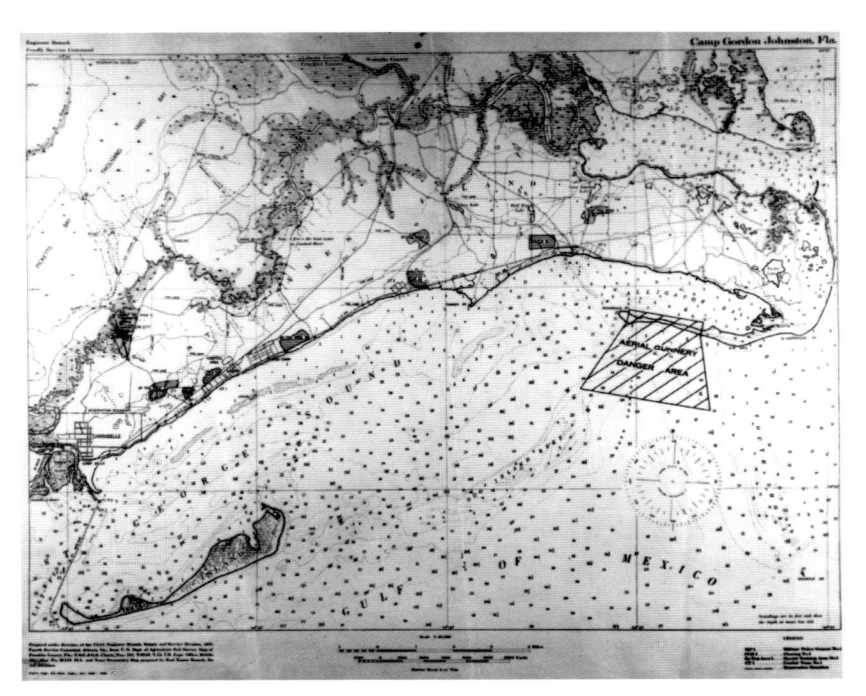

Government agents purchased 10,000 acres from private land owners and leased another 155,000, mainly from St. Joe Paper Company and on July 8, 1942, ground clearing began for Camp Gordon Johnston. Courtesy of the Florida State Archives.

invasions. Government agents purchased 10,000 acres from private land owners and leased another 155,000 (mainly from the St. Joe Paper Company). William H. Wilson, the primary owner of St. George Island, signed over control of his property to the government. The rent per annum amounted to $599. Construction on the camp progressed so rapidly that it seemed miraculous. Support units arrived on September 10 and soon a rigid program of instruction was ready to begin.

Living conditions were never comfortable at Camp Gordon Johnston but in the first year they were particularly bad. Barracks were made of cheap, prefabricated wood and the floors were simply dirt. The men ate their meals from mess kits because mess halls, defying Napoleon's theory that an army traveled on its stomach, were not considered a top priority. They were not even built until later. Understandably, members of the first brigade to arrive were appalled at the conditions. They quickly realized that the marshy Gulf coast did not fit their images of Florida.

The men were unaccustomed to the sheer volume of blood sucking insects that infested the region. It took time for them to get used to the reptiles and wild hogs that inhabited the swamps and forests surrounding the

Defying Napoleon's theory that an army traveled on its stomach, the men at Camp Gordon Johnston ate their meals from mess kits because mess halls were not considered a top priority. Courtesy of the Florida State Archives.

installation. Every day the population of critters and pests seemed to increase. Avoiding such nuisances did not fit the G.I.'s definition of recreational activities. Nor were they impressed when informed that special county regulations exempted them from the necessity of buying hunting licenses.

At first, traditional outlets for leisure time were non-existent. The young men found the nightlife of the two nearest towns, Carrabelle and Sopchoppy (in Wakulla County) lacking, to understate the situation. Apalachicola did not seem much better. One popular hang-out was located in Eastpoint. Known as a "juke" or "jook" in tribute to the inevitable music box it contained, the rustic setting had an unmistakable ambience. The multi-colored machine constantly played popular hits for a nickel a record; those wartime songs, considering the setting, gave the word "homesick" new meaning. The establishment, as its owner Homer Marks of Apalachicola recalled years later, was filled nightly with

Living conditions were never comfortable but in the first year they were particularly bad. Barracks and other facilities were made of cheap, prefabricated wood, and the floors were simply dirt. Courtesy of the Florida State Archives.

servicemen. "Jukes" were common and popular across the South.

The relentless heat and lack of basic amenities aside, the primary concern of the men was the severity of the training. Part of the commando-style instruction included swamp maneuvers, live-fire obstacle courses, street-fighting, and water survival. An article in *Newsweek* magazine (March 1934) featured the "Spartan" training at Camp Gordon Johnston: "the assignments specifically call for the conditioning of the soldiers mentally and physically...[and] that involves many toughening-up exercises, ranging from rope climbing and obstacle scaling to the best methods of throat cutting and strangling." In addition, there were the many exercises performed to perfect amphibious landings. While the camp regimen was brutal and overall conditions desolate, Camp Gordon Johnston served its purpose of helping to prepare men for the demands of battle, and it gave them the skills necessary to prevail. A further look at Camp Gordon Johnston was provided through *"Amphibious Fighters,"* a Grantland Rice Pictures film produced locally and at Wakulla Springs and distributed nationally.

Meanwhile, the activity at the Amphibious Training Center was not the only physical evidence of the massive global fight that took place in Franklin County. On the night of June 28, 1942, the *H. M. S. Empire Mica*, a British Liberty ship, was twenty-five miles south of

Orange flames burned for eight hours after the British Liberty ship, **Empire Mica**, *was torpedoed by a German U-boat. The Coast Guard vessel* Sea Dream *and another vessel, the* Countess *were dispatched to investigate and found fourteen sailors treading water. The survivors were successfully rescued although one of the sailors did not live. Courtesy of the Florida Department of Commerce.*

Apalachicola. Commanded by Captain Hugh Bradford Bently, it was en route to Great Britain with a crew of forty-seven English, Scots, and Irish, and in its hold was a full load of high octane aviation gas. Even had Captain Bently wanted to, he could not have put in at one of the Gulf's shallow water ports because his heavy cargo prevented entry. He had cause to be worried about German submarines—since Pearl Harbor 317 Allied ships had been sunk. The *Empire Mica* was proceeding without any lights but the full moon and shining sea made the ship's silhoutte visible and it was spotted by a Nazi U-boat with the appropriate nickname of "Raider." Kaptinleutenant Gunter Muller-Stokheim, the commander, gave the order and two torpedoes were released, the first at about 1:30 A.M., Monday morning, June 29. Thirty-three seamen were killed, most of them burned to death in their bunks. There was a loud explosion as the ship caught fire and sank. The orange flames burned for eight hours and were spotted in Apalachicola by the crew of the *Sea Dream*, a Coast Guard vessel. The *Sea Dream* was a local pleasure craft designed and built by Willie Fred Randolph and Allie Camp and had been leased by the government for wartime duty. Another vessel, the *Countess*, was also dispatched to aid in investigating the explosion.

Arriving at the wreckage, the *Sea Dream's* crew found fourteen sailors treading water. Successfully rescuing the survivors, the *Sea Dream* and assisting vessels returned to Apalachicola. Rescuers were astonished at how young the British sailors were. By 1942, the war had taken its toll on the manpower of Great Britain. Boys between fifteen and sixteen-years-old were common aboard the *Empire Mica*. Back in Apalachicola, the surviving British seamen recuperated in the armory. They were attended by a local doctor, and the Red Cross supplied soup and coffee. One of the sailors did not live but the others recovered. Later, the dead bodies and pieces of bodies were brought in wrapped in sheets. Members of the Philaco Women's Club visited the sailors, comforting them and helping to raise their spirits. Gene Austin, owner of Austin's Department Store, assisted the Red Cross in supplying food and blankets.

Even on the home front there were always painful examples of how impersonal and unpredictable death could be. In March 1943, a medium bomber on a routine flight from Atlanta to Panama City crashed on St. George Island. The bodies of all six crew members were found in the wreckage.

Change came rapidly to Apalachicola and Franklin County. A quiet coastal region trying to make ends meet suddenly found itself an important player in the middle of a major war. Apalachicola, according to one person, had an electric atmosphere. Franklin countians felt a responsibility for the military personnel temporarily located with them. They were especially concerned with single men, and each Christmas and Thanksgiving many people invited servicemen to eat dinner with them. Beginning in 1942 the Apalachicola *Times* began running columns about the county's military personnel—by then there were hundreds of them. Columnists Don McLeod, a former lawyer and judge, and Farley Warren, kept the servicemen informed about the home front and the civilians appraised of how Franklin countians were faring in the military. Warren's column was called "Our Boys And Girls In The Service."

There was organized concern as well. Mrs. Joseph P. Hickey, better known as Rebecca to the townspeople and as "Mama" to the military personnel, was the indefatigable chairman, despite being in her high sixties, of the Apalachicola Servicemen's Club. It was officially called the Little United Servicemen's Organization (USO). The large, white-haired Rebecca was an excellent organizer. She was forever arranging dances at the armory for the military (civilians frequently attended), lining up the bands (usually from Camp Gordon Johnston or Tyndall Air Force Base) to play, and keeping the cookie jar at the Servicemen's Club full. She was assisted by two sisters, Mabel and Molly Osburn, and Rophebe Mathis, a black woman whose superb sandwiches made her famous with the servicemen.

The Servicemen's Club was first organized in a small upstairs room in a wooden building on Market Street. Then it was moved down the street into larger quarters and finally found a home in the armory. The Servicemen's Club shared the all purpose building with the Red Cross and the local Rationing Board. The club opened early in the morning and closed late at night. Military personnel availed themselves of the club's books and magazines, lounging in chairs around tables. They socialized, wrote letters, and listened to the steady stream of songs coming from the juke box.

Despite wartime conditions, Rebecca Hickey saw to it that an almost Victorian decorum prevailed in the relations between the area's young women and the military. Mama Hickey and an organized group of escorts, formally named the Chaperons, oversaw social events that were attended by young women from Apalachicola, Carrabelle, and surrounding towns.

As early as August 1942, approximately one hundred young Apalachicola women were organized into two social groups: the Bombadears and the Victorettes. The two groups had a schedule of reporting for duty at the Servicemen's Club, and held regular meetings. Besides attending dances and other events and being present at the club, the women provided sandwiches and coffee for the military personnel. Several of the young women married servicemen stationed in the area. A Service Men's Wives Club was also organized.

Active throughout the war, the local Red Cross helped look after servicemen's needs. It served the vital function of being a communication link between the men in uniform and their families back home. Executive Secretary Mercia Montgomery, like Rebecca Hickey, served as a mother figure to the young men. Laurie McLeod Rivers, a teenager during the war, worked as Mercia Montgomery's secretary. In 1996 she remembered that the Red Cross directed volunteer knitting projects for the town women at the armory. She recalled other Red Cross services there: "In the big hall, there would be these long tables and all the women would be in there wrapping bandages."

By 1943 Camp Gordon Johnston had grown beyond its primitive origins. Its Special Service Division provid-

Mrs. Joseph P. Hickey, known as Rebecca at home and "Mama" to the servicemen, was an excellent organizer who arranged dances, lined up bands, was the chairman of the Apalachicola Servicemen's Club, and made sure the cookie jar there was always full. This dance was at a Camp Gordon Johnston hall about 1944. Courtesy of the Florida State Archives.

ed dances on the base with music furnished by groups such as the 112th Infantry Dance Band. The military furnished the transportation for girls from the surrounding area, including the Bombadears and the Victorettes. The events were coordinated with women such as "Mama" Hickey and Mary Butera, president of the USO in Sopchoppy. By then the large post had several theatres, a library, Enlisted Men's (EM) clubs, noncommissioned officers clubs, and an officer's club. Ultimately, there were six chapels. The base organized baseball and basketball leagues, and boxing matches were presented. In the camp's waning days, a football team, the Hell Drivers, was formed. Coached by a serviceman, a former scout for the New York Giants, the team played at least one game on their home field against an air force team from Homestead, Florida. At the smaller Apalachicola air base, entertainment was on a much smaller scale.

Local people enjoyed the all soldier show "Talk It Up" in April 1943. An original production, including its music, "Talk It Up" drew large audiences on base and at Chapman High School and Carrabelle. Despite the lack of entertainment facilities at first, the base made a concerted effort later to provide for the soldiers' leisure time. As was true elsewhere, black soldiers suffered from discrimination.

In Apalachicola the Gibson Inn, opened as The Franklin in 1907 and renamed in the 1920s, served the war effort in several capacities. In 1942 the government took control of the hotel to use as an officers' club. It

Education suffered during the war from lack of supplies, teachers, and physical deterioration of buildings. Segregation, which was legal, continued with the Alvan W. Chapman High School for whites and Dunbar High School for blacks. Courtesy of the Florida State Archives.

was not needed for that purpose, and after three months, was returned to civilian operation. For four dollars a day the Gibson provided a room and included three "all-you-can-eat" meals as part of the package. Of necessity, the arrangement was abandoned as a permanent offer. The hotel faced bankruptcy as the result of feeding ravenous soldiers whose other meals were the mess halls' unappetizing offerings. Throughout the war soldiers frequented the inn as a place to relax on weekend leaves. In Apalachicola military personnel also visited the Fuller Hotel, a black owned establishment that catered to a white clientele.

Early on, a Franklin County Defense Council was appointed and divided into various committees. Throughout the war the citizens, with few exceptions, reacted patriotically to its demands in a fashion similar to that of other Americans. In November 1942, there was a scrap metal drive. That year Apalachicolans sacrificed outside and inside Christmas lights to conserve electricity for the war effort. Their voluntary action was in line with War Production Board (WPB) policy. Later, local authorities shut off street lights year-round. It was done as part of the war effort and was an unconscious tribute to local safety conditions. Some groups, such as the local Jaycees, lost so many members to military service that they shut down from 1943–1945. By 1943 Chapman High School's football team had been reduced to the six-man variety and sporadic schedules (they defeated Port St. Joe 21–6 in November 1943).

Education suffered during the war (lack of supplies, physical deterioration of buildings, difficulties in obtaining teachers). School segregation, which was legal, continued. Alvan W. Chapman High School was for whites and Dunbar High School, with its inferior facilities, was for blacks. Dunbar had existed since 1900 but did not graduate its first twelfth grade class until 1936. The Dunbar school was famed for its beautiful grounds which were skillfully landscaped under the direction of its principal, Gaddis C. Hall, a native of Louisiana and a graduate of Florida Agricultural and Mechanical College at Tallahassee. People with no connection to the school visited it to view Hall's shrubbery, grass, and walkways. In February 1943 a defective flue caused a fire that destroyed Dunbar. Wallace M. Quinn, the white owner of the menhaden plant, gave twenty-one acres to the school board for a new facility. Despite wartime shortages and priorities, Franklin County build a new black school. The first graduating class at the appropriately named Wallace M. Quinn High School was that of 1945–1946.

In 1945 Apalachicola had two other schools. Both were Catholic and neither offered instruction beyond the elementary school level. The Holy Family Catholic School for blacks and the Mary Star By The Sea for whites were small but prepared their charges well for advanced educational training.

Sacrificing on the home front to help American servicemen on the fighting front was an axiomatic commitment but it also included enforcement. That came from various agencies spread out from Pennsylvania Avenue in Washington to Market Street in Apalachicola. Despite overlapping of authority and name and personnel changes, the vast bureaucracy worked surprisingly well. The Office of Price Administration (OPA) was in charge of rationing. In December 1942, long lines of automobiles were reported at local service stations. They were filling up before gas coupon books went into effect. Civilian goods, everything from sugar to shoes and from coffee to tires, were rationed. Many products appeared irregularly or disappeared entirely. The next automobile model after 1941 came out in 1946. Harry Buzzett, son of William D. Buzzett who opened Buzzett's Drugstore in 1905, remembered years later how difficult it was to obtain certain items. "When my father would receive Kleenex in his store," Buzzett noted, "the whole town was alerted, 'There's Kleenex at Buzzett's'!"

Chief Air Raid Warden Jay A. Shuler and his six assistants helped coordinate a statewide blackout in January 1943. The results in Apalachicola, as in the rest of Florida, were a mixed success. The next month embarrassed citizens hastened to remedy a discovered deficiency: Apalachicola was the only city between Key West and Port Arthur, Texas, that did not have a twenty-four hour lookout to spot airplanes. The women of Apalachicola came to the rescue with a voluntary airwatch effort. Looking for Axis planes and even more improbable Japanese planes, they scanned the skies from a platform located at the top of the existing tower above the armory. Their mission was to report enemy

Franklin Countians, like other Americans, endured rationing and bought War Bonds. Courtesy of the Florida State Archives.

aircraft to Tyndall Air Base. Much later, Laurie McLeod Rivers recalled with humor that the task was not easy. She said, "My mother used to go with me—and she was pretty old at the time. I don't know how she did it. We used to climb the tower and watch for planes and try to recognize them by [our] chart and report any unfamiliar ones. It was hard because they used to go by so fast! We thought we were very important! We never identified any enemy planes though." Without a doubt, Franklin countians, like other Americans, were united in their determination to win the war.

As a spur of Tyndall Air Field, the field at Apalachicola was part of the large base of operations for the Army Air Forces Training Command (AAFTC). Roughly five hundred men were stationed in Apalachicola at various times. As mentioned, the field functioned to develop aerial artillery gunners. The airmen were drilled to man machine guns mounted within B-17, B-24, and B-25 bombers. Routine training missions involved target practice on flights over the Gulf of Mexico. Aerial warfare had advanced dramatically since World War I, and Gulf coast air fields were integral parts of an entirely new method of warfare. Clark Gable, assigned to Tyndall for training in aerial gunnery, was also in and out of the Apalachicola base.

From the first class on, trainees at the Apalachicola gunnery base scored high in their air-to-air firing. In 1944 over $190,000 was spent on the base—the runway apron was extended and the taxiway was widened. The Apalachicola gunnery school was active for thirty-three months. In July 1945, when training was suspended, locals and the men trained there took pride in the official description of their performance: "Outstanding." The installation was finally used as an auxiliary base by Maxwell Air Force Field, at Montgomery, Alabama. It remained under the administration of Tyndall Field. Lieutenant Richard H. Schrantz assumed duties as commanding officer and a minimum number of enlisted men were assigned there for maintenance duties.

Many units passed through ATC's rigorous regimen. In January 1943, the best known and highly decorated soldier to train at Carrabelle was assigned to the camp. General Omar N. Bradley, who went on to distinguished military service in North Africa and Europe, and his Twenty-eighth Infantry Division arrived during an unseasonably cold winter. They found the installation both miserable and invaluable. Bradley specifically noted that the practice of storming the beaches of Dog Island taught him the complicated nature of amphibious landings. Ill-prepared for the freezing panhandle winter, Bradley recalled, "Every exercise was a numbing experience."

In March 1943, the dangerous maneuvers enacted at the camp finally resulted in a deadly accident for Bradley's Twenty-eighth Division. During a final landing exercise, an unanticipated heavy storm destroyed a large amount of equipment. One of the boats in the Second Battalion of the 112th Infantry Regiment hit a sandbar. The collision caused the confused coxswain to believe the designated point of entry had been reached. Ordered to abandon the boat, the men quickly found themselves surrounded by deep water. Several soldiers were saved, but fourteen drowned.

Shortly afterwards, Army officials decided to discontinue the Amphibious Training Center, although the

General Omar N. Bradley inspected Camp Gordon Johnston during an unseasonably cold winter. He noted that the practice of storming the beaches of Dog Island taught him the complicated nature of amphibious landings. Courtesy of the Florida State Archives.

In September of 1943 Carrabelle was selected as a location for training men in the operation of the "1942 Amphibian, All-wheel Drive, Dual Rear Axle" trucks. Lt. Nagel and Lt. Howard Friedman are in one of the pioneering vehicles, a "DUKW", that revolutionized amphibian warfare. Courtesy of the Florida State Archives.

determination was not motivated by the losses sustained by the Twenty-eighth Division. It was decided that the U.S. Navy would become the branch of service responsible for this manner of attack. On June 10, 1943, the ATC disbanded, leaving Camp Gordon Johnston with an unknown identity. The war effort was too crucial to allow the large facility to lie idle. In September, Carrabelle was selected as a site for the Army Service Forces Training Center (ASFTC). Its new mission was to serve as a location for training men as harbor craft companies (small boat crews) and as amphibian truck companies. The latter became adept in the operation of the "1942 Amphibian, All-wheel Drive, Dual Rear Axle" trucks. The pioneering "DUKW," as the vehicle quickly became known, revolutionized amphibian warfare.

The ASFTC also trained units on port construction and instructed repair and maintenance sections.

The majority of the troops that passed through the ASFTC were blacks. While the African-American soldiers adjusted to the rigorous elements of North Florida, they were outspoken regarding the unequal recreational facilities. Initially, such comforts (limited at best) were available to whites only. The black troops voiced their objections in the camp's newspaper, the *Amphibian*. Later, construction was completed on a guest house and service club for the black troops.

Weekend passes enabled the soldiers to go as far away as Tallahassee, already bulging with soldiers in transit through the city and pilots training locally at Dale Mabry Field. On weekends other bases in nearby towns added to the congestion when their servicemen depart-

A year after V-J Day the army was completely gone. Franklin County slowly forgot the G.I.'s, housing shortages and the fast pace of wartime existence. Courtesy of the Florida State Archives.

ed for the capital city. Obtaining lodging became almost impossible, although some local citizens with every bedroom taken let soldiers sleep on their porches. As time passed there were difficulties between black servicemen and white civilians and questions of who had authority over military personnel allegedly behaving illegally. The issues usually concerned one or more of the Jim Crow segregation laws.

Before the end of the war four separate racial incidents broke out in Tallahassee. No one was seriously injured and property damage was minimal. The potential for worse results was avoided but the incidents created bad feelings. For weeks Tallahassee was declared off limits to all Camp Gordon Johston personnel. In retrospect, it is clear that as the United States attacked tyranny abroad, there were racial problems at home, including such places as segregated north Florida.

On April 12, 1945, President Roosevelt died at Warm Springs, Georgia. Apalachicolans canceled a dance scheduled for the armory that night and joined other Americans in mourning his loss. Harry S. Truman became president and the war wore on and down. By June 1945, many servicemen were getting discharges and coming home to Franklin County and to Apalachicola, Eastpoint, and Carrabelle. Each bore the proud title of "veteran."

Fourteen men from Franklin County lost their lives during the war; eleven of them were in the army, two in the navy, and one in the marines. It was the duty of Estelle Marshall, local Red Cross caseworker, to inform the servicemen of family news, and that of the federal government, by the less personal means of a telegram, when a serviceman was killed. Each death was a tragedy and none more than that of First Lieutenant Julian R. Buzzett who was known as Rex. Lieutenant Buzzett entered the service with the local national guard in 1940 and was one of five brothers who served in World War II. He was killed on D-Day, June 6, 1944, during the invasion of France. His brother, Harry Buzzett, graduated from the United States Military Academy on that same day. Buzzett, who remained in the military after and war and retired as a colonel, remembered in 1996 that "When my brother was killed, the whole town mourned."

The end of the war in Europe came on May 8, 1945, VE (Victory Europe) Day, and was followed by the end of the war in the Pacific on August 15, 1945, VJ (Victory Japan) Day. Local affirmation came in an emotional sense with joyous celebrations for soldiers and civilians and in a material sense with the lifting of rationing. Gasoline, fuel oil, canned goods, and other products became available without restrictions. The Jaycees resumed holding meetings, and the War Price and Ration Board closed on December 15.

Military training at the Carrabelle camp continued well after VE Day. Even though part of Camp Gordon Johnston served as a German and Italian prisoner of war camp from early 1944 until the end of the war, no hostility erupted there after Germany fell. Japan fought on with renewed ferocity and the course of the war was unpredictable. The tone of the installation grew even more serious after an accident at East Pass. At the opening there between Dog and St. George islands some paratroopers attempting to land on Dog Island were blown off course and into the channel. Strapped in heavy equipment, the men were unable to tread water. Ten of them drowned in the incident. They were the first fatalities out of over one thousand successful drops on the islands.

Even after the Japanese surrender in August and Americans celebrated V-J Day, the soldiers at Camp Gordon Johnston were in a state of disbelief. Once the fact was confirmed, alcohol became a major beverage

A 1960 aerial view looking northwesterly from south of the Gorrie Bridge. Courtesy of the Apalachicola State Bank.

of celebration and happy soldiers had no qualms about drinking the warm beer that was available. Never intended to be a permanent installation, Camp Gordon Johnston no longer served a purpose for the military. After a brief period as a deployment base, its functions were terminated in February 1946. In an article on the installation, historian David Coles concluded, "Without the realistic training and the experience gained at Camp Gordon Johnston...the blood spilled on numerous beaches might have been greater, and the length and cost of the war much greater."

A year later the army was completely gone. Most of the land was returned to the St. Joe Paper Company with a fee of $37,000 for restoration of the area. St. Teresa, Alligator Point, Dog Island, and St. George Island quickly went back to their pre–war status as weekend retreats and isolated beaches. Franklin County slowly forgot the memories of G.I.s enmeshed in severe training routines, of young men longing for home, of housing shortages for families, and of the fast pace of wartime existence.

Apalachicola and Franklin County returned to a peacetime economy and existence (Lanark would become a retirement community). The following decades became the most affluent times in American history but Franklin County did not share immediately in the bounty. A large portion of the money invested in Franklin County disappeared and part of the depletion was because Camp Gordon Johnston closed. Even so, the climate was still the same, the beaches were still pristine, and the area was about to be discovered by non-natives who realized why locals might move away, but, if they could, always came home. As newcomers whose numbers would steadily increase, they wanted to share the good life of the Gulf coast and Franklin County.

Car and passenger ferry service from Catpoint at Eastpoint to East Hole on St. George and from Carrabelle to Dog Island began in 1955. The first ferry, Georgia Boy, was replaced by the state-owned Sirius (serving St. George) and the Spica (serving Dog Island). Courtesy of the Florida Department of Commerce.

Twelve

To the End of the 1900s

IN 1945 THE WAR WAS OVER AND THE people of Apalachicola and Franklin County began adjusting to a peacetime world that had the ironic potential of being blown up by an atomic explosion. The 1950s have been characterized as unimaginative (other than being the incubator of rock and roll), a money-making decade of superficial goals, a time of a shooting war in faraway Korea and the cold war in diplomacy. The turbulent sixties are seen as a time of youthful rebellion, the rising consciousness of women, sexual freedom, civil rights expansion, environmental awareness, and an unpopular war in Vietnam. The seventies, eighties, and nineties are still being defined. During those decades trends from the preceding thirty-five years continued, and the nation grew more conservative. A federal government that could guarantee what President Lyndon B. Johnson (1963–1968) called the "Great Society" seemed impossible. Yet history can never be reduced to neat bundles of time and explained in generalities. The people of Franklin County were as confused as the rest of the nation about what it all meant and what should be done or not done.

Space limitations prevent a detailed study of local events from 1945 to the twenty-first century, but some developments can be noted. After unsuccessful attempts to sell St. George Island, William H. "Bill" Wilson conveyed half of it in 1945 to Clyde W. Atkinson. Clifford C. Land subleased the island from the 1930s to the early 1950s (except for the war years), but several individuals owned lots and Franklin County acquired property there for delinquent taxes. Planning development through lot sales, Wilson and Atkinson formed a company in 1951 known as St. George Island Gulf Beaches, Inc. (made up of themselves and their friends and relatives, most of them from Tallahassee). They sold the island to the corporation which quieted the title, ceded certain rights to Franklin County and took over in August 1952.

As St. George Island Gulf Beaches, Inc. went about platting the island into units and selling lots, questions arose that were crucial to the company, Apalachicola, and the county. Franklin County commissioners were aware that the island's development would attract people and improve the depressed economy. Ferry service to St. George and Dog islands, a bridge, and a channel through St. George were all concerns.

In 1951 Bryant G. Patton, the county's representative in the legislature and a member of the Company, helped pass legislation authorizing toll bridges. In a countywide referendum the voters agreed by 98 percent to fund construction with the 80 percent surplus of the secondary gas tax. The money was distributed across the state and was a vital source for poor counties such as Franklin. The proposed bridge from Eastpoint to St. George Island was centrally located and would provide access to many miles of beaches

Acting for the Company, Representative Patton won county agreement to establish ferry service. St. George Island was represented in the negotiations by Wilson and Atkinson and Dog Island by Ivan Munroe. State monies were secured for the ferries and for the proposed ship channel site. Besides the use of gas tax and funds from the State Road Department (SRD), the federal government appropriated money for the ship channel, with Franklin County and Apalachicola making up the rest.

A $4,000,000 bridge to St. George Island was announced in 1962. The work went forward and the bridge opened without fanfare on Friday morning at seven o'clock, December 17, 1965. Courtesy of the Florida Department of Commerce.

Despite delays, car and passenger ferry service from Catpoint at Eastpoint to East Hole on St. George and from Carrabelle to Dog Island began in 1955. The first ferry, *Georgia Boy*, was replaced by the state-owned *Sirius* (serving St. George) and the *Spica* (serving Dog Island). Managed by the county, the ferries performed their function but there were problems over schedules and fares. After losing money, they were operated by the owners of the islands. The *Sirius* made its last run on December 14, 1965 and within days the Bryant Patton bridge opened. The *Spica* continued to serve Dog Island for twenty-seven years, closing in April 1982.

From 1955 on there were engineering surveys and monetary grants from the SRD and St. George Island Gulf Beaches, Inc. for the bridge. In 1962 State Road Commissioner William T. Mayo announced that a $4,000,000 bridge would be financed by the sale of bonds by Franklin County and from the Florida Development Commission's pledging gas tax monies. The work went forward, and the bridge was opened without fanfare on Friday morning at seven o'clock, December 17, 1965. The fare varied depending on the size and weight of the vehicle, but the basic charge for passenger cars was $2 each.

As early as 1947 Apalachicolans requested local harbor improvements providing a 30 by 300 foot ship channel to run eight miles from John Gorrie bridge across the bay and through St. George Island to the open Gulf. Among the expected benefits were: increased trade with both the river valley system and the Caribbean and South America; a shortened route to fishing and shrimping grounds; and the improvement of sediment problems (silt-ridden river water would empty into the Gulf). City Manager W. N. Creekmore led the campaign. In 1949 the legislature established a Port Authority at Apalachicola and a special tax district to support it. Local officials, aided by Congressman Sikes secured congressional authorization in 1954. The federally owned cut was completed in April 1957, at a cost of $606,299 and named the Robert L. Sikes Channel.

In the 1970s suggestions to deepen the cut were beaten back by ecologists and environmentalists. Heavily salinated water seeping into the bay was seen as a threat to the balance of plant and marine life. Yet, when the cut was made, it was considered a positive economic benefit.

With the bridge open, St. George Island Gulf Beaches, Inc. increased its lot sales and their prices. For a large number of affluent Americans, the idea of owning a beach home had become an obtainable reality. Even so, many people opposed the development of Florida's remaining unspoiled lands. Words such as "ecology," "environment," and "preservation" had assumed powerful meanings and protecting the American landscape became important as never before. The stockholders decided to sell their part of the island.

As the sixties ended, John Stocks came forward. In his thirties, tall, powerfully built, and blond-haired, Stocks was an Alabamian and a self-made man. He

For many years Apalachicolans had requested a 30 x 300 foot ship channel to run eight miles from John Gorrie bridge across the bay and through St. George Island to the open Gulf. Authorization was received in 1954 and the federally owned cut was completed in April 1957, at a cost of $606,299 and named for congressman Robert L. Sikes. Courtesy of the Florida Department of Commerce.

With the bridge open, St. George Island Gulf Beaches, Inc. increased its lot sales and prices. For a large number of affluent Americans, the idea of owning a beach home had become an obtainable reality. Courtesy of the Florida Department of Commerce.

differed in personality and looks from William Lee Popham but the two men had the same propensity for taking economic gambles and the same determination to develop St. George Island.

With the death of Bill Wilson on October 9, 1969, Atkinson became the company's most influential member. Negotiations began and Stocks signed a mortgage for the island in November 1971. In December Leisure Properties (LP) (originally called St. George Island, Ltd.) was formed. The general partners were Stocks and Leisure Properties and the limited partners were the St. George Island Development Corporation and twenty individuals, mostly Tallahasseans. The latter group owned 40 percent of LP but Stocks's majority interest gave him control. In the spring of 1972 he mortgaged part of the island to obtain operating money.

Popham would have been proud of the audacious Stocks. All the developer had left to do was pay off his limited partners, acquire an able business associate (he got one in Gene Brown, a young Tallahassee lawyer), turn a profit for himself, and persuade a rising chorus of opposition to accept St. George's limited commercial development.

To succeed Stocks needed money and in May 1973, he found a buyer: the state of Florida. What followed was complicated and controversial. Claude Kirk (1966–1970), Florida's first Republican governor since Reconstruction, carved an impressive record in the area of conservation. His successor, Democrat Reubin Askew, continued and expanded the movement, as state government allied itself with individuals and private agencies that championed environmentalism.

Led by state officials and legislators (Robert Graham in the senate and Richard Pettigrew and Jack Shreve in the house), new agencies were created in 1972 to supervise land development and protect water resources. One act provided for a bond issue permitting the state to purchase acreage for parks and environmentally endangered lands. The Florida Environmental Land and Water Management Act allowed local and state agencies to regulate "developments of regional impact" (DRIs) that affected the people of more than one county. The governor and cabinet could designate "areas of critical state concern" and allow local and state agencies to formulate special environmental regulations. The Department of Natural Resources (DNR) was given broad regulatory powers over state waters. The governor was made the state's chief planning officer, and a Division of State Planning was established within the Department of Administration. These vanguard laws were expanded by future legislation. Major executive decisions were made by the Trustees of the Internal Improvement Fund (the governor and his cabinet).

The state already owned 318 acres on the island's eastern tip (ceded by St. George Island Gulf Beaches, Inc.), and on May 1, 1973, Florida's cabinet voted five to zero to purchase 1,883 acres on the eastern end of St. George Island with five annual payments. Anxious to protect the oyster beds and Apalachicola Bay, the state got several developmental concessions and certain inspection rights from LP.

The state's purchase of land on St. George Island did not go uncontested in Tallahassee. Soon the controversy involved Governor Askew, his election bid to succeed himself, the cabinet, an appointee to high office, and officials of Leisure Properties. There were accusations that the state paid too much money and of improper influence having been exerted. The controversy was followed closely in the press. Investigations revealed no conspiracies and concluded that nothing illegal had occurred. The purchase was carried out, and Askew was renominated and reelected governor. Actually, the state had made an excellent real estate deal. Florida acquired land and beaches of unsurpassed beauty and the public was provided with a recreational area free of commercial development.

Aside from the purchase issue, various state agencies and later the Franklin County Commissioners would have questions about Leisure Properties's DRI. They included sewage, drainage, runoff problems, density of housing units and pollution harmful to the bay and the seafood industry. LP helped finance investigations of water conditions surrounding St. George Island. Professor Robert Livingston of Florida State University headed the project and became an expert on the island and the bay. Inevitably, though, differing concepts between LP and Franklin County over development emerged.

The detailed steps necessary to gain approval of a DRI involved numerous agencies and committees. The final decision rested on the recommendation of the county commissioners. A storied battle ensued between LP, as represented by Stocks and Brown and their lawyers and experts, and the county commissioners and their lawyers and experts. It became a struggle of developers versus a combination of environmentalists and seafood industry people. Both sides made impressive arguments.

There were many actors in the DRI drama, but county commissioners Cecil Varnes and I. D. "Ikie" Wade were particularly prominent. Statements by Professor Livingston were significant, as was the work of County Attorney Al Shuler and Robert Ingle of the local planning commission. Close auditors included then Clerk of the Circuit Court Bobby Howell; John Lee, manager of the Apalachicola *Times;* and businessman Wesley Chesnut.

In the final analysis Stocks and Brown were outsiders. Franklin countians, economically dependent directly or indirectly upon the seafood industry, and their county officials were not convinced by LP's arguments. Nor were environmentalists. The Company's point—controlled growth was better than uncontrolled growth, county schools would benefit from increased tax money, the labor problem would be eased, overall income would rise—were not enough. Yet, growth had become inevitable once Bryant Patton bridge was opened and the question was how to deal with it. The public hearings in May and June 1975 ended with the placement of restrictions unacceptable to the Company. For the time being, Leisure Properties abandoned its efforts.

In 1975 another environmental controversy caused ongoing debate in Franklin County and elsewhere. The

Jim Woodruff Dam, under construction for several years, was opened at Chattahoochee in 1957, and, according to its proponents, oyster production increased in Apalachicola Bay. The claim was strongly disputed in Apalachicola. Now, in 1975, the United States Army Corps of Engineers proposed to build a low level navigational dirt dam on the river between Bristol and Blountstown. The Franklin County Commissioners, the Apalachicola Bay seafood industry, Florida's state officials, and numerous conservationists statewide joined forces to oppose the dam. Favoring construction were various interests in Florida's Gadsden, Liberty, Jackson, and Gulf counties, plus farmers and their agricultural allies in Georgia and Alabama. The Tri-Rivers Waterway Development Association carried out extensive public relations efforts.

Opponents countered that the dam would bring more pollution. The river's role as a natural and vital food chain for the seafood industry would be diminished. The dam could destroy the livelihoods of thousands of north Floridians, as well as an important national heritage. The dam was not built but other serious questions involving the water supply from the north developed in the century's last decade.

The high stakes on St. George Island forced a resumption of the debate. In 1977 LP got a DRI. Included was a development order that covered the island, including Nick's Hole, Sikes Cut, and Sunset Beach as conceptual commercial areas. Stocks and Brown dissolved their partnership, with Stocks getting their property's commercial portions and Brown obtaining the residential areas. Both men sold their holdings but before Brown bowed out he developed The Plantation, a privately owned area of luxury homes.

Meanwhile, individuals continued to build their private homes on the island. A growth surge followed the removal of the $2 toll on the bridge to the island. Some argued in 1986, the year that the bonds were paid off, that the toll should be removed. The Department of Transportation (DOT), successor to the State Road Department, argued that retaining the fee was justified to pay the high costs of bridge repairs. Restoration had been expensive following the damage done in the 1980s, especially the destructive results of hurricanes Elena and Kate in 1985. Some Franklin countians insisted that at least some kind of pass system should be inaugurated and pressure was put on the DOT and the legislature. As a result, the DOT suddenly removed all tolls on July 1, 1992. Despite the loss of revenue and predictions of increased crime on the island, the decision stood. During this time other developers came in, there was commercial expansion, and continuing questions and debate over the intensity of development.

The price of preserving the blessings of water has been that of eternal vigilance. A crucial problem of the 1990s involves the tri-river system and its flow of water. In 1992 Alabama entered a lawsuit against Georgia and was joined later by Florida. The issue concerns water quantity more than water quality. Georgia wants to hold Chattahoochee River water and release it slowly in order to preserve the Atlanta area's water supply and the water level of Lake Lanier, a major recreational area at Gainsville, about fifty miles northwest of Atlanta. The United States Army Corps of Engineers supports Georgia. Alabama wished more water for industrial and agricultural purposes. Florida's concern is for the quantity of river water that empties into Apalachicola Bay. Periodic floods are part of the river system's pulses and bring nutrients necessary to the bay area's marine life. Florida wants to be recognized as a "user" of fresh water along with Georgia and Alabama. The state and particularly Franklin County are vitally affected by what happens to the water north of the bay.

An interstate Coordinating Committee is at work on the problem. Some kind of basin authority will be established to work out a solution but the task will not be easy. Whatever compacts are reached, they will require legislative sanction in the three states and must be approved by Congress.

People in post World War II Apalachicola and Franklin County, while mindful of the large questions of policy and the issues of politics, were personally concerned with their daily lives. The absorbing requirement of making a living occupied most of their time. In numerous ways the area remained unchanged after 1945. The military bases closed, leaving the area commercially dependent upon the seafood business and, to a lesser extent, timber. There was little industry to provide steady payrolls. Apalachicola remained a true commercial center. Within a block or two of Market Street—between Austin's Department Store, Nichols's Economy Store, the Apalachicola 5 & 10 Cents Store, and a few

In many ways Franklin County remained unchanged after World War II. After the military bases closed, the area returned to dependence upon the seafood business and, to a lesser extent, timber. Courtesy of the Florida Department of Commerce.

others—most goods could be purchased. Besides, the ride over Highway 98 to Panama City or to Tallahassee was uncomfortable and took hours. The town's isolated location benefitted area merchants, but increasingly, highways were improved as were affordable automobiles. Area residents began shopping elsewhere. Such fiscal habits finally proved too much for downtown stores and many of them closed.

Fortunately, by the late 1970s the trend was reversed, as the county was discovered by new people and rediscovered by natives. Beginning in the 1960s John B. Meyer, Director of Community Development, worked hard to obtain funds for various city improvements. Attractive and imaginative specialty stores opened and prospered. Private individuals such as newcomer Kristin Anderson, with the aid of others, opened the Apalachicola Maritime Museum and brought a restored 1877 schooner, the *Governor Stone,* to Apalachicola to moor permanently at the Battery Park Basin.

Apalachicola and the county never encountered the racial problems that disrupted parts of the post–war South. Before the Supreme Court's historic Brown decision of 1954, the county had a legally segregated school system. In Apalachicola Chapman High School for whites and Quinn High School for blacks were separate but unequal. Yet, the disparities were less inequitable than in much of Florida. When implementation of the

Apalachicola remained a true commercial center. Looking west from water's edge of Avenue E, 1960. Courtesy of the Apalachicola State Bank.

desegregation ruling proved unacceptably slow in the South, the Civil Rights Act of 1964 applied additional pressure. Finally, during the 1967–1968 school term integration began in Apalachicola. New schools were constructed and old ones improved. In Apalachicola and Carrabelle racially inspired disturbances were few and none were of major proportions. Evidence of good relations came two years after integration was achieved when a black was elected student body president at Carrabelle High School.

Blacks and whites agreed that integration was relatively smooth because of both towns' interracial demographics. Differing from the usual southern pattern, Apalachicola did not have a community segregated along strictly geographical lines. Most blacks lived in the northern end of town in a section called "the Hill." Still, other blacks lived in predominately white neighbor-

Seafood wholesalers and retailers began selling their products elsewhere and refrigerated trucks revolutionized the industry. Courtesy of the Florida State Archives.

Seafood people buy shrimp, oysters, and scallops off the boats, clean and pack them, and send their products via eighteen-wheelers throughout the country. Courtesy of the Florida Department of Commerce.

hoods. In addition, the Hill was home to white residents as well as blacks. Historically, Apalachicola never had a large slave economy, and race relations, if short of what they should have been, were never virulent. The pattern continued to the twentieth century. For example, the Fuller Hotel, owned by a black couple, Spartan and Belle Jenkins, was one of the town's most thriving businesses when it burned in 1945.

As the county's largest employer the seafood industry engaged people in oyster and shrimp harvesting on the water, as dock workers and other laborers, and as wholesalers and retailers. Locals began selling their products elsewhere, and refrigerated trucks revolutionized the industry. As mentioned above, two men—Joseph Taranto of Sicily and Belton Tarantino, another Italian, iced their products and used trucks in the 1930s. Another means of transporting seafood came from the

Tourists, in 1956, examine and sample oysters fresh from the banks. Pictured left to right: Buster Licidello, Richard Hillman, Louise Barkster and Susan Hillman. Courtesy of the Florida Department of Commerce.

Along the Carrabelle River, Carrabelle has a marina for pleasure seacraft and an even larger commercial section for boats. Courtesy of the Florida Department of Commerce.

Apalachicola Northern railroad (known locally as the "Doodle Bug"). The line's track paralleled Water Street so that its cars could take on loads. The drawback was that rail shipment was slow.

Currently, seafood people buy shrimp, oysters, and scallops off the boats, clean and pack them, and send their products via eighteen-wheelers throughout the country. With contracts from supermarkets, restaurant chains, and other major buyers, a number of local businesses prosper. It is now an efficient operation, one complete with market research and technology that make possible precision orders and distribution. Cyclic in annual production totals, the local oyster industry has problems both natural and man made. Yet, the bay area had seven hundred registered oyster harvesters in 1977. Apalachicola produces over 90 percent of Florida's oysters and over 10 percent of the national total. Properly managed, the oyster, shrimp, and other seafood enterprises have a solid economic future.

A major blow came locally and to other coastal regions in 1994 when a state constitutional amendment banned gill nets larger than a specified size. The effect was disastrous for the lucrative mullet and speckled trout markets. Florida voters agreed by over 70 percent that the entangling nets damaged the ecology of Florida's waters. Critics countered that voters were ill-informed by the advertising blitz favoring the amendment. Because grouper, the area's most consumed fish, are caught by rod and reel along offshore reefs, they are unaffected by the net ban.

The twentieth century importance of the sea for leisure and for the economy is seen in Apalachicola at the city-owned Battery Park Basin where a variety of yachts and pleasure boats owned by locals and visitors are always at anchor. John Ruge's will in 1931 deeded the property (where his seafood business was located at Ten-Foot Hole) that became the basin and Battery Park to the city. He stipulated that it always be used as a recreation area. Part of Battery Park also came from the Florida Promenade, as it was called in the nineteenth century, an area located west of Ruge's property.

Commercial boats take advantage of Scipio Marina north of town. The marina began as a staging area in the nineteenth century by lumber companies that floated their logs there before transhipping them. As time passed, shrimpers and crabbers made increasing use of the facility. It became a modern working marina in the 1980s and has a Harbormaster House, completed in 1988 with a Department of Community Affairs (DCA) grant. The House is headquarters for the St. Vincent National Wildlife Preserve and contains a small environmental museum. Eastpoint has an occasional pleasure craft, but is predominantly the home of "working" boats. Along the Carrabelle River, Carrabelle has a marina for pleasure seacraft and an even larger commercial section for boats.

Apalachicola's Water Street is a name unmistakably identified with its geography and its purpose. Marked by its eclectic architecture, Water Street is a colorful mixture of restaurants, a drive-in by land or float-in by water motel, seafood houses, bars, businesses, and restoration projects. Lee Willis, II, and Lou Hill, Jr., of

The Florida Seafood Festival was begun in 1963. In 1970 John "Jimmy" Nichols, Kathy Nichols, Valerie Ralstead and Mayor Jimmy Nichols hold up welcome signs. Courtesy of the Florida Department of Commerce.

One of the activities of the 1970 Seafood Festival was the blessing of the fleet. Courtesy of the Florida Department of Commerce.

Tallahassee are restoring the J. E. Grady & Co. building constructed in 1884. It was destroyed by fire in 1900 and immediately rebuilt. The building is on the site of an 1837 cotton warehouse, one of several multi-storied brick warehouses that once lined the street and dated from the Apalachicola Land Company. Water Street also houses the Apalachicola Fire Department. Shrimp boats and other vessels ride anchor in the river by the street.

Apalachicola annually attracts people to its Florida Seafood Festival. Borrowed in concept from early twentieth century Mardi Gras festivals, it was begun in 1963. It has the dual purpose of helping promote the seafood industry and of having the industry advertise Franklin County. At first the event was mostly a community fish fry that attracted few visitors. It has long since grown, and is now an extended weekend that includes live music from nationally known performers, an arts and crafts fair, a variety of food, and thousands of visitors. The oyster eating contest, conducted yearly since 1973, is the most popular event. "King Retsyo" (oyster spelled backwards) presides over the event and is chosen annually as someone who has helped the industry. In the great tradition of American festivals there is a queen. Miss Florida Seafood is typically a high school student.

The paramount importance of water to the area's life is given valuable focus by the Apalachicola National Estuarine Research Reserve. It is part of the national reserve system established by a congressional act of

The City of Apalachicola's float in the 1970 parade. Courtesy of the Florida Department of Commerce.

1972. The Reserve was opened in 1979 through a cooperative agreement among the National Oceanic and Atmospheric Administration, the state of Florida, and Franklin County. Woody Miley was the first staff person in 1981, and in 1997 presided over a fulltime staff of thirteen. The agency performs its mission of conserving estuarine resources through field research and through education from its headquarters located in Apalachicola. With nearly 194,000 acres of land and water in Franklin, Liberty, and Gulf counties, the Reserve makes its scientific work available to the public through informative and attractive publications that are distributed without charge. Its printings include booklets on shells, amphibians and reptiles, fishes, birds, and mammals.

Florida, hoping to cope with the problems of runaway population growth, passed a law in the 1980s known as the Growth Management Plan. It required each county and municipality to adopt a "Comprehensive Plan" that laid out policies for future growth with specific plans regarding land regulations, zoning, and so on. Franklin County moved to conform. Overseeing the Comprehensive Plan statewide was the Department of Community Affairs (DCA), headed by Tom Pelham who was appointed by Governor Bob Martinez (1987–1991). According to local historian George Chapel, everybody had a plan. One local noted that Larry Capune, laying over in Apalachicola from hand paddling a surfboard from Maine to Texas, was the only adult in Franklin County who neither knew nor cared about a plan.

As noted, in 1985 Franklin County and Apalachicola were badly hit by hurricanes Elena and Kate. The disasters promoted the governor and the cabinet to declare the region an Area of Critical State Concern (ACSC). A law dealing specifically with Franklin County authorized Governor Martinez to appoint a Resource Planning and Management Commission (RPMC). The RPMC was to oversee the administration of the legislative mandate to recommend funds that would improve Franklin County and Apalachicola's infrastructure and economic situation. The RPMC was also charged with protecting the area's natural resources. It was made up of people appointed by the governor from state and local agencies, as well as local government officials and citizens. Broken down into committees with specific tasks, the RPMC worked out recommendations on a variety of environmental, economic, and social issues.

As part ot the ACSC mandate, the RPMC also helped formulate the county's Comprehensive Plan. County Planners James Floyd and especially Alan Pierce, county commissioner Jimmy Mosconis, and others, including George Chapel, helped draft Comprehensive Plans for the county. The Plans for Franklin County, Apalachicola, and Carrabelle were adopted in 1991. Franklin County and Carrabelle were removed from the ACSC that same year but Apalachicola remained a part of it in 1997. Drafting, implementing, and later revising the proposals required a great deal of time and effort. Both detailed and general in content, the Comprehensive Plans were not perfect but they answered critical needs.

As complicated plans and proposals were debated and adopted, Franklin County was undergoing a visible and esthetic cultural and economic transition. The restoration and reopening of the Gibson Inn was a major catalyst in Apalachicola's downtown revitalization. Three investors from out of state—Michael J. Koun, Neil Koun, and Michael Merlo—decided that tourism held the area's greatest potential for growth. Apalachicola and the surrounding area had the attractions to lure visitors but they needed a place to stay. The entrepreneurs purchased the deteriorated Gibson Inn in 1983. After a twenty-three-month restoration, the early twentieth-century structure was restored to its original authenticity and grandeur and reopened for overnight accommodations in November 1985.

Part of the crowd at the 1973 Seafood Festival. Courtesy of the Florida Department of Commerce.

Avenue E looking east toward Water Street. The restaurants and shops display the variety of the city's facades.

An aerial view of the Apalachicola River and Bay estuarine with the new Gorrie Bridge under construction, 1990. Courtesy of the Apalachicola State Bank.

In 1988 the John Gorrie bridge that had stood since 1935 was replaced. There were some nostalgic remarks but locals were pleased that the new structure still bore the John Gorrie name and that it was a state of the art elevation bridge. Descending from it into town, motorists see first the blue painted Gibson, and both structures—the bridge and the hotel—symbolize the old and the new Apalachicola.

The newcomers, as well as locals, were drawn to Apalachicola's variety of large and small homes with architectural distinction. The older homes were usually frame structures. Many of them were renovated and new ones were built. Some former private residences such as Adolph Flatauer's, built in 1908–1909, were converted for commercial usage. In the 1980s Flatauer's renovated home became the offices of the Gulf State Bank. Downtown, older buildings were restored and sometimes used for their original purposes. For example, George W. Saxon of Tallahassee established a branch of his Capital City Bank at Apalachicola in 1897. Local businessmen bought him out in 1906 and it became the Apalachicola State Bank. After extensive renovations in the mid-1990s the bank still operates at its Avenue E address, and in 1997 entered its one

The 1961 destruction of the Lovett home, which had been the property of James Holland, and was one of the oldest residences in Apalachicola (1828), caused alarm among townspeople and concern about the destruction of landmark buildings. Courtesy of the Florida Department of Commerce.

hundredth year of operation. By the century's end, Apalachicola's thriving real estate market was referred to by some as a boom.

Apalachicola has benefitted from a national reaction to crowded streets, mindless rush, inconvenience, pressure, inefficiency, and crime (to name a few objections) that accompany urban living. Instead, Apalachicola offered and offers small town life in an attractive setting, one that is rich in tradition and history. More and more, artists and craft specialists have moved to the area.

LaFayette Park is one point of appeal. Located in the western part of town, it was in the original plat, and at one end contained a cemetery that was later closed. During the lumber boom of the nineteenth century's last decades, houses were built along Bay Avenue to take advantage of the view and the park began to take more distinctive form. The present expanse—with its gazebo, grass carpet, shrubs, flowers, weather-bent live oaks and other trees, walkways, and pier—is the late twentieth century work of local architect Willoughby Marshall. Local boosters also point out the numerous historic churches and other landmarks, and despite the citizens' reputation for being independent-minded and having strong convictions, most now agree that much of the late William Lee Popham's hyperbole was pure gospel. They are ready for a new century.

The new Bryant Patton bridge from Eastpoint to Saint George Island was opened in February 2004. It is 4.1 miles long and is the third longest continuous span in Florida. The old bridge is being demolished for use as an artificial reef, but both ends of it are being kept as fishing piers.

Thirteen

The Beginning of a New One-Hundred-Year's Cycle

From the mid-1990s to the middle of the new century's first decade Apalachicola and Franklin County experienced significant growth and change. The census figures of 2000 revealed some important facts. Franklin County had 11,057 people (4,816 females and 6,240 males) with a median age of 40.8. The county's white population was 8,983 and its blacks numbered 2,074. Apalachicola had 4,506 people, Carrabelle 3,710, and Eastpoint 2,642. Apalachicola's African Americans totaled 1,804, with Eastpoint's 68 constituting the fewest of the county's three towns. The white population made up 79.9 percent of the total population.

Franklin County's educational status for residents twenty-five years and older, a total of 8,202 persons, demonstrated a rise from 1990. Of these citizens 68.3 percent were high school graduates or higher, and 12.4 percent had a bachelor's degree or higher. The county had 1,555 workers who were drawing salaries, and in Apalachicola the median salary was $25,101 with Carrabelle and Eastpoint being roughly comparable. In 2000 Franklin County had 1,654 people or 17.7 percent of its population whose incomes were below the poverty level. Home values had increased since 1990 and the curve was continuing to climb. The median value was $105,300. There were 2,053 homes in the county occupied by owners. In the lowest category, 281 owners had homes worth $50,000 to $99,999 and in one of the higher categories, homes worth $200,000 to $200,999, there were 262 owners. There were 362 owners in the largest category of homeowners, those whose residences were valued at $150,000 to $199,000.

The entire county profited from the opening of a new bridge in 2004. The Florida Department of Transportation (FDOT) has the responsibility of maintaining bridges in Florida. Regular inspections by the FDOT revealed that the Bryant Patton bridges to Saint George Island were ideal candidates for replacement. More than thirty years old, the span (two bridges connected by a central causeway) required frequent and costly maintenance, and its narrowness inhibited expeditious evacuations of the island during hurricane season. In addition, the causeway had become a sensitive nesting area for rare birds, namely the American oystercatcher and the black skimmer. Traffic to and from the island threatened the future of the endangered species. The necessary procedures and approvals were obtained, and in July 1999, construction on a new bridge began.

Before building commenced, the FDOT also considered the project's potentially damaging economic and environmental impact. Traversing a wide arc to the west of the previous route, the new bridge bypasses sensitive oyster beds—a habitat critical to both the bay's ecosystem and to the livelihood of many families in Franklin County—while also maintaining the same landfall sites.

Concerned for the oyster's fate, proponents of some early proposals called for building the new bridge as far as four miles to the east. Yet planners ultimately decided against the move when they anticipated the devastating result that such a route would cause existing businesses that depended upon bridge traffic for commerce. The new bridge was also economically feasible because it would be cost-effective for taxpayers in the long run. The $78 million price tag was far less than the funds that would have been required to pay for continuous work to offset corrosion and deterioration on the old bridges. Built and designed by the team of Boh Brothers Construction and Jacobs Civil, Inc., the

Bob Sikes Cut, which divided Saint George Island from Little Saint George Island and creates an opening from Apalachicola Bay to the Gulf of Mexico, is a popular gathering place for fishermen and pelicans alike.

new bridge gave promise of requiring little maintenance during the new century.

After the new bridge opened in early 2004, the FDOT converted portions of the old bridges into fishing piers for both the mainland and the island while the rest of the pilings and roadway were dismantled and donated to any artificial reef project in the Gulf of Mexico. The former causeway was converted into an island bird sanctuary managed by the Florida Department of Environmental Protection. Measuring 4.1 miles, the new toll-free Bryant Patton Bridge is the third longest bridge in the state.

The twenty-first century accelerated the transformation of Franklin County and the entire Florida Panhandle. As a result of large land sales to the state and purchases of land from the state the region would never be the same. At the same time, private individuals and smaller real estate agencies were part and parcel of the

This is a view of Market Street, Apalachicola's main thoroughfare, looking north. It continues to be the busy center of shops, restaurants, and various other stores.

The new **Apalachicola Times** *office on Market Street. The newspaper recently moved from its headquarters in one of the old ice exchanges on Water Street.*

changes that came to Apalachicola and the region. When the St. Joe Company shut down its paper company at Port St. Joe in 1998 it was Florida's largest private landowner with one million acres. It was also the largest owner of land in Franklin County where 60 percent of the county was owned by the government, and of the remaining 40 percent, half was owned by St. Joe. As the nation entered the new millennium the company negotiated a series of land sales and land purchases from the state of Florida. In October 2001 the state paid the company approximately $6.4 million for 3,406 acres in the county. The purchase was negotiated by The Nature Conservancy, Inc. (TNC) and had been approved by Governor Jeb Bush earlier in the summer. The Florida Forever program provided the funds, and Florida's Division of Forestry became the property manager. The land is located in Tate's Hell State Forest which borders Apalachicola National Forest in the north and Apalachicola Bay in the south. It is an area with large areas of flatwoods, wet prairies, cypress swamp, and contains numerous rivers and streams that flow into the bay. The continuing protection of the land is necessary to the commercial and recreational fisheries on the bay's estuary, and the exchange of the land from private to public ownership marked an important step.

Woody Miley of the Apalachicola National Estuarine Research Reserve, said, "Protecting these areas is just as much an economic concern as it is an environmental concern." The Nature Conservancy headed by Bob Bendick, director of the Conservancy's Florida Chapter, had acquired nearly 100,000 acres of Tate's Hell State Forest. Now The Conservancy and Peter S. Rummell, chairman and CEO of St. Joe, and Governor Bush with his interest in environmental issues all played important

A new building in downtown Apalachicola contains a variety of stores. Included are Verandas, a restaurant and wine bar, as well as Sirens, a clothing store. The building conforms with the older downtown architectural patterns.

parts in the negotiations. Although Florida became the owner of the land, local government also profited because 15 percent of the income received from the state forest's resource management was set aside for Franklin County's School Board Program.

Another large purchase occurred in October 2002 when Governor Bush and the state cabinet approved the purchase of 2,851 acres of land on Franklin County's Bald Point. The purchase price was $10 million dollars, or $3,613 per acre. The sale helped ease the concerns of some environmentalists who opposed Arvida, the St. Joe Company's development arm, in its proposal to develop SummerCamp, a project that included construction of homes, a sixty-room inn, and stores on 786 acres near St. Teresa. Some residents and state officials feared the development would threaten Alligator Harbor's sea life.

The Bald Point property was acquired through a multiparty agreement with TNC as part of the state's Florida Forever land acquisition program. The acreage stretches from Ocklockonee Bay to Alligator Harbor, and has considerable frontage along both estuarine bodies that connect to the Gulf of Mexico. It is composed of high quality upland and wetlands that provide impressive vistas and highly developable water frontage. The tract contains wetland ponds and tidal creeks, especially Tucker Lake and Big Chairs Creek, which support numerous fish species, and the estuarine-influenced water bodies also provide habitat for a variety of waterfowl. The coastal location serves as a resting site for migratory birds before and after their flight across the Gulf of Mexico. The property also provides a foraging habitat and corridor for Florida black bears that migrate back and forth from the coast to upland swamps on the northern part of St. James Island. Bordered by the Ochlocknee Bay, Carrabelle and Crooked Rivers, and the Gulf of Mexico (and including the rural communities of Alligator Point, St. Teresa, Lanark Village, and the City of Carrabelle), St. James

Island contains about sixty thousand acres primarily owned by the St. Joe Company.

"This is the best thing that could happen to this property," according to Roy DuVerger, president of the Apalachee Ecological Conservancy (APECO), an Alligator Point–based nonprofit environmental organization. DuVerger expressed interest in working with the St. Joe Company and the DEP to establish links between future communities in St. James Island with Bald Point State Park by way of trail and greenway connections. Those greenways, according to DuVerger, could "provide people and wildlife a corridor to the coast and other wild places so they may both live better in harmony with the environment."

Within St. James Island, St. Joe proposed its SummerCamp development. The project proved controversial, and prompted a standing-room-only attendance at a public meeting of the Franklin County Commission in January 2003. Billy Buzzett, director of strategic planning for St. Joe, explained that when the project was started in the fall of 2001 and presented to the State Department of Community Affairs, that body raised no objections: Back at the drawing board and working with state and local environmental groups, St. Joe presented its new plans to the public hearing. The company scrapped its intent to move U.S. Highway 98 and abandoned plans for a marina, favoring a single ten-craft dock and ten community piers with no boat slips. SummerCamp would have no boat ramps, and the only watercraft would be canoes and kayaks.

Continuing its outlines, the company noted that the Florida State University marine laboratory, situated in the middle of the acreage, was not threatened. St. Joe created a conservation easement and access to Turkey Creek and thus protected the significant research site there. The company pledged to support the labs programs. The company also agreed to manage its own water, build an advanced wastewater treatment plant, and offer the community of St. Teresa the option of switching off septic tanks. The company

Utilitarian and beautiful, Lafayette Park (formerly a cemetery) fronts Apalachicola Bay. It boasts wind-bent trees and a gazebo designed by Willoughby Marshall.

assumed responsibility for treating its own storm water. As a result various influential environment groups that had previously opposed SummerCamp dropped their objections.

There was not 100 percent unanimity among those at the meeting. John Hedrick of the Panhandle citizens coalition expressed his belief that St. Joe planned to build "a new city" of St. James Island and raised the issue of "hidden costs." Buzzett replied that the company had no immediate plans to develop St. James Island, but that its future was a company concern. The Commission voted 5–0 to adopt a comprehensive plan amendment enabling the St. Joe Company to take the necessary steps toward turning the 784 site into a residential community.

This view of historic Chestnut Street Cemetery shows the Ruge family and the Messina family plots. The cemetery is located on Avenue E which is also U.S. Highway 98 and is distinguished by its moss-draped live oaks and Coontie palms.

The sale to the state of fifty thousand acres in the Panhandle was another project of the St. Joe Company. In June 2003 Florida's Acquisition and Restoration Council added the land to a priority list for state land purchases. As it was planned this St. Vincent Sound to Lake Wimico ecosystem would become part of the "St. Joe Timberlands" project. It included tens of thousands acres of company-owned lands which straddled Franklin and Gulf Counties. One sale went through, and negotiations continued between the state and the company.

In November 2003 the St. Joe Company purchased Timber Island. Sitting in the mouth of the Carrabelle River where it empties into the Gulf of Mexico, the forty-nine-acre island had been part of a land swap in 1985 that saw the state take possession and then lease the property to the Carrabelle Port Airport Authority. Plans to turn Timber Island into a seafood industrial park failed to materialize, though a portion of it was subleased, and the island reverted to state ownership in 2001. The state put the property up for sale in 2003, and the St. Joe Company was the only bidder. The purchase price was $6.8 million.

Led by Franklin County environmental officials and state representative Will Kendrick (Democrat-Carrabelle), there was wide support for the purchase. Tim Edmund, president of the capital region for Arvida/St. Joe Company, quieted any fears that the company planned a high-rise development. The company planned to build a commercial marina and develop a residential area according to market demands and conservation efforts.

In November 2003 the St. Joe Company sold the state over thirteen thousand acres along Crooked River in eastern Franklin County. The purchase price was $14.5 million which came from Florida Forever funds. Standing to gain were Florida's bears and its citizens—the bears and other wildlife receiving protection and the public gaining access to the land for hunting, fishing, boating, and picnicking. The parcel expanded Tate's Hell into the state's largest state forest. It also added twenty miles of Crooked River shoreline to the state's property.

Located on Bay Avenue, the Grady-Hodges home was built circa 1870 and purchased by J. E. Grady in the 1880s. Inherited by Joseph and Alice Hodges in the 1930s, the house was restored in the late 1980s.

In all of the activity that took place and will continue to come forward the Franklin County Community Planning Process has been important. It engaged property owners, interested citizens, business interests, responsible government agencies, and others in discussing plans that addressed common concerns. Interest has been high and participation spirited in the workshops that have been held and have involved many groups, including citizens and such corporate bodies as the St. Joe Company.

In the twenty-first century "dramatic change" were the key words for Franklin County, its cities and towns of Apalachicola, Carrabelle, and Eastpoint, its barrier islands and interior regions, and its people. For lifetime residents and newcomers alike, rising to the challenge would have to be met. Keeping in mind the old admonition that even "the best laid plans" can bring unintended results, it seems reasonable and rational to hope that Franklin County will have a prosperous future. Who knows, perhaps the dreams of its most optimistic citizen, William Lee Popham, can come true.

Select Bibliography

Boynton, Walter Raymond. "Energy Basis of a Coastal Region: Franklin County and Apalachicola, Florida." Ph.D. dissertation, University of Florida, 1973.

Cushman, Joseph D., Jr. "The Blockade and Fall of Apalachicola, 1861–1862," *Florida Historical Quarterly*, 41 (July 1962), 38–46.

Ingle, Robert M., and Whitfield, William E., Jr. *Oyster Culture in Florida*. Tallahassee: State of Florida Board of Conservation, 1968.

Jahoda, Gloria. *The Other Florida*. New York: Charles Scribner's Sons, 1967.

Key, Alexander. *The Wrath and the Wind*. Indianapolis: Bobbs-Merrill, 1950.

Knauss, James O. *Florida Territorial Journalism*. Deland, Florida. Florida State Historical Society, 1936.

Livingston, Robert J. *Resource Atlas of the Apalachicola Estuary*. Tallahassee: Florida Sea Grant College Program, 1983.

Nixon, Eugene L. "A Doctor and an Island," *Journal of the Florida Medical Association*, 63 (August 1972), 45–53.

Owens, Harry P., "Apalachicola Before 1861." Unpublished doctoral dissertation, Florida State University, 1966.

Rogers, William Warren. *Outposts on the Gulf Saint George Island and Apalachicola from Early Exploration to World War*. Pensacola: University of West Florida Press, 1987.

Sherlock, Vivian M. *The Fever Man: A Biography of Dr. John Gorrie*. Tallahassee: Medallion Press, 1982.

Turner, Maxine. *Navy Gray: A Story of the Confederate Navy on the Chattahoochee and Apalachicola Rivers*. Tuscaloosa: University of Alabama Press, 1988.

Upchurch, John Calhoun. "Aspects of the Development and Exploration of the Forbs Purchase," *Florida Historical Quarterly*, 48 (October 1969), 117–139.

Willis, Lee. "Bellwether Parish: Trinity Episcopal Church of Apalachicola, 1835–1914." Unpublished master's thesis, Florida State University, 1998.

Willoughby, Lynn. *Fair to Middlin' The Antebellum Cotton Trade of the Apalachicola/Chattahoochee River Valley*. Tuscaloosa: University of Alabama Press, 1993.

Ziewitz, Kathryn and June Wiaz. *Green Empire: The St. Joe Company and the Remaking of Florida's Panhandle*. Gainesville: University Presses of Florida, 2004.

Index

A

Abbot, Trevett, 47
Abbott, James J., 96, 106, 109, 111, 114, 117, 119, 121
Adams, John Quincy, 16
Adams-Onis treaty, 7, 15, 16, 19
Adela, 51
Advertiser, the, 26
African Methodist Episcopal Church, 63, *105*
Alabama railroad line, 38
Alabama, 7, 8, 9, 13, 16, *16*, *23*, 42, 46, 47, 53, 60, 71, 82, 154
Alafia River, 96
Alaqua Guards, 32
Albany, Ga., 13, 24
Alexander, Edward P., 55
Allen's Negro Minstrels, 90
Alligator Harbor, 170
Alligator Point, 135, 147, 170, 171
Allison, Albraham K., 52
Altha, *125*
Alvin W. Chapman High School, 86, 133, 141, 142, *142*, 155
Amelia Island, 41
American Exchange Bank, 114
American Revolution, 16
Amphibian, 135, 145
Amphibious Fighters, 138
Amphibious Training Center, 135, 138, 144
Amphibious Training Command Military Reservation, 135
Anderson, Charles, 78, *79*
Anderson, James Patton, Colonel, 42, *42*
Anderson, Kristin, 155
Anderson, W. W., 106
Apalachee Bay, 88
Apalachee County, *13*, 15, *15*
Apalachee Ecological Conservancy, 171
Apalachee Indians, *12*, 14, 15
Apalachicola 5 & 10 Cents Store, 154
Apalachicola Academy, 31
Apalachicola and Alabama Railroad, 59
Apalachicola and Columbus Deep Water Association, 60
Apalachicola Army Air Field, 9, 134, *134*
Apalachicola Bay, 7, 9, 11, 12, 13, *14*, 15, 17, 21, 22, 27, 68, 72, 78, *112*, 125, 130, *131*, 153, 154, 168, 169, *171*
Apalachicola Board of Trade, 60
Apalachicola Chamber of Commerce, 116
Apalachicola *Commercial Advertiser*, 32
Apalachicola Defense Rental Agency, 136
Apalachicola Fire Department, 159
Apalachicola Guards, 32
Apalachicola Indians, 7, 12, 14
Apalachicola Land and Development Company, 113
Apalachicola Land Company, 7, 26, 27, 28, 29, 35, 36, 39, 159
Apalachicola Maritime Museum, 155
Apalachicola Mission, 32
Apalachicola National Estuarine Research Reserve, 160, 169
Apalachicola National Forest, 169
Apalachicola Northern Railroad, 83, *84*, *85*, 156
Apalachicola Packing Company, 74
Apalachicola River, 8, 9, 12, *12*, 13, 14, 15, *15*, *17*, 19, *20*, 21, 23, 24, 25, 26, 27, 35, 45, 59, *64*, 69, 71, 78, 83, *84*, *101*, *108*, 111, 126, 137, *164*
Apalachicola Servicemen's Club, 140, *141*
Apalachicola State Bank, *102*, 162
Apalachicola Temperance Society, 32
Apalachicola *Times*, 85, 93, 98, 99, 132, 133, 135, 140, 153, *169*
Apalachicola Women's Auxiliary of the Chamber of Commerce, 136
Apalachicolan, 31
Appomattox Courthouse, 52
Area of Critical State Concern (ACSC), 161
Army Air Corps, 134
Army Air Forces Flexible Gunnery School, 134, *134*
Army Air Forces Training Command, 143
Army of the Tennessee, 53
Army Service Forces Training Center, 144
Arriola, Andres, 15
Arvida, 170, 172
Asboth, Alexander, General, 52, 53
ASFTC, 145
Asia, 9, 133
Askew, Reubin, 152, 153
Atkinson, Clyde A., 127, 128
Atkinson, Clyde W., 149, 152
Atlanta *Journal*, 106
Atlanta, Ga., 96, 109, 121, 140, 154
Atlantic and Gulf Railroad, 57
Atlantic Coast Line Railroad, 83, 123
Austin's Department Store, 139–140, 154
Austin, Gene, 123, 139
Austria, 93
Automobile Association of America, 116
Avenue D., *88*, *93*
Avenue E., *163*, *172*
Avenue F., *98*
Aviles, Pedro Menendez de, 15

B

Bahamas, 74
Bainbridge *Argus*, 35, 38
Bainbridge, Ga., 8, 24, 57, 84
Bainbridge, *Southern Spy*, 21
Bald Point, 170
Bold Point State Park, 171
Ball, Ed, 9

Baltimore, Md., 75, 76
Bank of Apalachicola, 29
Baptist church, 32
Barkster, Louise, *157*
Barrow, W. G., 83
Bartlett's *Gazette*, 31
Bartlett, Cosam Emir, 27
Battery Park Basin, 155, 158
Battery Park, 137
Battle of Horseshoe Bend, 16
Battle of Mariana, 52
Battle of Natural Bridge, *49*, 52
Battle of Olustee, 8, *48*
Bay Avenue, 165, *173*,
Bay City Packing Company, 74, *74*, 78, *79*,
Bay County, 9
Bay Croft syrup, 9
Beall, Phillip, 118, 119
Bendick, Bob, 169
Benjamin, Judah P., *42*, 44
Bentley, Hugh Bradford, Captain, 138
Beveridge, Robert, 25
Big Chairs Creek, 170
Big Clitty, 95
Birmingham, Timothy, Reverend, 32 *106*
Black Baptists, 32
Black, Ed, *128*
Bloodworth, B. Frances, *123*
Blountstown, 50 *125*, 153
Bob Sikes Cut, 11, *168*
Boh Brothers Construction, 167
Bombadears, 140
Bowles, William Augustus, 17, *19*
Bradley, Omar N., 144, *144*
Bragg, Braxton B., General, 41
Brash, Henry, 57
Brash, M., Mrs., Sr., *85*
Brazil, 114
Breakers, The, 98
Bristol, 153
Britain, *17*
British East Florida, 16
British West Florida, 16
Broadway Melody, The, 123
Broughton, George, Mrs., 85, *87*
Brown decision, 155
Brown family, 9
Brown, David H., *64, 65, 66, 67*, 68
Brown, Gene, 152, 153, 154
Brown, Herbert G., 68
Brown, Joseph E., Governor, 52, 53
Brown, Rebecca Wood, 68
Brown, Thomas, 9
Brunson, Mrs., *133*
Bryan, Samuel J., 31
Bryan, William Jennings, 113, 119
Bryant Patton Bridge, 9, *102*, 150, 153, *166*, 167, 168
Buck, James Fulton "Jeff", *84*, 97

Buck Lumber Company, L. B., 129
Buffalo, New York, 8, *55*, 56
Burke-Wadsworth Act, 133
Bush, Jeb, 169, 170
Butera, Mary, 140
Butler-Lindsay Riparian Act, 113
Buzzett's Drugstore, 143
Buzzett, Harry, 143, 146
Buzzett, Julian R., 146
Buzzett, Rex, *123*, 146
Buzzett, William D., 143, 171, 172

C

Cabeza de Vaca, Alvar Núñez, *13*, 14
Calhoun County, 27
California, 129
Call, Richard Keith, *24*, 26
Calvary Baptist Church, 116, 117, *119*
Camp Blanding, 133
Camp Carrabelle, 134, *135*
Camp Edwards, 135
Camp Gordon Johnson, 9, 135, *135*, *136*, 137, *137*, 138, *138*, 140, *141*, 144, *144*, 146, 147
Camp Retrieve, 44
Camp, Allie, 139
Campeche, Mexico, 78
Canada, 16
Cape Canaveral, 43
Cape Florida, *20*, 21
Cape San Blas, 29, 82
Cape St. George, 8, 11, 29, 36, 37, *37*, 43, 53, *103*, 103
Capital City Bank, 87, 96, 162
Capune, Larry, 161
Caribbean, 150
Carnochan and Mitchel, 19, 21
Carolinas, 125
Carrabelle High School, 155
Carrabelle Ice Company, 88
Carrabelle Land and Lumber Company, 82
Carrabelle River, 8, 63, *63*, 65, 104, 158, 159, 170, 172
Carrabelle, 8, 9, 11, *36*, 59, 60, 63, *63*, 64, *64*, 66, 68, 69, 75, 83, 85, 88, *88*, 96, 99, *101*, *102*, *103*, *104*, *112*, *114*, 117, 119, 126, 129, 133, 135, 136, 137, 140, 141, 144 145, 146, *148*, 150, 155, *158*, 159, 161, 167, 170, 172
Carrabelle, Tallahassee and Georgia Railroad Company, 8, *63*, 68
Carrabelle Port Airport Authority, 172
Castelnau, Conte de, *17*
Catholics, 32, 57
Catpoint, 68, *148*, 150
Catts, William J., 116, *116*
Cedar Key, 47, 49

Chaires, Benjamin, 26
Chapel, George, 161
Chaperons, 140
Chapman, Alvan W., Dr., *28*, 29, 30, 48, *107*, 113, *114*
Charleston and Apalachicola Line, 37
Charleston, S. C., 15, 41
Chase, William, 41
Chattahoochee (gunboat), 45, 49, 50, 51, 52, 53
Chattahoochee arsenal, 42, *42*
Chattahoochee River Valley, 22, 23
Chattahoochee River, 9, 13, *23*, 24, 25, 38, 41, *65*, 69, *84*, 137, 153, 154
Chesapeake Bay, 72
Chesnut, Wesley, 153
Chestnut Street, 28
Chestnut Street Cemetery, *101*, 106, *172*
Chipola Canal Company, *24*, 26
Chipola River, 13, 25
Choctaw, 12
Christ Church, *31*, 32
Christian Commonwealth, 9, 68, 69
Cide San Blas, *10*
Cincinnati, Ohio, 55
Citizen's Band, 90
City Cavalry, 32
City Cornet Band, 84
City Dragoons, 32
City Hospital, 33
City Hotel, 32
City of Carrabelle (tugboat), *89*
Civil Aeronautics Authority, 134
Civil Rights Act of 1964, 155
Civil War, 7, 32, 39, 41–53, 56, 68, 72, *101*, *104*, *107*
Civilian Conservation Corps, 126
Clay County, 133
Climax, Ga., 83
Club House, *89*, 89, *90*
Co-Worker' Fraternity, 9, *65*, 69
Coacoochee, *22*, 23
Cobb, Howell, 49 53
Coe, John M., 119
Colbert County, Ala., 81
Coles, David, 146
Collier, William H., 106, 109, 111, 113, 114, 117, 119, 121
Colored Odd Fellows, 84, *85*
Columbus Ga., 8, 9, 13, 21, 24, 26, 29, 32, 38, 42, 49, 50, 52, 53, 57, 60, *64*, 68, 131, *131*
Commerce Street, *93*
Commercial Advertiser, 31
Commercial Bank of Apalachicola, 29
Commonwealth, 69
Company E, 129, 133
Company L, First Florida Infantry, *92*

Comprehensive Plan, 161
Confederate States of America, 7, 8, 41–53, 101
Congregational church, 69
Connecticut, 24, 72
Connor, Doyle F., 128
Constitutional Convention of 1838, *25*, 27
Cook, John, 61
Coombs family, *58*
Coombs Hill, *89*
Coombs, J. P., 134
Coombs, James N., 57, 59, 82, *83*
Core, George, *123*
Cottonton, 7, 21
Countess, *139*, 139
Counts, George M., Sr., 89, *90*, 127, 128
Courier, 31
Covington, Hampton, *64*, 68
Crawfordville, *136*
Creek Indians, 7, 16, *17*, 22, *23*, 24
Creek War, 16
Creekmore, W. N., 151
Creekmore, W. N., Jr., 133
Cresent City (steamship), *66*, 69, 81, *81*
Crooked River lighthouse, 8, *62*, 65, *103*
Crooked River, 63, 170, 172
Cropp, William F., Captain, 42
Cuba, 36, 43, 68
Cubberly, Fred C., 118, 119
Cultivated Oyster Farms Corporation, *112*, *118*, 124, 125, *125*
Cummings, Harry, 114
Cummings, Reaver, *90*
Curtis House, *60*, 61
Curtis, Benjamin, 8, 55, 68
Cuyler, R. R., (steamer), 43
Cypress Lumber Company, 57, 59, 81, 82, *83*

D
Dade County, 16
Darien, Ga., 19
David, E. T., 118
David, Fred H., 118
Davis, Jefferson, President, 41, *42*, 49, 119
Decatur County, Ga., 24, 45
Dechant, C. M., 114
DeCosmo, Jimmie, *92*
Delaware, 109
Democrats, 7, 8, 68
Dempsey, Jack, 123
Developments of regional impact (DRIs), 152, 153, 154
Dewey, Thomas E., 133
District of Apalachicola, 21
Dixie Theatre, 90, 100, 111, 113, 123, 136, *136*

Dog Island Cover, 59
Dog Island, 7, 8, 11, 12, *13*, 14, 36, *37*, 39, 42, 43, 46, 53, 55, *62*, 63, 65, 68, 71, 74, *86*, *103*, 135, 144, *144*, 146, 147, *148*, 149, 150
Dreamland Theatre, *88*, 89, 90, 93
Duff, Charles R., 83, *84*
DUKW, 145, *145*
Dunbar High School, 142, *142*
Duval, William P., 21, *22*
DuVerger, Roy, 171

E
East Bay, 12 97
East Gulf Coast Blockade Squadron, 8, *42*, 43, *44*, 49, 50, 53
East Hole, *148*, 150
East Pass, 8, 11, 51, 55, 59, 63, 142
Eastpoint post office, *66*
Eastpoint, 8, 9, 64, *64*, 65, *66*, 68, 69, *102*, 109, 126, *127*, 135, 138, 146, *148*, 149, 150, 159, *166*, 167, 172
Edmund, Tim, 172
Edwards, Mr., *92*
EGCBS, 46
Eighteenth Amendment, 111
Eighty-Second U.S. Colored Infantry, 53
Elena (hurricane), 154, 161
Empire Mica (British ship), 138, 139, *139*
England, 15
Episcopalians, 32
Estes, Clare, 124
Estes, Maude Miller, 95
Estes, Silent Jim, 113, 124
Eufaula, Ala., 24
Europe, 133, 144
Evans, W. A., 128
Everglades, 7, 23

F
Fanny (steamboat), 21
Farley, W. F., 86, 88
Farmers' Alliance, 68
Fashion, 50
Federal Deposit Insurance Corporation, 126, *127*
Federal Emergency Relief Administration, 126
Federal Housing Agency, 136
Feldman, J. P. H., Dr., 117, *119*
Fernandina, 45, 47, 75, *77*
Field, Dale Mabry, 145
Fifth Street, *98*
Finland, 44
First Seminole War, 16, *17*
First United Methodist Church, 97
Flatauer Building, *67*
Flatauer, Adolph, 162
Flint River, 13, 24, 38, 137

Flora of the Southern United States, 31
Florida Acquisition and Restoration Council, 172
Florida Agricultural and Mechanical College, 142
Florida Co-Operative Colony, 111, 113
Florida Commercial Fisheries Association, 132
Florida Department of Administration, 153
Florida Department of Agriculture, 71
Florida Department of Community Affairs, 158, 160, 182
Florida Department of Environmental Protection, 168
Florida Department of Game and Fish, 71
Florida Department of Natural Resources, 153
Florida Department of Transportation, 154, 167
Florida Development Commission, 150
Florida Division of Forestry, 169
Florida Division of State Planning, 153
Florida Environmental Land and Water Management Act, 152
Florida Fishing Commission, 71
Florida Forever, 169, 170, 172
Florida Fourth Infantry, 44
Florida Goat, Sheep, and Turkey Farms, 127, 128
Florida House of Representatives, 116
Florida Industrial Commission, 137
Florida Keys, 74
Florida Oyster Farms, Incorporated, 125
Florida Promenade, 158
Florida Road Department, 149, 154
Florida Seafood Festival, 159
Florida Senate, 52
Florida State University, 153, 171
Florida Sunland Farms, 125
Florida Wholesale Land Company, Inc., 114, 119
Florida-Canadian Farms Company, 98
Floyd, Gabriel I., Colonel, 27, 36, 45, 46, 47
Floyd, Mr., *92*, 161
Floyd, Richmond F., 44
Forbes Purchase, 7, 16, 21, 22, 23, *24*, 26, 28
Forbes and Company, John, *18*, 19
Forbes, John, 17, 19
Forbes, Thomas, 16, *19*
Fort Clinch, 41
Fort Davis, 44

Fort Hughes, 24
Fort Marion, 41
Fort Sam Houston, 135
Fort Sumter, 41
Fortunas, Alex, 136, *136*
Fourth Florida regiment, 46
Fowler, R. G., 59
France, 15, 93, *94*, 98, 99
Franklin, The, 141
Franklin Bank, 29
Franklin County Commercial Seafood Dealers Association, 136
Franklin County Commission, 153, 171
Franklin County Community Planning Process, 172
Franklin County Courthouse, 39, *100*, 100
Franklin County Defense Council, 142
Franklin County, 7, 8, 9, 12, *12*, 21, 27, 28, 31, 32, 38, *40*, 41, *47*, 53, 55, *57*, 58, 59, 68, 71, 74, 75, *76*, 81, 82, 87, 93, *94*, *96*, 97, 98, *98*, 100, *103*, *105*, *112*, *113*, 114, 116, 119, 123, *126*, 128–129, 131, 132, 133, 134, 135, 137, 140, 142, 146, *146*, 147, 149, 153, 154, *155*, 159, 160, 161, 162, *163*, 167, 168, 169, 170, 172
Franklin Course, 32, *33*
Franklin Hotel, *84*, *97*, *124*
Franklin Volunteers, 42
free blacks, 35, *35*
Freedman's Bureau, 56
French and Indian War, 15
Friedman, Howard, *145*
Fry-Conter house, *98*
Fuller Hotel, *61*, 141, 156
Fuller, Mary Aldin, *61*, 63

G

Gable, Clark, 143
Gadsden County, 25, 83, 153
Gainesville, 127, 154
Galveston, Tex., 7, 39
Garden of the Gods Romance, 96
Gazette, 27, 68
George W. Miller (steamer), 131, *131*
Georgia Boy (ferry), *148*, 150
Georgia railroad line, 38
Georgia, 7, 9, 13, 15, 16, *16*, 17, 21, 23, *23*, 24, 42, 45, 46, 47, *65*, 68, 69, 71, 88, *88*, 113, 125, 154
Georgia, Florida, and Alabama Railroad, 68, 83–84, 88, *88*
Germany, 57, 93, 134, 146
Gex and Lenin Lumber Company, 133
Gibbs, Richard, 81
Gibson Hotel, *126*

Gibson Inn, *97*, *124*, 141, 162
Gibson, Annie, *124*
Gibson, Gip, 92
Gibson, Mary Ellen Sunshine, *124*
Gift, G. W., 51, 52
Giles, S. J., 117
Gilmore & Davis, *67*
Godley's Bluff, 69
Gorrie Bridge, John, 9, 126, *127*, 130, *147*, 150, 151, 162, *164*
Gorrie, John, Dr., 29, *29*, 30, *31*, 59, 85, *87*, *100*, 107
Governor Stone (schooner), 155
Grady, Elizabeth, 59
Grady, H. L., 61
Grady & Company, J. E., *99*, 159
Grady, J. E., *59*, 173
Grady, John F., 60
Graham, Robert, 152
Grange, 8, 65, 68
Grant, Ulysses S., 8, 52
Grantland Rice Pictures, 138
Grayson, John B., Colonel, 44, 45
Great Britain, 16, 93, 138, 139
Great Depression, 9, 100, 123, 125, 126, 131, 134
Great Fire of 1900, 85
Great Lakes, 15
Great Plains, 68
Growth Management Plan, 160
Grubb, W. I., 119, 121
Gulf County, 9, 154, 160, 172
Gulf of Mexico, 7, 8, 11, 12, 14, 19, 39, 43, 55, 68, 69, 71, 74, 78, *101*, 136, 143, 150, 151, *168*, 168, 170, 172
Gulf Squadron, 45
Gulf State Bank, 162

H

Hagans, James, 133
Hall, Carolyn Aarrabelle, 8, *63*, 68
Hall, Gaddis C., 142
Hall, William Henry, 63
Hampton, Charles N., 106, 109, 119, 121
Hannah's Court H. J. J., No. 11, *61*
Hanover, Germany, 73
Harbormaster House, 158
Hardee, Cary Augustus, 116, *116*
Hardin County, Ky., 95
Hardtimes (steamship), 38
Harvard, 69
Haskew, Peter, 32
Hatch, George, 55
Havana, Cuba, 14
Heart Poems, 124
Hedrick, John, 172
Hell Drivers, 141
Hell State Forest, 169
Hendrickson, Corey, 135
Henry County, 96
Henry, James M., 133

Hickey, Joseph P., Mrs., 140, *141*
Hiles, Ed., 123
Hiles, George, *123*
Hiles, Joe, *123*
Hill family, 99
Hill, Lou, Jr., 159
Hill, Sam, 63
Hill, the, 156
Hillman, Richard. *157*
Hillman, Susan, *157*
Hitchiti, 7, 12
Hobart, Charlie, 92
Hodges, Alice, *173*
Hodges, Grady, *173*
Hodges, Joseph, *173*
Hodges, T. R., 71, 74, 115, 116, *116*, 117, 118, 119, 121
Hodges, William C., *120*, 127, 128
Hoffman, Earl, 118, 119
Hoffman, V. M., *190*
Holland, James, *165*
Holland, Mercedes, *88*
Holley, Frank, *90*
Holy Family Catholic School, 142
Home Owners Loan Corporation, 126
Homestead, Florida, 141
Hoover, Herbert, 126
Hopkins, Edward, Colonel, 44, 45
Hoppe's Jewelry Store, *60*
House of Bourbon, 15
Houston, John, 92
Howell, Bobby, 153
Hudson River, 24
Huggins, Charles, 133
Humphries, Horace H., 58, 81, 87
Hun Hammer, 99
Hunter, J. N. G., 46
Hunter, Sadie, *88*
Huntsville, Ala., 74

I

Indian Pass, 11, 12, 43, 71
Indian Removal Act, 23
Ingle, Robert, 153
Innerarity, James, 17
Innerarity, John, 17
Intracoastal Waterway, 123
Iola, *17*, 38
Irishtown, 28
Island House hotel, 8, *63*, 68
Isle St. Catherine, *10*
Isle St. George, *10*
Isles Aux Chiens, 11

J

Jackson County, 21, 25, 41, 60, 153
Jackson River, 26
Jackson, Andrew, 16, *17*, *24*, 26, 33
Jacksonville, 47, 51, 68, 98, 99, 123, 127, 132, 133
Jacobs Civil, Inc., 167

Jafnbar (bark), 86
James A. Garfield, (schooner), 86
James N. Coombs, 83
Japan, 134, 146
Jenkins, Belle, 156
Jenkins, Charles, 21
Jenkins, Dan, 88
Jenkins, Edna, 88
Jenkins, Fred, 88
Jenkins, Harry, 88
Jenkins, Sadie, 88
Jenkins, Spartan, *112*, 157
Jesse Mae, *129*
Jews, 57
Jim Crow segregation laws, 145
Johnson, Lyndon B., 149
Johnson, Greene S., Jr., 123
Johnson, Henry Walker, 61, 117
Johnson, Herbert K. "Duke," 63
Johnson, Joseph E., 53, *123*
Jones, Charles, Reverend, 32
Jones, Theodore, 63

K
Kate (hurricane), 154, 161
Kelley, Oliver Hudson, 8, *63*, 65, 68
Kendrick, Will, 172
Kenney, Jefferson D., 119, 121
Kevan, William P., Jr., 134
Key West, 41, 45, 74, 75, *100*, 143
Kimball Lumber Company, 59, 87
King, F. R., 81, 86
King, Imogene, 82
King, Paul S., 81, 82
Kingfisher, 44
Kirk, Claude, 152
Korea, 149
Koun, Michael J., 162
Koun, Neil, 162

L
La Salle, Cavelier Sieur de, 15
Lady Popham (boat), 116
LaFayette Park, 165, *171*
Lake City, *48*, 51
Lake Wimico and St. Joseph Canal and Rail Road Company, 24, *25*, 26
Lake Wimico, 26, 172
Lakeland, 98
Lanark Hotel, 135
Lanark Inn, 88
Lanark on the Gulf, 88
Lanark Springs, 88
Lanark Village, 88, 170
Lanark, 135, 147
Land, Clifford C., 127, 149
Langston, Mose, 133
Latava (bark), 86
Lawrence, Joseph S., 38
Lee's Bus Line, *125*
Lee, John, 103, 153

Lee, Robert E., General, 8, 46, 52
Lefevre, A. N., Mrs., *133*
Legislative Council, 21, *22*, 27, *31*, 32
Leisure Properties, 151–152, 153, 154
Leon County, 114, 119, 153, 160
Leroy's, 38
Leslie, John, 16, *19*
Liberty County, 114, 119, 153, 160
Licidello, Buster, *157*
Lights and Shadows of Itinerant Life, 44
Lincoln, Abraham, President, 7, 41, 42, 43,
Little St. George Island, 8, 11, 36, 37, *37*, 49, 53, 55, 81–82, *82*, 89, 92, 123, *168*
Little St. George Lighthouse, *103*
Little St. Marks River, 12
Little United Servicemen's Organization (USO), 140
Liverpool, 36, *36*
Livingston, Robert, 153
Los Angeles, 129
Louis XIV, 15
Louisiana, 15, 142
Louisville *Happy Home and Fireside*, 95
Louisville, Ky., 95
Love's Rainbow Dream, 96
Love, E. C., 118, 132
Lovett home, *165*
Lovett, Francis, 114
Lower Creek, 12, 24
Loxley Lumber Company, 82
Luckey, W. S., 90

M
Macon, Ga., 53
MacRae, William A., 113
Maddox, Fred, *92*
Maddox, Montgomery, *92*
Maine, *57*, 72
Malcolmson, John, 98
Mallory, Stephen M., *42*
Mammoth Cave Romance, 96
Mansion House, 32
Manteo (steamer), *114*
Marianna, 8, 25, 48, 136
Marine Hospital, 33
Marine Insurance Bank of Apalachicola, 29
Marine Street, 89
Market Street, 88, 115, *115*, 140, 143, 154, *168*, *169*
Marks, Harry, Mrs., *133*
Marks, Homer, 114
Marks, Willoughby C., Lieutenant, 99
Marks, Willoughby, Mrs., *133*
Marshall, Estelle, 146
Marshall, George H., 59, *83*

Marshall, H. O., 133
Marshall, John, 25
Marshall, Rudolph, 116
Marshall, Willoughby, *98*, 165, 171
Martin, A. E., *88*
Martina, Frank, *92*
Martinez, Bob, 161
Mary E. Morse (schooner), 86
Mary Emeline (steamer), 24
Mary Star By The Sea, 143
Maryland, 135
Masonic Hall, *93*
Massachusetts, 30, 65, 135
Mathis, Rophebe, 140
Maxwell Air Force Base, 144
Mayo, William T., 150
McClay, Charles, *92*
McClay, John, *92*
McCook, Edward M., *50*, 53
McCormick, George W., 86
McDonough, Ga., 96
McGillivray, Alexander, 17, *19*
McIntosh, McQueen, *40*, 41
McLaughlin, August, 44
McLeod, Don, 133, 140
McLeod, Martha Norris, 137
McLeod, Roderick D., *51*
McRae, William A., 125, 127
Mechanics & Merchants Exchange, 32
Mediterranean Sea, 72, 74
Mediterranean fruit fly, 123
Memminger, C. S., *42*
Mercedita (steamer), 46, *47*
Merlo, Michael, 162
Messina family, *172*
Messina and Company, Joseph C., *72*, 72
Messina, Joseph C., 74
Messing, Joe, Mrs., *133*
Methodist church, 86, 87
Methodists, *31*, 90
Mexico, 14, 59
Meyer, A. F., 60
Meyer, John B., 154
Meyer, Lonnie, *92*
Miami Beach, 116
Miami, 116, 118
Middle Atlantic States, 37
Middle District of Florida, 49
Middle Florida, *12*, 14, 68
Miley, Woody, 160, 169
Miller, Father, 47
Miller, John, 38, 72
Million Dollar Bond Plan, 113, 114, 118
Milton, John, 8, 41, 42, 43, 44, 45, *45*, 46, 47, 48, 49, 50, 52, *128*
Minnesota, 65
Miss Florida Seafood, 160
Mississippi, 41
Mississippi River, 15, 23, 38
Mississippi Valley, 15

Mitchel, Colin, 19, 25
Mobile, Ala., 7, 16, 39, 83
Mohr, A. S., *57*, 59
Monroe, James, *20*, 21
Montgomery (steamer), 43
Montgomery, Ala., 41, 53, 88, 90, 144
Montgomery, Mercia, 140
Montgomery, Rosa V., *92*
Montgomery, W. E., 86
Moore, E. R. L., 119
Moore, James, Governor, 15
Moorings, The, 104
Morton, Carl, *123*
Mosconis, Jimmy, 161
Muller-Stockheim, Gunter, Kaptinleutenant, 139
Munroe, Ivan, 149
Murat, A. J., 60
Murray, Allen, *90*
Muscogee (ironclad), 51, 52
Muskogean Indians, 7, 12
Muskogee County, 38
Myhoff, Fred, *90*

N

Nagel, Lieutenant, *145*
Naiad, 84
Napoleonic wars, 16
Narvárez, Pánfilo de, *13*, 14
National Guard, 133
National Oceanic and Atmospheric Administration, 160
Natural Bridge, 8
Nature Conservancy, The, 9, 169
Nebraska, 9, 68
Nedley, Bud, *90*
Nedley, Mike, *92*
Neel, Daniel O., 81
Neel, William H., 81
Nesmith, Thomas J., *84*, *128*
New and Enlarged Plan, 114
New Deal, 126, 132
New England, 37
New Inlet, 11
New Jersey, 24
New Orleans, La., 7, 16, 39, 57, 59, 68, 121
New Pace Vaudeville theatre, 89
New River, 63
New York, 24, 28, *31*, 32, 36, *36*, 57, 74, 75, *76*, 101
Nichol's Economy Store, 154
Nichols, Jimmy, Mayor, *159*
Nichols, John "Jimmy," *159*
Nichols, Kathy, *159*
Nick's Hole, 81, *82*, 89, 134, 154
Nickmire, Hazel, *92*
Norris, H. A., 28
North Africa, 144
North Carolina, 53
Nourse, Hiram, 36

O

Ocean Pond, *48*, 51
Ochlockonee Bay, 170
Ochlockonee River, 78, 88
Office of Price Administration, 143
Oglethorpe, James, 15
Ohio River, 38
Oliver, H. L., 89
106th Engineers, 129, 133
112th Infantry Dance Band, 140
112th Infantry Regiment, 144
Ordinance of Secession, 40
Original Broadcasting Band, *90*
Orman, W. Thomas, 8, 49, 55, 59
Ormond, Thomas G., 39
Osborne, Mabel L., 118, 136, 140
Osburn, Molly, 140
Osceola, *22*, 23
Our Boys and Girls in the Service, 140
Owl Cafe, *93*
Ownes, Bill, *123*
Oyster Farm News, 113
Oyster Growers' Co-Operative Association, 109, *110*, 113, 114, 117, 119
Oyster Nip, 125
Oyster shuckers, *111*
Oystermen's Protective Association, 85

P

Paisley, William A., 128
Panacea Springs, 88
Panama City, 134, *134*, 140
Panton, Leslie, and Company, 17, 19, *19*
Panton, William, 16, 17, 19, *19*
Parlin, Charles H., 59
Partington, Cleo, 100
Partington, Rex, 100
Patrons of Husbandry, 65
Patton, Bryant G., 9, 102, 149, 150, 153
Patton, Mattie, Miss, *133*
Pearl Harbor, 133, 138
Pelham, Tom, 161
Pennsylvania Avenue, 143
Pennsylvania Tie Company, *57*, 59
Pensacola and Atlantic Railroad, 60
Pensacola, 15, 16, 17, *19*, 21, *22*, 41, 52, 53, 83, *83*, 90, 118, 119
People's or Populist Party, 68
Perry, Madison Starke, Governor, 41, *41*
Pettigrew, Richard, 152
Philaco Women's Club, 84, 132, *133*, 140
Philadelphia (steamer), 83
Philippine Insurrection, 135
Phillips, Herbert S., 128
Pichard, Alphonse, 128
Pickett's Harbor, 63

Pickett, McGregor, 63
Pierce, Alan, 161
Pierce, Ray V., Dr., 8, *55*, 56, *56*
Pineda, Alonzo de, 14
Pinhook, 26
Posser, W. M., *90*
Popham Trust Estate, 119, 123, 124
Popham, Clara, 95, 113, 129
Popham, Maude, 96, 99, 117, 118, *119*, 124, 127, 128, 129
Popham, Virgil, 95
Popham, William Lee, 11, 90, 95, 96, 98, 106, 109, *110*, 111, *112*, 113, 114, *114*, 115, 116, 118, 119, *120*, 121, 124, *125*, 126, 127, 128, 129, 151, 152
Popham, William Lee, Jr., 9, 99, 113, 124, 127, 129, 173
Population, 8, 167
Port Arthur, Texas, 143
Port St. Joe, 83, *125*, 131, *131*, 136, 142, 169
Porter, 82, *82*, 89, 123
Porter family, 7
Porter, Edward G., 81, *82*, 88, 89
Porter, Eleanor, *82*, *92*
Porter, Ethel, *82*
Porter, Harry, *83*
Porter, Jo, *82*
Porter, Josephine, *82*, *92*
Porter, Mary Tibbitt Salter, 81
Porter, Pearl, 82, *82*, *92*
Porter, R. G., 118
Porter, R. H., 61
Porter, Red, *123*
Porter, Richard, *123*
Porter, T. F., William G., 39
Posey, Annie Haddock, *136*
Post Office, *93*
Prison Poems, 124
Prospect Bluff, 17
Public Works Administration (PWA), 126, *127*, 132

Q

Quakers, 69
Quincy, 25, 57, 132
Quinn High School, 155
Quinn, Wallace M., 132, 142

R

Raider (U-boat), 139
Ralstead, Valerie, *159*
Randolph, Willie Fred, *123*, 131, 139,
Raney House, *104*
Raney, David Greenway, 36, 39, *39*, *104*
Rationing Board, 140
Reagan, John H., *42*
Rebecca Everingham (steamship), 64
Red Cross, 139, 140, 146

Register, W. A., 116, 117
Republicans, 8, 68
Resource Planning and Management Commission (RPMC), 161
Rhode Island, 39
Rhodes, Ola, 82, *82*
Ricco's Bluff, 47, 49, 52
Rice Brothers Packing Plant, 126
Rice, Emmalee, 81
Rice, Rob Roy, 74
Rice, S. E., 131
Rice, S. E. Jr., 118
Rice, S. E., Mrs., *133*
Rice, Samuel E., 81
Rice, Samuel E., Sr., 68, 69
Rice, Stephen Ewing, 74
Rice, Stephen E., Jr., 74
Rice, Steppie, Miss., 85
Richards, Fred, *123*
Richardson, Simon Peter, 44
Richmond, 44, 52
Rio Carrabelle, 68
River Junction, 83
Rivers, Laurie, McLeod, 140, 143
Road to Success: The Best Book in the World, The, 95
Roat, William, 90, 98, 109, 113
Roberts, William C., *128*
Robinson, Charlie, *90*
Rocco, Leon A., *90*
Rodgers, Mr., *92*
Roosevelt, Franklin D., 126, 131, 132, 133, 146
Roux, Audrey, 136
Ruff, D. J., 89
Ruge Brothers Canning Company, 74, *74*
Ruge family, *172*
Ruge, George H., *58*, 59, 74
Ruge, Herman, 73, 74
Ruge, John G., *58*, 73, 74, 113, 117, 121, 158
Ruge, John R., 59
Ruge, John, Mrs., *133*
Ruge, J. D., Mrs., *133*
Rummell, Peter S., 169

S
Sadie J. (boat), *112*
Saffold, Ga., 42, 45, 49
Sager, Arthur N., 119
Saint George Company, 98
Salvador, Mark, 75, 76, 77
Salvatore, Sollecito, 75
San Francisco, Ca., 75, 76
San Jorge, 12
Sangaree, Veto G., *92*
Savannah, Ga., 19, 46, 57, 68
Saxon, George W., 87, 89, 90, 96, 98, 99, 109, 162
Saxon, Sarah Bell, 88
Schoelles, Philip, 60

Schrantz, Richard H., 144
Scipio Creek, *108*
Scott, George Washington, *46*
Sea Dream (Coast Guard vessel), 139, *139*
Seafood Festival (1970), *160*
Seafood Festival (1973), *162*
Second Seminole War, *22*, 23, 28, 32
Segras, Joseph, 72
Selective Training, 133
Selma, Ala., 53
Seminoles, 7, 16, *16*, 22, *22*
Service Act, 133
Service Men's Wives Club, 140
Seven Years' War, 15
Shaw, T. Darrah, 43
Shell Fish Commission, 71
Sheppard, William B., 118
Sheridan, Reverend, *90*
Sherman, William T., 53
Shotwell, Alexander, 24
Shreve, Jack, 152
Shuler, Al, 153
Shuler, Jay A., 143
Siberia, 14
Sicily, 156
Sikes Cut, 154
Sikes, Robert L. F., 11, 134, 151
Sikes Channel, Robert L., 151
Simmons, William H., Dr., 21, *22*,
Sinclair, George, 8, 55, 58
Sinclair, William, 55
Sirens, *170*
Sirius (ferry), *148*, 150
Smith, C. H., 81
Smith, Helen Brooks, 98
Smith, Mary F., 81
Smith, Walter E., 135
Snow, Richards, and Harris, 58
Somerset, 51
Sopchoppy, 137, 140
Soto, Hernando de, 14, *14*
South America, 150
South Carolina, 17, 29, 41, 46, *97*
Southern, Baptist Theological Seminary, 95
Southern Co-Operative Association, 69
Spain, 7, 15, *15*, 16, 17
Spanish-American War, 135
Spanish influenza, 99
Spartan Jenkins Hotel, 63
Spencer, Samuel W., 36
Spica (ferry), *148*, 150
St. Andrew Bay, 26, 43, 49, 83
St. Augustine, 15, *15*, 16, 17, *19*, 21, *22*, *41, 47*
St. George Co-Operative Colony, 99, 106, 109, *110*
St. George Co-Operative Company, 109
St. George Island Club, 89

St. George Island Company, 88, 98
St. George Island Development Company, 90, 152
St. George Island Gulf Beaches, Inc., 149, 150, 151, *152*, 153
St. George Island, 7, 8, 9, 11, 12, *13*, 14, 29, 33, 36,37, 39, 42, 46, *47*, 49, 50, 51, 55, 58, 60,63, 68, 71, *80*, 81, *81*, 82, *82*, 85, 86, 87, 88, *88*, 89, *89*, 90, 95, 96, 98, 99, *102*, 109, 113, 114, 115, 118, *121*, 124, *125*, 127, 128, *128*, 129, *131*, 134, 135, 137, 140, 146, 147, *148*, 149, 150, *150*, 151, 152, 153, 154, *166*, 167, *168*
St. George Sound, 8, 12, 35, 43, 51, 59, *62*, 63, *63*, 68
St. James Island, 88, 170, 171, 172
St. Joe Company, 9, 169, 170, 171, 172
St. Joe Paper Company, 9, 137, *137*, 147, 169
St. Joe Timberlands, 172
St. Johns Shipyard, 99
St. Joseph Bay, 26, 27
St. Joseph Station, 32
St. Joseph to Iola rail line, 27
St. Joseph, 7, *10*, 22, *25*, 26, *27*, 36, 83
St. Lawrence River, 15
St. Louis, Mo., 69, 75, *76*
St. Marie d'Apalache, *10*
St. Marks River, 12
St. Marks, 14, 21, *22*, *44*, 49, 52, 75, 99
St. Patrick's Roman Catholic Church, 32, *106*
St. Teresa, 88, 135, 147, 170, 171
St. Vincent Island, 7, 8, 11, 12, *13*, 14, 39, 42, 44, 45, 46, *47*, 49, 55, *55*, *56*, 70, 74, 89
St. Vincent National Wildlife Preserve, 159
St. Vincent Sound, 11, 43, 172
Star of the West, 31
Starke, 133
Stellwagen, H. S., 46, 47, 48
Stephens, Alexander H., *42*
Stocks, John, 151, 153, 154
Stokes, John P., 118, 119
Storrs, C. L., 59
Storrs, James C., 89
Strum, Louis W., 127, 128
Suber, George, *123*
Sumatra, 63
SummerCamp, 170, 171
Summerford, Ramsey, *92*
Sunset Beach, 154
Suwannee, River, *12*, 14
Sylvania plantation, 8, 41

T

Talk It Up, 141
Tallahassee *Democrat*, 118
Tallahassee *Floridian*, 28
Tallahassee, 9, 14, *14*, 21, *22*, 26, 39, *50*, 52, 53, 57, *67*, 68, 84, 87, 88, 96, 98, *99*, 106, 116, 118, 119, *120*, 121, 123, 127, 128, 135, 142, 145, 147, 149, 152, 153, 162
Tampa Bay, *13*, 14, *14*
Tampa, 90, 96, 106
Tarantino, Belton, 132, 156
Taranto, Joe, 132, *132*, 156
Tarpon Springs, 74; 75
Tarpon, *83*
Tate's Hell, 8, 63, 169, 172
Tate, Cebe, 63
Teague, J. J., *123*
Teague, Samuel E., 87, 89
Telegraph, 27
Tent and Awning plant, 135
Texas, 78, 135
Thomasville, Ga., 8, 68
Tift, Nelson, 24
Timber Island, 172
Times, 27, 109, 117, 129
Toombs, Robert, *42*
Tortugas, 78
Trapier, John H., 45
Treaty of 1763, 15
Treaty of Fort Gibson (1833), 23
Treaty of Fort Jackson (1814), 16, 24
Treaty of Ghent (1814), 16
Treaty of Moultrie Creek (1823), 22
Treaty of Payne's Landing, *22*, 23
Tri-Rivers Waterway Development Association, 154
Trinity Episcopal Church, 32, *107*
Tripler, A. B., *57*, 58
Truman, Harry S., 146
Truman, Ivan, *123*
Trumbull, Sidney E., 98
Tucker Lake, 170
Tunney, Gene, 123
Turkey Creek, 171
Twenty-eighth Infantry Division, 144
Tyndall Air Field, 134, *134*, 143, 144
Tyndall Air Force Base, 140, 143

U

U.S. Army Corps of Engineers, 11, 60, 153, 154
U.S. Department of Agriculture, 8, 65
U.S. Highway 98, 154, 171, *172*
U.S. Navy, 144
University of Florida, 127
Upper Anchorage, 59
Upper Creek, 24

V

V-E (Victory Europe) Day, 146
V-J (Victory Japan) Day, 146, *146*
Vale (bark), *86*
Varnes, Cecil, 153
Venice Island, 113
Venice, 111
Verandas, *170,*
Victorettes, 140
Village by the Sea, The, 96
Virginia, 52, 68
Vivette (barkentine), *86*
Vrooman, Harry C., 9, 65, 69

W

Wade, I. D, "Ikie," 153
Wakefield, John, Mrs., *133*
Wakulla County, 71, 117, 137
Wakulla River, 19
Wakulla Springs, 138
Walker, Leroy Pope, *42*, 43
Wall Street, 123
War of 1812, 16, 19
War Price and Ration Board, 146
War Production Board, 142
Warm Springs, Ga., 146
Warren, Farley, 85, 86, 140
Washington County, 21
Washington, D.C., 68
Washington, George, *66*
Watchman of the Gulf, 31
Water Street, *26*, 28, *34*, *54*, *96*, *99*, 156, 159, *163*, *169*
Waybright, Edgar W., 127
Waybright, Roger J., 127
Weatherspoon, Raymond, *90*
Wefing, George F., 55, 61
Wefing, George, Mrs., *133*
West Gap, 11
West Pass, 8, 11, 12, *20*, 21, 35, 36, 43, 47, 51, 55, 59, 63, 132
West Point Military Academy, 146
West Point, 7, 21
Westcott, Dinsmore, 26
Western Bank of Apalachicola, 29
Wewahitchka, *125*
Whigs, 7
White Plains, New York, *107*
Whiteside, W. H., Mrs., *133*
Wilkie, Wendell L., 133
Williams, John Lee, 21, *22*
Willis family, 99
Willis, Kathy, *173*
Willis, Lee, II, 7, 159, *173*
Wilson, Edward, 133
Wilson, James H., 8, 53
Wilson, William H. "Bill," 128, 137, 149, 151
Wilson, Woodrow, President, 98
Wing, Andy, Captain, 81, *81*
Wise, G. D., *37*
WJAX, 123
Women's Reading Club, 132
Woodruff Dam, Jim, 154
Works Progress Administration, 126, *127,* 132, 134
World War I, 9, 89, 98, 134, 135, 143
World War II, 9, 129, 134, 135, 154, *155*
World-Wyde Oyster Puree, 125
World-Wyde Products, Incorporated, 125

Y

Yearty, George, *92*
Yearty, Walter, *92*
Yent and Alexander, 72
Yerkes, Damon O., 127
Yosemite Valley Romance, 96
Yucatan Channel, 43

Z

Zulavsky, S. S., 53

About the Authors

William Warren Rogers

Lee Willis III

Joan Morris

Bawa Satinder Singh

WILLIAM WARREN ROGERS is Emeritus Professor of History at Florida State University. He earned his Ph.D. at the University of North Carolina at Chapel Hill. A native of Alabama, he has published a number of books and articles about the South. Among co-authored works of related interest to this book are his *Favored Land, Tallahassee: A History of Tallahassee and Leon County* and *The Croom Family and Goodwood Plantation: Land, Litigation, and Southern Lives*. His particular fields of interest are the history of Florida, Alabama, and Georgia.

LEE WILLIS III is a doctoral candidate in History at Florida State University. After receiving his master's degree in American and Florida Studies from F.S.U. in 1998, he taught high school in Tallahassee for four years. He has published in the *Florida Historical Quarterly* and is currently working on a dissertation about religion and political culture in nineteenth-century Florida.

JOAN MORRIS lives in Tallahassee where she retired in June 2003 after thirty-three years as curator of the Florida photographic collection in the Florida State Archives. She earned her undergraduate and master's degrees at Florida State University. Morris is the photographic editor of seven books on Florida and since 1995 has compiled *The Florida Handbook*, a biennial reference of Florida government, history, and statistics,

BAWA SATINDER SINGH was born in India and received his undergraduate degree at the University of Panjab. His doctorate is from the University of Wisconsin. A professor of history at Florida State university, he is the author of several books, including *The Jammu Fox* and *The Hardinge Letters*. Interested in photography since his teenage years, Professor Singh has taken pictures in many countries.

at Apalachicola Fla